K·I·S·S

DK

The Only Guides You'll Ever Need!

THIS SERIES IS YOUR TRUSTED GUIDE through all of life's stages and situations. Want to learn how to surf the Internet or care for your new dog? Or maybe you'd like to become a wine connoisseur or an expert gardener? The solution is simple: Just pick up a K.I.S.S. Guide and turn to the first page.

Expert authors will walk you through the subject from start to finish, using simple blocks of knowledge to build your skills one step at a time. Build upon these learning blocks and by the end of the book, you'll be an expert yourself! Or, if you are familiar with the topic but want to learn more, it's easy to dive in and pick up where you left off.

The K.I.S.S. Guides deliver what they promise: simple access to all the information you'll need on one subject. Other titles you might want to check out include: Playing Guitar, Living With a Dog, the Internet, Microsoft Windows, Astrology, and many more to come.

K·I·S·S

GUIDE TO

Cat Care

STEVE DUNO

Foreword by **Christopher Walken**

Academy Award-winning Actor

DK

A Dorling Kindersley Book

**LONDON, NEW YORK,
MUNICH, MELBOURNE, DELHI**

DK Publishing Inc.
Senior Editor Jennifer Williams
Editor Beth Adelman
Copyeditor Christy Wagner
Category Publisher LaVonne Carlson

Dorling Kindersley Limited
Project Editor David Tombesi-Walton
Project Art Editor Simon Murrell

Managing Editor Maxine Lewis
Managing Art Editor Heather McCarry

Production Heather Hughes
Category Publisher Mary Thompson

Produced for Dorling Kindersley by Design Revolution Limited
Queens Park Villa, 30 West Drive, Brighton, East Sussex BN2 2GE
Project Editor Julie Whitaker
Designer Lucie Penn
Design Assistant Katie Walmsley

2 4 6 8 10 9 7 5 3 1

Published in the United States by
DK Publishing, Inc.
375 Hudson Street, New York, NY 10014

Library of Congress Cataloging-in-Publication Data

Duno, Steve.
    Kiss guide to cat care / Steve Duno.
      p. cm. -- (Keep it simple series)
    ISBN 0-7894-8012-3 (alk. paper)
    1. Cats.   I. Title. II. Series.
  SF447 .D86 2001
  636.8'0887--dc21

                                    2001001486

Color reproduction by Colourscan, Singapore
Printed and bound by MOHN media and Mohndruck GmbH, Germany

See our complete product line at
www.dk.com

Contents at a Glance

CONTENTS

PART TWO Cat Basics

APPENDICES

Foreword

IT SEEMS TO ME *that we humans sometimes forget that we are animals too; in the best sense – the pure sense of the forest where our first memories were made. And there are as many kinds of us as there are of them: solitary, gregarious, monogamous; the beach master with his harem; those who meet once and move on; the hunters; the vegetarians.*

We have domesticated many animals, but cats seem to have retained a sense of the forest. Their cleanliness is famous. They have grace in so many ways. From the tintinnabulation of their walk, to the way they tend to leave a small amount of food in the bottom of their bowl in what looks to me like an offering. Their self assurance and ability to articulate their needs to us with such clarity and insistence. They pose for us as naturally as Garbo because they are entitled to.

When it comes to dogs, size does not matter. Cats are fearless. They are fierce and nice – a wonderful combination of qualities. I can think of no other familiar animal with such natural confidence. And self confidence sounds like self awareness. These things combined with inquisitiveness and communication skills suggest genuine intelligence. They seem to possess an independent mind. And what about that purr? No one knows the mechanism of it. It is as mysterious as human laughter.

I've heard that the symbol we use to signify a question (?) is, in origin, an Egyptian hieroglyph that represents a cat as seen from behind. I wonder if the Egyptians were expressing suspicion or an inquiring mind . . . or something else?

I had a cat who lived a long time. Long enough to enjoy a number of places my wife and I had lived in, finally settling in the country, where he hunted, played, groomed, slept, ate. Then it came time to die. He grew very thin and fragile over the course of a few months. He kept his chin up, but it was sad to see the good nature of his spirit struggling. I work at home a lot, often in the kitchen, which has a large window looking out over a long driveway full of trees. One morning, having coffee, I felt a familiar bump against my leg. My old cat was looking at me in a powerful way. I rubbed him for a while. He purred. He drooled. I got up and gave him what he wanted, and then

I let him outside and went back to my coffee. For the next 10 minutes I watched him creak his way down the long driveway. He was almost out of sight when my wife walked into the room. "Look," I said to her. "Isn't it wonderful? He knows it's time to die. He said goodbye and now he's back off to the woods to be by himself, listen to the birds and the wind, and go to sleep. Nature is so pragmatic, so amazing . . . ."

My wife took a long look at him, then at me. She went to the front door, flung it open, and yelled, "Pookie, get back in here." My ancient cat stopped in his creaky tracks, looking exactly like a question mark from my angle (though in my mind's eye I could see his face). He looked confused, then suddenly determined, energized, victorious. He bumpily made a 180-degree turn and headed back toward the house. My wife waited out the whole journey, standing at the open door. He reached the stairs, and, with a sudden burst of youth, mounted them and ran into the house. He placed himself in the middle of the living room rug, which seemed odd since he had a favorite chair. He cleaned himself for a while and took a nap.

He was up and down that day a few times for a bite of turkey baby food and a drink from his bowl. Later, a demand to be rubbed; then back to his nap, in the middle of the rug. My wife and I kept him company as we watched TV, then we left him there and went to bed. The next morning, he was dead: as if he'd said, "That was good. I was brave. Time to go . . . . See you again???"

He had spent his last days hunting, playing, grooming, sleeping, eating – being a cat, being happy. What more can we want for our feline friends?

CHRIS WALKEN

CHRISTOPHER WALKEN
Feb 2001
NYC, USA

Introduction

WELCOME! YOU ARE ABOUT to enter the exciting
fellowship of cat lovers, a group of feline aficionados growing by
leaps and bounds each year. Already the world's most popular home
companion, the cat is a beautiful, intelligent, captivating animal that
may soon have you wondering just who the owner and who the
owned really is.

Anyone who has lived with cats knows they are mysterious creatures.
They have their own language, their own ways of perceiving the
world, their own reasons for the things they do. They have us figured
out pretty well, but we have a long way to go before we really
understand them.

That being said, there's a lot about cats that we do know. The intent
of this book is to take a person who knows very little about cats and
turn him or her into a veritable cat expert. To accomplish this, the
K.I.S.S. Guide to Cat Care is arranged from the most fundamental
cat facts to the more advanced, making it most effective for you to
start reading from the beginning and slowly work your way through
to the more complex chapters. If you do so, I promise that you will
quickly become a connoisseur of cats in no time at all. Really!

Like many of you out there, I have gone through periods of living in
a cat-less world; how sad and boring! Luckily, if done correctly, you

should be able to incorporate a cat into your life no matter what your present living arrangement. Whether you live in a chateau or a shoebox, you should be able to enjoy the refined company of a feline, provided you read this book first!

If you are a beginner, prepare to have a new window on the world opened up to you, one that leads to a wilder, more seductive side of nature than you might otherwise have experienced with other pets. The cat, though serene and delicately mannered, remains less of a pet and more of an artistic experience, ever-changing, with one foot in the wild and another in our hearts and homes.

Hopefully, this book will also encourage you to go beyond what you find here and seek out additional sources of cat information – other books, magazines, web sites, or other media sources. The cat world, you see, is ever-expanding, due to our elegant feline friends' increasing worldwide popularity.

STEVE DUNO

What's Inside?

THE INFORMATION in the K.I.S.S. Guide to Cat Care *is arranged from the simple to the more advanced, making it most effective if you start from the beginning and slowly work your way to the more involved chapters.*

PART ONE

Part One of this book helps ease you into the feline world by discussing the cat's rising popularity, evolution, and historic relationship with human beings over the millennia. Additional information covers the fundamentals of feline physiology and psychology, breed information, how to choose a cat, and just how the cat measures up to the dog as a pet in today's increasingly urban world. You'll want to have this information on hand so you can establish a good feline perspective and know what cat aficionados out there are talking about.

PART TWO

Part Two gives you vital information on what to do during the first few days after bringing kitty home and on how to teach your new kitty the house rules. I'll also cover what to feed, how to groom, and how to keep your kitty happy and well adjusted.

PART THREE

Part Three talks about preventive care, and then provides you with a complete primer on the most common cat maladies and their treatments, discusses how best to care for an aging or injured cat, and offers practical solutions to the most troublesome behavioral problems your cat might exhibit. The section ends with a short discussion on how to deal with the passing on of a beloved pet. I hate to mention it now, but it's best to be prepared.

PART FOUR

Part Four takes you beyond the realm of the house cat. The practical realities of breeding and showing pedigreed cats are discussed. I'll talk about the benefits of networking with other cat fanciers and how to learn the latest info on your favorite breed or cat topic. You'll also find a chapter on how to teach your cat a few tricks. Trust me: It's simple!

The Extras

THROUGHOUT THE BOOK, *you will notice a number of boxes and icons. These are meant to emphasize certain points that I want to be sure you pay attention to. They'll help you really understand what I'm talking about. Look for:*

Very Important Point

This icon will point out a bit of information I believe deserves your careful attention. You really need to know this before continuing.

Complete No-No

This is a warning, something I want to advise you not to do or to be aware of.

Getting Technical

When the information is about to get a bit technical, I'll let you know so that you can read carefully.

Inside Scoop

These are special suggestions that come from my own personal experience. I want to share them with you because they helped me when I was learning the game.

In the margins you'll also find additional information that I think you will enjoy. Look out for:

Trivia...

These are simply fun facts that will give you an extra appreciation for the history and uniqueness of the cat.

DEFINITION

*Here I'll **define** words and terms for you in an easy-to-understand style. You'll also find a glossary at the back of the book with all the feline lingo.*

INTERNET

www.dk.com

I think the Internet is a great resource for cat owners, so I've scouted out some web sites that will add to your enjoyment and understanding of cat care.

PART ONE

THE CAT IS A TRUSTING AND AFFECTIONATE FRIEND

THE FABULOUS FELINE

As the opening section of this book, Part One's job is to ease you into the *exciting* world of cats as gracefully as possible. As the world's most popular pet, the cat has captured the hearts and minds of millions of die-hard fans, including you! More and more people are *discovering* just how easy cats are to own, how *fascinating* they are, and how big a part of their owners' lives they become.

Being a cat owner isn't as easy as just finding a lonely cat and giving it a home. There's more you need to know. As with any major decision you make, you should first *educate* yourself about what cat choices are available and exactly which would make the most sense for you, your family, and your lifestyle. So, sit back, put your feet up, and start reading.

Chapter 1

Welcome to Cat Club

YOU HAVE TRIED to resist the urge for years, but your time as a cat owner has finally come. No grumpy landlord is forbidding you to have one. No cat-hating dog is around to give chase. You are not allergic. Although you live a hectic life, you are home often enough to care for an animal as adaptable as a cat. No, you have absolutely no reason to resist at all, do you? Let me welcome you to a very special club – one whose members have learned to relish the company of a mysterious animal capable of great physical feats and heartwarming affection. Dues to belong to this club are quite inexpensive: All you need do is own and love at least one furry feline.

In this chapter...
✓ The most popular pet
✓ Feline globetrotters
✓ Is the cat domesticated?
✓ Are domestic cats like wild cats?

The most popular pet

TODAY'S DOMESTIC CAT has become the pet of choice for millions of people around the world. In the United States alone, more than 30 million pet cats now eclipse the dog population by several million, with the gap growing even wider each day. Why has the household feline become so popular? What is it about this puzzling creature that appeals to so many of us?

THE DOMESTIC CAT

The feline personality

Part of the answer certainly has to be the enigmatic personality of the cat. Highly intelligent, it possesses a remarkable combination of characteristics not found in other domestic pets. Captivating and quiet, poised and self-sufficient, athletic and fastidious, the cat is rarely needy and always right. It loves company but is also content to go it alone for hours at a stretch. This independent streak, a result of felines in nature living a largely solitary life, gives the domestic cat a slightly cavalier attitude about life; for them, the sun does not rise and fall around humans, although they will take us when they can get us, thank you very much.

The ability cats have to survive with or without humans may just be one of the main reasons why we like them so much. Emotionally needy pets (or people) tend to grate on the nerves after a while; cats are charming narcissists. This, combined with their beauty, grace, dignity, and ease of care, makes them always desirable.

The feline detachment

We also like cats for their ability to say, "I am your roommate, not your servant," and for their ability to recognize the value of a good nap. And who doesn't appreciate the cat's clean, fastidious nature and built-in toilet training? Try getting a Schnauzer puppy to use a *litter box*!

Cats enjoy all the attention we humans lavish upon them, though they will, I think, never confess it. They are content to stay with us because we love them and provide for them, but if we vanished from the Earth tomorrow, chances are the cat would

> **DEFINITION**
>
> *A rectangular plastic container filled with an absorbent granular material, a **litter box** provides your cat with a place to relieve itself properly.*

mourn a bit, meow some, and then get on with the business of finding a furry little meal – all the while lampooning the millions of rudderless, heartbroken dogs wandering around aimlessly, wondering what to do next.

In my experience, I have always developed closer ties with a cat when I allow it to decide for itself when and where it wants affection from me.

In other words, don't pester your cat all day in an effort to pet it or show it love. One reason cats often shy away from children is that they usually don't know when to leave a cat be. Instead, let the cat come to you when it wants some close attention. That way, you will always be assured that it truly wants your undivided attention. When your kitty does approach you, reinforce this offering of affection by stroking and massaging the cat and with some quiet, gentle conversation.

The feline mystique

Cats are popular not only because of their desirable characteristics, but because of that intangible, seductive something they provide – a primal feeling longed for by those of us who sometimes regret being so civil, orderly, and responsible. Owning a cat opens up a small window onto the mystery and power of the natural world. Cats are elusive, unpredictable, and beautiful, as well as alarmingly efficient, from a rodent's point of view. Cats sit atop a bridge that connects the civil world to the untamed, casually grooming themselves while pondering the question: "Which way shall I go today?"

We choose to share our homes with cats because they are good companions and also because they represent independence, competence, and self-sufficiency – qualities that we all strive to attain. Cats don't have to strive; they simply have these characteristics within them. They are animated masterpieces here to befriend and beguile, but never to serve. No wonder so many millions of people have chosen to share their lives with a feline.

■ **Your cat will seek attention** *when it feels the need for some loving cuddles. Never try to force your pet to accept your affection – it will generally shun your efforts.*

Feline globetrotters

THE DOMESTIC FELINE *can be found in nearly every corner of the globe, from the frigid steppes of Asia to the searing heat of the Egyptian desert. Indeed, cats can endure and prosper in the most unlikely places due to their supreme powers of adaptation. Whatever the climate or conditions, chances are a cat is there – and doing very well at that. Cats with long coats can tolerate frigid weather, while cats with short, close coats do just fine when the mercury soars. Because of this ability to prosper in nearly any environment, cat lovers across the globe can enjoy a feline's company.*

THE RIGHT TEMPERATURE

Even though the cat has an incredible ability to adapt to a wide range of climates, you should try to keep its living environment at a comfortable temperature, and always provide it with plenty of water when the mercury soars. Keeping your home at a temperature between 62°F (17°C) and 72°F (22°C) should work just fine. If you allow your cat access to the outdoors (something I do not recommend), first decide if the outside temperature is manageable for your pet.

Don't let your cat out when the temperature falls below freezing or soars above 90°F (32°C). Also, be sure to leave a large bowl of water outside on hot days so your cat can cool off with a long drink.

■ **Keep your cat hydrated.**
Make sure that it always has access to a bowl of clean, fresh water, especially in hot weather.

A cat for all regions

Although the domestic cat probably first appeared in southern Europe or northern Africa, it quickly found itself being distributed all over the known world by merchant sailing vessels, whose crews would almost always take along a few cats to help keep the rodents on board to a minimum. As a result of being adopted by humans, shorthaired cats from hot climates ended up in more temperate regions, while longhaired cats from cooler climes eventually found their way to warmer havens. Because of their great intelligence and adaptability, transplanted cats did just fine.

Today, mixed-breed and pedigreed cats of all shapes and sizes can be found wherever cat lovers live. Whether it be an apartment in New York City, a farmhouse in Burgundy, a bed & breakfast in Toronto, or a tavern in Glasgow, there's bound to be a cat lover quietly stroking a placid, regal feline.

■ **Shorthaired cats** *probably originated in hot climates, but they migrated to more temperate regions and are now found all over the world.*

Is the cat domesticated?

*UNLIKE THE TRUSTY DOG, whose history of **domestication** goes back thousands of years longer than the cat's, felines didn't really begin to develop a working relationship with humans until we began growing crops and storing them. Once the grain ended up in storehouses, so, unfortunately, did the rodents – breaking into granaries and other storage areas in an attempt to eat the contents. In doing so, these vermin reduced our available food surpluses and spread disease.*

But with every problem there happily comes a solution. In this case, it was the cat that came to the rescue. Instinctively adept at hunting, killing, and eating rodents, the introduction of several cats into a farm's ecosystem helped curb the vermin population, thereby preserving food stores and minimizing rodent-borne diseases. Tough barn cats just did their thing, much to the relief of farmers everywhere.

> **DEFINITION**
>
> **Domestication** *means taming and selectively breeding wild animals for the purpose of accommodating humanity in some fashion, whether for food, service, or companionship.*

Cats just do their thing

As I've already mentioned, cats have also been welcome aboard merchant ships, especially those carrying cargoes of grain or other foodstuffs. Their use on ships and on the farm, however, did not require any special training or breeding; the cat instinctively knew what to do – get the mice. Because killing rodents was the only thing we needed cats for, they were never selectively bred to the extent that dogs were. So many breeds of dogs have been developed to enhance the characteristics needed to serve us in many different ways, from guarding and tracking to herding, hunting, racing, and even as couriers. Because of all the genetic manipulation done to dogs over the millennia, they have become much more varied in appearance and less in touch with their

■ **The domestic cat** *was popular with merchant sailors and farmers who valued the animal for its natural hunting skills and ability to kill vermin.*

wild sides. Cats, on the other hand, never needed special breeding or training to kill vermin, and so we left them pretty much to breed as they pleased, and they kept most of their wild instincts intact.

Not one of the gang

The pack-oriented mindset of dogs also enables us to control them more efficiently than cats, who are, by and large, loners in the wild.

As a result, the cat has remained an aloof, independent animal. This does not mean that domestic cats would prefer to live in the wild, though. The process of domestication has certainly changed our cats and has created an animal that generally likes the idea of having a warm couch (or lap) to curl up on. Still, if I were forced to answer the question "Are cats domesticated?" I would have to say, yes – as long as it pleases them!

Trivia...

In addition to being used as ratters, cats have also been kept as pets for thousands of years. In some cultures they were even worshiped and deified. The ancient Egyptians, for example, identified the cat with Bastet, the Egyptian goddess of fertility and maternity. Love and reverence for the cat was so strong among them that some felines were mummified and entombed with great ritual, just as many Egyptian aristocrats were.

Are domestic cats like wild cats?

THE HOUSEHOLD CAT WE KNOW and love has more in common with its wild relatives than you might think. Like the domestic cat, wild cats can be found in nearly every climate zone, except in Australia, the polar regions, and on the tundra. Also like the house kitty, they tend to sleep up to 18 hours each day and are often more active at night than during the day. Most wild cats are loners, choosing to live life by themselves, coming together only to mate or to engage in disputes over territory. Lions, who live in small packs led by a dominant male, are, of course, the exception, as are cheetahs, who sometimes hunt in small groups.

All in the family

Your affectionate house cat hasn't changed its habits much from its wild brethren over thousands of years. Both wild and domestic cats eat a mostly meat diet. The way house cats hunt is very similar to the methods that jaguars, leopards, bobcats, and ocelots use. Tact, stealth, superior sensory abilities, and incredible athleticism abound in both the wild cats and your own feline friend at home.

The household cat shares the same basic reflexes with its wild counterparts, though some wild cats tend to have better hearing. The serval, for instance, hears more acutely than other cats due to its larger outer ears and longer neck, which enables it to crane its head up above the tall savannah grasses.

Trivia...
The Asian tiger is the largest cousin of your house cat. At over 11 feet long and more than 600 pounds, this magnificent animal has had a reputation of being a man-eater, and with good reason. During the 18th and 19th centuries, hundreds of humans were killed and eaten by tigers in India, Burma, Singapore, and other Southeast Asian countries.

All cats, be they wild or domestic, belong to the same family of animals called felidae. All animals in this family have retractable (or semi-retractable) claws, eyes with slit irises, and whiskers.

THE WILD CATS

The small wild cats of the world include:

- African wild cat
- Black-footed cat
- Bobcat
- Canadian lynx
- Caracal
- European lynx
- European wild cat
- Fishing cat
- Flat-headed cat

- Geoffrey's cat
- Iriomote cat
- Jaguarundi
- Leopard cat
- Marbled cat
- Margay
- Ocelot
- Oncilla
- Pallas' cat

- Pampas cat
- Rusty-spotted cat
- Sand cat
- Serval
- Spanish lynx
- Temminck's cat

BOBCAT

The large wild cats of the world include:

- Cheetah
- Clouded leopard
- Cougar
- Jaguar
- Leopard
- Lion
- Snow leopard
- Tiger

■ **The male lion** *is truly king of the beasts. Although the female lions do most of the hunting, it is the male who will eat first after a kill.*

INTERNET

www.discovery.com

Log on to this web site and click on the "Animals & Pets" link for many informative and entertaining articles on nature's most interesting creatures, including the wild cats.

The differences

Size among the wild cats can vary tremendously, unlike the more petite domestic cat, whose size remains relatively constant in comparison. Some wild cats are about the same size as the domestic cat, though, including the African wildcat, the margay, the jaguarundi, and the sand cat.

In comparison to its wild cousins, the domestic cat's coat varies quite a bit, due largely to selective breeding for desirable coat traits. A Norwegian Forest Cat, for example, has a much longer coat than does a Siamese, even though they are the same species. All leopards, however, apart from some color variations, have the same basic coats.

Never ever obtain and keep as a pet any wild cat.

These undomesticated, dangerous animals hunt and kill by necessity and can seriously hurt or kill you or a loved one without warning. In addition to the danger to yourself, the future of all the wild feline species is jeopardized whenever someone foolishly attempts to take one from the wild and confine it to a home, yard, or enclosure. These animals were meant to live free from human control – period!

Trivia...

Unlike the lion, tiger, jaguar, and leopard, your house kitty cannot roar. Be very thankful for that. The big cats can roar because of the unique structure of their larynxes and skulls.

A simple summary

✔ Cats have become the world's favorite domestic pet, not only because they are easy to care for, but because their mystique and competence, as well as their capable, dignified personalities, enthrall us.

✔ The house cat maintains the ability to survive if placed in a less-than-domestic situation, thanks, in part, to a much less intense history of selective breeding by humanity than its canine cousins have endured.

✔ The domestic cat has adapted extremely well to nearly every climate and location in the world, enabling cats aficionados worldwide to enjoy and appreciate them.

✔ Our domestic cat resembles its wild feline relatives behaviorally, as well as physically. Although many wild cats are much larger than the domestic feline, many are about the same size.

Chapter 2

The Cat Defined

Now LET'S LOOK at the cat's long, colorful history, including how it has, over the course of time, fallen in and out of favor with human societies around the world. Few animals on earth can claim to have the physical attributes and the psychological profile of the domestic cat, who for centuries has amazed us with its athletic prowess, imperturbable mindset, and incomparable beauty. It is a perfect hunting machine, thanks to its well-designed body and its superb senses.

In this chapter...

✓ A simple feline history
✓ The love-hate relationship
✓ The cat's amazing body
✓ The feline senses
✓ Cat psychology
✓ One species, many breeds

A simple feline history

CATS HAVE BEEN around for a very long time – certainly longer than we have. About 50 million years ago there lived a mammal with a fairly long body and short legs named Miacis. The oldest ancestor of the cat yet found, it was similar in form to today's weasels and lived in the forest. Miacis had retractable claws, making tree-climbing an easy task. Over the millions of years, Miacis evolved into many other catlike creatures, including the saber-toothed tiger, perhaps the most famous cat of all.

■ **The saber-toothed cats** *had canine teeth that extended well below their lower jaws. They used them to stab at their prey.*

Not much has changed

The oldest fossils found of animals closely resembling today's domestic cat date back about 10 million years, predating the existence of modern humans and even dogs. Known as Dinictis, these fossils show that today's cat has changed very little from those ancient ones. This means that the cat achieved its nearly perfect design millions of years ago and has since needed few changes to succeed and prosper.

About one million years ago, cats divided into the three modern groups we know today: the large cats (including the lion and tiger), the small cats (such as the lynx and the African wildcat), and the cheetah, which is different enough from other cats to merit its own group. The large and small cats distributed themselves around the globe, from the frigid Canadian north to the jungles of India.

Trivia...

Saber-toothed cats had long, dagger-like canine teeth, enabling them to kill animals as large as a mastodon. Numerous forms of unique, specialized saber-toothed cats existed; some lithe and agile, others huge and bulky. One form of saber-toothed cat actually fed only on the blood of its victims, while another walked upright on the soles of its rear feet. The saber-toothed cats became extinct when the huge animals they preyed upon were forced into extinction by the great Ice Age. The ponderous cats could not move fast enough to prey upon the small animals that survived.

The love-hate relationship

TODAY'S DOMESTIC CAT *is thought to have evolved from the African and European wildcats, small felines living in temperate and semi-arid climates. Over 5,000 years ago, the Mesopotamian and Egyptian cultures in the Middle East began farming on a large scale, growing crops not only for immediate consumption, but for storage as surplus. These cultures were most likely the first to adopt the cat as a pet and helper, to keep down rodent populations that threatened to destroy grain crops being kept in large storehouses.*

Cat worship

Some cultures even worshiped the cat. The Vikings did, as well as the Thais, the Burmese, and the Japanese. None did so more than the Egyptians, however, who deified the cat. Anyone caught injuring a cat was severely punished, and when a cat died, the family mourned, often shaving off their eyebrows as part of the process.

Cat fear

Trading vessels eventually distributed the cat to all four corners of the earth, where it became both pet and rodent controller. However, some time in the Middle Ages, Europe's love affair with the cat came to a halt due to the influence of religious zealots who began to claim that a link existed between the cat and the devil. Paranoia over witchcraft and devil worship, the role of the cat in pagan religions, and a profound reliance on superstition caused church officials to condemn the poor cat, resulting in burnings, sacrifices, and abominable mass killings of cats.

Trivia...

Native South Americans were first introduced to the domestic cat by Spanish explorers during the 16th century. The Aztecs affectionately referred to the cat as Mizton, or "Little Lion," because of its close resemblance to the indigenous mountain lion.

There was a price to pay, though. The Plague swept across Europe and parts of Asia in the 14th century, caused by a contagion carried by the fleas infesting rats. This disease killed millions. Faced with such a catastrophe, church officials and commoners alike quickly sang a different tune about the cat – the only effective vermin killer around. By the 17th century, the domestic cat was once again welcome all over the world.

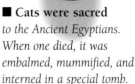

■ **Cats were sacred** *to the Ancient Egyptians. When one died, it was embalmed, mummified, and interned in a special tomb.*

The cat's amazing body

THE CAT IS ONE *of nature's greatest success stories. Apart from its fascinating personality, what makes it so successful is its unique, high-tech body. Its flexible musculature and skeleton enable it to perform incredible physical feats. Few animals are capable of moving like the cat, who can leap incredible distances or heights, silently stalk a hapless mouse, effortlessly climb a tree, or land on its feet no matter what the height of the fall. Let's take a closer look at the feline body, so that you can better understand just why the cat is so special and why it behaves the way it does.*

A FINE BALANCE

The feline circulatory system

The cat's circulatory system moves blood throughout its body to nourish all its cells and remove waste from the system. The cat's four-chambered heart beats about 120 to 130 times a minute, pumping blood through arteries and capillaries to distribute nutrients and oxygen to all parts of the body. Then the blood is returned to the heart and lungs by a system of veins, to be replenished with more life-giving nutrients and oxygen.

THE CIRCULATORY SYSTEM

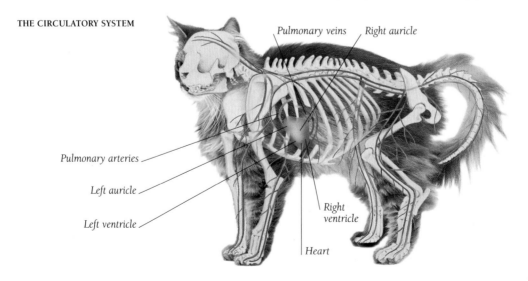

Pulmonary veins

Right auricle

Pulmonary arteries

Left auricle

Left ventricle

Right ventricle

Heart

The feline digestive system

Like all living things, your cat needs to eat to survive. Nutrients from its food supply the cat with energy and enable it to grow and to repair injured tissues. To extract those nutrients from the food, however, the cat (or any animal, for that matter) must ingest the food and let the digestive tract do its job. Essentially a tubular food-processing plant running from the cat's mouth to its anus, the digestive tract ingests and breaks down food into essential nutrients that can be absorbed by the cat's body. The entire digestive tract consists of the mouth, pharynx, esophagus, stomach, small and large intestines, and anus.

THE DIGESTIVE SYSTEM

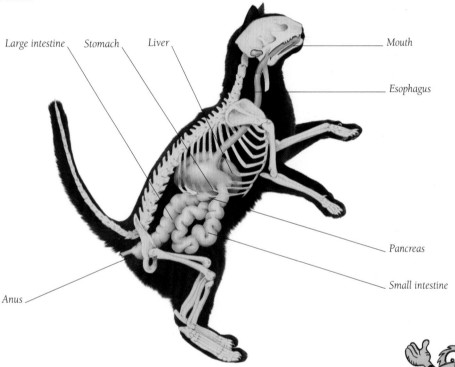

Large intestine   Stomach   Liver   Mouth

Esophagus

Pancreas

Small intestine

Anus

Working in conjunction with the digestive organs are the digestive glands, whose secretions help break down and process food. These include the salivary glands, liver, gallbladder, and pancreas.

Because cats are carnivores, their digestive tracts are designed to efficiently process meat into energy. The cat's specialized, highly acidic digestive juices break down meat fairly quickly, so its digestive tract is proportionally shorter than our own.

INTERNET

www.lookd.com/cats/ anatomy.html

Log on to this web site for great information on the anatomy of the domestic cat.

The feline respiratory system

The lungs, bronchial passages, and diaphragm make up the respiratory system. The function of this vital system is to provide oxygen to the cat's body and remove carbon dioxide, a waste product of respiration. The respiratory system also helps the cat stay cool by enabling it to breathe faster, or pant, and also aids the cat's sense of smell. A normal rate of respiration for a cat is about 20 to 25 breaths per minute.

THE RESPIRATORY SYSTEM

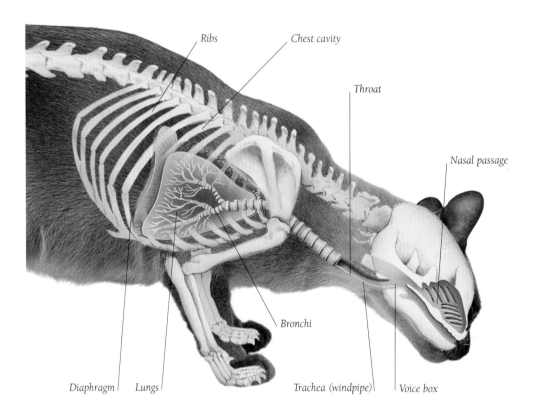

Ribs

Chest cavity

Throat

Nasal passage

Bronchi

Diaphragm | Lungs |

Trachea (windpipe) | Voice box

The feline nervous system

The cat's nervous system is a marvelous apparatus, allowing the feline to react almost instantaneously to external stimuli, such as a mouse, or to commands from the cat's brain. The nervous system controls the cat's body, gathers information about the environment, processes that information, and decides what to do next. The brain and spinal cord are the master controls for the nervous system; they take in data from the senses then send out commands to the muscles and other systems in the body via nerves that run through the entire animal.

The autonomic nervous system controls involuntary actions such as breathing and heartbeat, while the somatic nervous system takes care of all voluntary functions.

THE NERVOUS SYSTEM

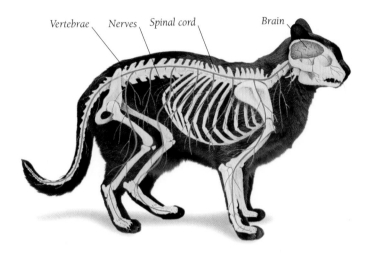

Vertebrae   Nerves   Spinal cord   Brain

The feline musculoskeletal system

All **vertebrates** have a skeleton, and the cat is no different. The skeleton serves as a framework for the body, a support for the muscles and skin, and a protector for the brain and internal organs. With about 244 bones (the number varies according to the length of the tail), the cat has 38 more than us. The cat's skeleton gives it great flexibility. With 30 vertebrae in its spine (five more than us), your favorite feline can exhibit an amazing range of movement. Interestingly, the cat has no real collarbone – a bone that, in humans, tends to limit shoulder movement. Its shoulder blades are positioned close in to its chest as well, so the cat can slip into skinny spaces.

The cat's musculature enables it to move about in its environment, breathe, eat, and circulate blood. The muscles are attached to the bones by ligaments and tendons; when a particular muscle contracts, the bone or bones it is attached to moves. When properly choreographed, this action enables the cat to move about in nearly any direction. The muscles themselves consist of minute, parallel fibers that function whenever a nerve impulse is sent from the brain.

> **DEFINITION**
>
> *Any animal with a backbone is a **vertebrate**. Invertebrates, such as insects and octopi, have no backbone. Insects make do with a hard outer casing called an exoskeleton, while the octopus has no hard structural support at all.*

The feline reproductive system

The male's reproductive organs consist of the testes (the sperm-producing structure) and the penis. The female reproductive system is comprised of the ovaries (the egg-producing structures), the fallopian tubes, the uterus, the cervix, the vagina, the clitoris, and the vulva, as well as the mammary glands.

The female cat experiences a cyclical reproductive interval called the estrous cycle, during a part of which she can become pregnant. Female cats are *induced ovulators*, meaning that the female readies an egg upon mating with the male. An egg is released by the ovaries, whereupon it travels through a fallopian tube and down to the uterus, by which time it has already been fertilized by the male's sperm. It then embeds in the wall of the uterus and develops. Unlike other mammals, the female cat can remain in heat almost continuously, as long as males are around. This remarkable fact explains why an unspayed female can produce such a large number of kittens during her life.

DEFINITION

An **induced ovulator** *like the cat releases an egg in response to the act of copulation.*

THE REPRODUCTIVE ORGANS

Trivia...
A single cat and her offspring can produce 420,000 kittens in just 7 years! That's a very good reason to spay or neuter your cat.

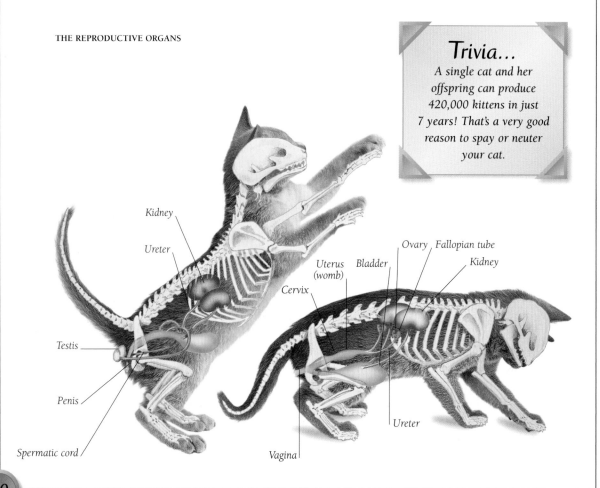

Kidney

Ureter

Uterus (womb)

Bladder

Cervix

Ovary   Fallopian tube

Kidney

Testis

Penis

Ureter

Spermatic cord

Vagina

The estrous cycle

The female cat's estrous cycle is the cyclical reproductive period. It consists of four main stages:

1 Proestrus. The beginning of heat, during which the female's behavior begins to encourage mating.

2 Estrus. Actual heat, during which ovulation occurs.

3 Metestrus. A period of normal behavior that follows estrus if no breeding has occurred. This can last two to three weeks, after which the cat can again enter the proestrus phase.

4 Anestrus. A period of inactivity that follows metestrus after several cycles. This is when the cat goes out of heat.

The feline senses

THE FIVE BASIC SENSES are vision, hearing, smell, taste, and touch, and here is where the cat shines. The cat's sensory system is responsible for gathering information about the cat's world and then delivering it to the brain for analysis. Its sharp hearing and sense of smell enable it to locate the most elusive prey animal. It is the cat's powers of vision, however, that are perhaps its most amazing tool, enabling it to see in just the tiniest amount of light.

The cat's sight

The cat's amazing eyes take moment-to-moment pictures of the world around it. The feline eye is perhaps the most important of the cat's sensory equipment. In daylight, the cat's pupils close to narrow slits to limit the amount of light entering the eye. In dim light, the muscles of the iris relax to open the pupil wide, allowing all available light to

■ **In darkness** *the cat's pupils dilate. This enables the cat to make efficient use of any available light, which is why a cat has superb night vision.*

stream in. Being basically nocturnal, the cat has superb night vision, due largely to a reflective coating behind the cat's retina called the *tapetum*.

Cats do not see color the way we do, but can distinguish between reds and blues to some degree. They do not see individual objects directly in front of them very clearly, but can spot movement much more effectively – a handy tool for a predator. They tend to also be somewhat far-sighted, and, like us, have stereoscopic vision, the result of having two eyes arranged in the same plane. Stereoscopic vision enables the cat (and us) to better judge depth and distance.

The cat's hearing

The cat's hearing is also a very important ingredient in its sensory make-up. Its ears can pick up sounds too high for us to hear, sounds that small creatures such as mice or birds might make. The *pinna* can be rotated in an arc of 180 degrees to help pinpoint the direction of a sound.

In addition to gathering sounds, the cat's ears help keep it balanced and properly oriented in its environment, usually a much more three-dimensional world than ours. Three semicircular canals inside the ear are arranged at right angles to one another, enabling the cat's brain to determine precisely any change in direction or speed. This helps the cat right itself in midair and always land on its feet. In addition to the semicircular canals, the inner ear of the cat has millions of tiny motion-detecting hairs called *cilia* that, when affected by a change in the cat's direction, signal the brain to report the change.

> **DEFINITION**
>
> A mirror-like apparatus located behind the retina, the **tapetum** consists of various proteins and zinc. Its job is to reflect back onto the retina as much available light as possible, including light that wasn't absorbed by the retina the first time around. Although the cat cannot see in total darkness, the tapetum enables cats to see in light levels that are so low they would seem to us to be completely dark. The tapetum is what makes cat's eyes glow when you shine a light on them or when you take a flash photograph.

> **DEFINITION**
>
> The **pinna** is the external part of the cat's ear – the triangle that sticks up. The two pinnas can rotate independently of one another. The semicircular canals are fluid-filled chambers inside the cat's ears that help it precisely determine its motion. **Cilia**, microscopic hairs that line the cat's inner ear chambers, also help the cat determine its exact position in space.

■ **A cat can hear** *high-frequency sounds up to two octaves higher than a human, and can distinguish noises made by small prey animals such as mice and birds. It can also turn its ears quickly and precisely to locate sound.*

The cat's smell

The cat's sense of smell is working almost immediately after birth (compare this to its vision, which takes at least 5 to 6 days to engage). Special receptor cells lining the nasal cavity gather and analyze molecules of air in an attempt to locate possible prey or something potentially dangerous, like a dog or another predatory animal. Though not as acute as a dog's nose, the cat's sense of smell is much sharper than our own.

DEFINITION

*The **papillae** are hook-shaped protuberances covering the cat's tongue, used by wild cats to strip meat from a bone. The papillae also help the domestic cat groom itself, by pulling loose hair out of the coat. You can feel the raspy papillae on your own cat's tongue whenever it licks you.*

The cat's taste

The cat's sense of taste is also important to its survival because it enables the cat to determine between palatable and poisonous foods. The cat's tongue is covered with hook-like structures called *papillae*, on which the taste buds are located. Cats can detect bitter, acidic, and salty tastes but not sweet – a taste that carnivores have little need for.

Trivia...

In addition to regular scenting, the cat's nose has a special structure called the Jacobson's organ, located just above the hard palate. Also called the vomeronasal organ, it's a small, cylindrical organ that analyzes the molecules that make up smells. When a cat sniffs and seems to be grimacing, it's actually flehmening – panting rapidly to move scent molecules up to the Jacobson's organ.

The cat's touch

Last but not least is the cat's sense of touch, which helps give it additional information about all that it comes in contact with. Touch receptors cover a cat's skin, particularly its pads, mouth, and whiskers. You have probably seen a cat probing an object with a paw; this is its way of examining something, just in the same way that you or I would. Cats rely on the information from their paws more than do dogs, who tend to examine most objects with their mouths only.

The cat's whiskers, located on the muzzle, eyebrows, and elbows, are attached to bundles of sensitive nerves hooked up to its nervous system. The cat uses them to detect movement of prey and to examine its environment in the dark. The whiskers also can detect minute changes in the air currents, a technique that helps the cat maneuver in darkness by sensing tiny changes in air flow near objects such as trees, walls, or furniture.

■ **The cat is a very sensual animal.** *Its skin is rich in nerve endings. This enables the cat to gather a great deal of information about any animal or object that it touches.*

Cat psychology

WHEN IT COMES to the psychology of the domestic cat, the discussion is never-ending, simply because the cat refuses to be neatly categorized. The cat's mind basically remains a mystery to us humans, due in part to its isolated, independent bent. That doesn't stop us from trying to nail down some basic truths about the cat's psyche, however.

THE INSCRUTABLE SIAMESE

Ego rules

First and foremost, the cat is an independent soul who does things its own way and always for somewhat egotistical reasons. Several things can explain this. First, from the very beginning of the species, cats have been loners. Second, cats have never been forced by humans to take on behaviors that are contrary to their basic instincts; we've demanded that dogs stop hunting sheep and start herding them, but we've never asked a cat to herd a mouse. All we have asked domestic cats to do is kill vermin, an altogether natural behavior.

Because of this, the cat's natural psychology remains largely untouched. By not being forced into unusual behaviors or social situations, the cat stayed, well, a cat.

A memory like an elephant

The cat is extremely adaptable, always a plus for a predator. It also has a wonderful memory, a characteristic that can help or hurt the cat-owner relationship. If, for example, you show a cat kindness upon first meeting, it will generally think well of you in future meetings. If, however, you accidentally step on a cat's tail, it will carry that memory for a long time. Though repairable, the trust of this unfortunate cat will take a while to regain.

Never force a cat to do anything it does not want to do, as this will almost certainly upset it and cause it to distrust you, possibly for a very long time.

What can cats learn?

The cat's mind is not as predictable as that of the dog's. It may choose to sleep in one spot for a year, then abruptly change its favorite spot, with no rhyme or reason. It may prefer a certain brand of food for years, then suddenly refuse to eat it, with no explanation. It is consistent with its love for immediate family, however, and with basic behaviors such as litter box use (thankfully) and predatory yearnings.

Remember, a cat will only do something if it decides there is some advantage in doing so. In other words, the cat won't learn anything it doesn't want to learn. That means there has to be some advantage to adopting a new behavior, in the cat's mind. *Sit just because you asked me to? Fat chance. For a mouthful of delicious food? We'll see.*

Curiosity and the cat

Cats are insatiably curious about their environments. Anything out of the ordinary will certainly be investigated, be it a fast-moving toy, a parakeet, or an interesting scent. This quality is common among predators, whose keen investigative minds must always be intimately engaged with their surroundings if they are to survive. No cat worth its salt will want to investigate something that poses a potential threat, however, such as a Saint Bernard or a speeding Mack truck. Do you blame it?

This is my territory

The cat tends to be very territorial and will defend its territory from those it considers invaders. For example, a typical house cat, no matter how amiable with its family, will not take too kindly to a new cat or dog. New animals need to be introduced slowly to the resident cat if any kind of amicable relationship is to form. The cat will usually react to the newcomer with hissing, biting, scratching, or at the very least, righteous indignation. The reason for this is simple: In the wild, cats vigorously defend their territories from other cats in order to maintain access to a sufficient number of prey animals and mates.

■ **Hissing and spitting** *may greet any newcomer to the household. This show of aggression is designed to defend your cat's territorial rights against any usurpers.*

As domestic cats have, for the most part, held onto most of their natural instincts, the same rules will apply in your home as in the wild. Your resident cat probably won't be all that rude to human visitors; though it might choose to ignore them for a while until they, too, become familiar.

How to look fierce

If a cat feels threatened in any way, the hair on its body stands on end and its back arches tightly. The reason for these instinctive reactions is simple: They make the cat look much larger than it really is. This can often cause the threatening object (a dog or another cat) to rethink its approach. In other words, the larger an animal is, the less likely another animal will be to attack it.

■ **Arched back,** *bristling fur, and swishing tail – this young cat is pretending to be much braver and larger than she really is.*

Show your love

Longhaired cats (such as the Persian) tend to be less active and outgoing than shorthaired cats (such as the Siamese), who are often more active and usually a bit quicker to accept a stranger. Of course, these are generalizations, and there are plenty of exceptions.

In my experience, a female cat will often be more up-front with its affections than a male cat will. A male will generally be a bit more independent and bold and may take much longer to warm up to strangers.

■ **The female cat** *will generally show more affection than a male. They also tend to be less independent and more cautious by nature.*

One species, many breeds

MOST CAT OWNERS own mixed-breed cats. Some,
however prefer pedigreed cats. There are currently more than
40 recognized cat breeds, and each has very distinctive
physical and behavioral traits that set it apart. Some have
long hair and large, powerful bodies, while others have
shorter coats and thinner bodies.

Breed behavior

Behaviorally, each breed has its own distinct temperament, just as
dogs do, although the range of looks and temperaments is quite a
bit narrower than it is for the many dog breeds.

For example, the Abyssinian is an active, intelligent, graceful cat with a curious nature.
This shorthaired, athletic cat is hardly ever content to rest all day and prefers regular
interaction with its owner or another resident cat. It is just as likely to be found atop
your refrigerator or kitchen cupboard as anywhere else.

In contrast, the Persian is a docile, affectionate, somewhat reserved
cat, and tends toward the quiet side. Unobtrusive to a fault, this
breed does not need regular companionship and can easily amuse
itself during the day. Though sweet and loving to its owner, the
Persian can be somewhat aloof toward strangers and may not
deal well with lots of commotion or a group of active children.

■ **The passive Persian:** *On the
whole, the Persian personality is
docile and somewhat introvert.*

CAT BREEDS

The Cat Fanciers' Association (CFA), the largest breed registry in North America, currently recognizes 40 cat breeds. They are:

- Abyssinian
- American Bobtail
- American Curl
- American Shorthair
- American Wirehair
- Birman
- Bombay
- British Shorthair
- Burmese
- Chartreux
- Colorpoint Shorthair
- Cornish Rex
- Devon Rex
- Egyptian Mau
- Exotic
- Havana Brown
- Himalayan
- Japanese Bobtail
- Javanese
- Korat
- LaPerm
- Maine Coon Cat
- Manx
- Norwegian Forest Cat
- Ocicat
- Oriental
- Persian
- Ragdoll
- Russian Blue
- Scottish Fold
- Selkirk Rex
- Siamese
- Siberian
- Singapura
- Somali
- Sphynx
- Tonkinese
- Turkish Angora
- Turkish Van

INTERNET

www.cfainc.org

The Cat Fanciers' Association (CFA), found at the web address above, is not the only breed registry for cats, though, and the 40 breeds it recognizes are not the only cat breeds. You can also check out the American Cat Fanciers Association at www.acfacat.com and The International Cat Association at www.tica.org.volupat.

■ **Affectionate and intelligent,** *the elegant Abyssinian is one of the oldest breeds of domestic cats.*

A nice mix

Mixed-breed cats are a whole lot cheaper than pedigreed cats. A quality pedigreed cat can cost anywhere from $250 to well over $1,000 (depending on the breed and the quality of the cat), while a healthy mixed-breed kitten or cat adopted from a shelter will cost you little or no money. An added benefit of adopting one of these adorable pets is the satisfaction you will feel about saving the animal's life and giving it a loving home.

Although pedigreed cats are incredibly beautiful animals, mixed-breed cats are arguably just as beautiful, and at least as intelligent and affectionate.

A simple summary

✔ The rich, interesting evolutionary history and folklore of the domestic cat is the story of an incredibly adaptable animal finding its niche in an ever-changing world.

✔ The cat's ability to perform feats of incredible athleticism are due mainly to its fascinating body, designed for speed, stealth, and acrobatic feats.

✔ The behavioral profile of the domestic cat is largely one of an adaptable, independent, curious animal capable of a broad range of emotions and actions. Its behavior is driven primarily by enlightened self-interest; cats will only do what they think is immediately beneficial to them.

✔ Although the domestic cat is one species, there are many breeds within this species. Though not nearly as physically or behaviorally diverse as the many different dog breeds, the various different cat breeds do show quite a bit of physical and behavioral variation.

✔ Mixed-breed cats have their own charm. Don't overlook them.

Chapter 3

Today's Perfect Pet

MORE AND MORE, people are turning to cats as their pet of choice the world over. Besides being so darned charming, cats are relatively easy to care for, highly intelligent, and extremely adaptable to nearly any home environment. Plus, they won't eat you out of house and home like a certain other four-legged mammal that shall remain nameless (at least for now). Why has the cat become so popular? The growth of cities and our increasingly fast-paced lives come into play, as does the cat's more independent nature. Why a cat, and not a dog, rabbit, bird, or turtle? Read on.

In this chapter...
- ✔ Moving to the city
- ✔ City cats
- ✔ Kitty costs
- ✔ Training issues

CATS ARE EQUALLY AT HOME IN THE RURAL OR URBAN ENVIRONMENT

Moving to the city

OVER THE LAST 50 YEARS *the world's human population has grown enormously, both in developed and developing countries. Most of these billions of extra people live in large cities or their suburbs. The shift from an agricultural to an industrial economy has been the primary force behind this great migration – cities are where the work is. As much as we might regret leaving the more pastoral farm life behind, big-city living is, for the time being, here to stay.*

Shrinking space

INTERNET

www.fanciers.com

Check out the Cat Fanciers web site for all sorts of great cat info, including general info, breed descriptions, cat care advice, and articles on veterinary developments.

Unfortunately, most city dwellers don't live in large homes or even have backyards. Instead, they make do with small apartments, condos, or cooperatives, with little or no land attached. Even suburban dwellers rarely have as much land or home space as their rural ancestors did, and usually make do with a small home on, at most, a half-acre of land.

Just because we have moved to more densely populated areas doesn't mean we have lost our desire for pets. If anything, the fast-paced city life can make us feel even more isolated and lonely. Having a sweet, affectionate pet waiting for you at home can help ease all that.

Still, the reduction in available living space has affected our choice of pets. On the farm, pet lovers could have a couple of dogs, a horse or two, a few barn cats, rabbits, and lots more. The dogs and cats spent much of their time outdoors, made possible by the lack of close neighbors and the absence of dangerous traffic.

City dogs

Moving to more densely populated areas changed things. Cramped up in a small home or apartment, the dog must rely on its owner to take it out regularly. That owner, however, is an office or factory worker who must be away from home for upwards of 9 to 10 hours each day. Not many dogs (or humans, for that matter) can wait that long for a chance to go to the toilet and stretch their legs. In addition, dogs, being intensely social creatures, do not fare well being left alone for long periods. Some dogs will develop behavior problems from the stress, often resulting in destruction to personal property, housetraining woes, or even aggression. If given a choice, I am sure the dog would prefer to roll back the clock a few hundred years.

City cats

WHAT ABOUT THE CAT? *How has he (or she) dealt with the move to more densely populated areas? Certainly better than the dog, thank you very much. Remember, cats are extremely adaptable creatures who take care of themselves quite well and who can get their exercise in much smaller spaces than a dog. Let's take a closer look at the reasons why cats tend to do better in urban or suburban settings and have, therefore, become more popular pets than dogs.*

Time

Let's face it; life is much faster than it used to be. It seems as if we are always rushing, trying to do more than is physically possible. Between work, kids, and all the other responsibilities we foist upon ourselves, we hardly have time to sit back at home and relax, let alone care for a pet.

Most cats can do just fine left alone for 10 hours each day while you slave away at the office. Cats amuse themselves and sleep away much of the day anyway. You don't have to walk a cat or take it out to relieve itself several times a day. A cat will not become stressed at spending the day alone, making destructive behavior much less likely.

Although cats are better at being alone for long periods than are dogs, you should still not abandon your cat for extremely long stretches, because it will feel stress over your disappearance.

■ **Your cat will spend** *much of its life sleeping. Cats sleep, on average, 16 hours a day, though usually only for a few minutes at a time, hence the term catnapping.*

Trivia...

The Ernest Hemingway Home and Museum in Key West, Florida, is home to approximately 60 cats, all tended to by the staff. Normal cats have 5 front toes and 4 back toes, but about half of the cats at the museum are polydactyl, which means they have an extra toe on each front paw. Back in the 1930s, Ernest Hemingway was given a 6-toed cat by a ship's captain; some of the cats who now live on the museum grounds are descendants of that sea-faring cat.

If you plan on going on vacation, do not simply leave out a ton of food and water and an extra litter box and expect your cat to be fine. Instead, have a friend or neighbor come over once each day to check on the pet, clean out the litter box, and refresh the food and water. He or she should also interact with the cat, because cats do need attention every day.

Space

Most of us live in smaller homes than our ancestors, and the cat just adapts to this better than the dog. So urbanization, which puts a greater premium on living space, makes cat ownership a whole lot easier.

A cat needs far less room than a dog to feel happy. This is mainly because the average cat is much smaller than the average dog. A 50-pound retriever will probably go stir-crazy in a one-bedroom apartment, while a cat will be perfectly happy in the same space. But even small dogs need to get out and stretch their legs regularly; it's just part of their heritage to want to get out and run and play. Most cats will simply survey the space they are in and happily adopt it as their own. Even two cats can exist nicely in a small apartment. Try that with two big dogs and you will most likely come home to a scary mess each day.

■ **While a cat or two** *will happily adapt to your small apartment, you will need to think carefully before bringing a dog into such a small space.*

Easy care

Most of us have less leisure time than in the past. We spend long hours at work, attend classes, play sports, tend to our families, and sometimes even work a second job to make ends meet. The last thing we need in our busy lives is a pet who requires a large investment of our time each day. Smaller pets such as a turtle, rabbit, rat, or hamster can be fun at times, but they aren't nearly as intelligent, entertaining, or versatile as a cat. Birds can also be a lot of fun, but you just can't relate to a bird in quite the same way as you can to a four-legged critter. Plus, they can be loud and unfriendly – and you can't housetrain a bird.

Some animals are more intelligent than most people give them credit for. Parrots and crows, for instance, can both learn to speak and perform complex tasks. Cats are still much more intelligent, however, and can learn to perform tasks that few other pets could dream of performing.

A cat almost takes care of itself. It grooms itself each day, comes housetrained, and needs little supervision. It will usually get into far less trouble than a dog and doesn't need to be walked. What more could a busy person ask for? Of course, a cat probably won't bark if an intruder breaks in. We can't all be perfect!

One last point about ease of care: A cat happens to be much quieter than a dog (with the possible exception of a Siamese cat). This important fact makes the cat a much better choice for people living in apartments or in densely populated areas. Nothing will annoy your neighbors or landlord as much as a yapping, barking hound. No one will get any sleep, and you could get evicted. The most you might get out of a typical house cat is a happy meow or a throaty, affectionate purr.

■ **Using saliva as a face wash,** *this cat is performing part of its daily grooming routine. Your cat will clean itself from top to toe every day, keeping its fur in pristine condition.*

Kitty costs

THE ASPCA ESTIMATES *that it costs about $360 a year to keep a cat, including routine health care. Of course, if your cat has a health emergency or if you travel a lot and need to pay for cat care often, you'll spend more. But, in general, a cat is not an extremely expensive pet.*

Cats and dogs

Compare a cat to a dog and what do you have? Dogs eat more because they're bigger. They need collars and leashes and chew toys and an endless supply of tennis balls. Cats need some equipment, too, but not nearly as much. And they don't chew up their toys the way dogs do.

A big dog can do a lot more damage to a home than any cat – or any five cats for that matter. In addition, dog ownership often means taking one or more obedience classes in order to keep Fido from doing naughty things. Some nasty canines could even bite another person: Do you know what lawyers cost these days? When was the last time you read about a cat putting someone into the hospital?

Cats and other pets

Owning other types of pets can certainly cost less than a owning a cat. A rabbit, bird, rodent, turtle, or hamster will eat far less than a cat. But will they be as entertaining, seductive, and mysterious? An aquarium filled with fish will cost a pretty penny, not only for all that equipment, but also for the fish themselves, which can get very pricey. Money is no object for you? Then consider this: Fish are, well, just fish. We eat fish. We stare at them through glass. They can't purr or snuggle. Fish are low on the companionship scale, wouldn't you say?

■ **Rabbits and rodents make** *good small pets but are seldom as rewarding as a cat.*

Training issues

AS I'VE ALREADY MENTIONED, *you've got to train a dog. An untrained, pushy, chaotic dog will be impossible to live with; it will destroy your home, eliminate anywhere it wants, growl or snap at those it considers below it in the pack order, and generally make your life miserable. Doing the training yourself can often take a long time and cost a pretty penny in book or video purchases. Taking the pooch to a professional trainer will cost you even more. In addition, the training needs to be kept up for the rest of the dog's life.*

Quick cat training

A cat needs very little, if any, training. Toilet trained right out of the box, a cat will only need you to point it in the right direction. Obedience training? Hardly. The cat's normal behavior patterns usually fit nicely into your lifestyle. You'll have to

■ **Unlike dogs,** *the natural behaviors of cats need little or no alterations.*

teach your cat that certain places are off limits, but you can do that by putting down some double-sided sticky tape around the forbidden areas or by using a squirt from a water pistol. So, you don't have to teach your cat what to do, you just have to teach it what not to do.

Never attempt to train a cat in the same manner you would a dog.

A dog will want to please you simply out of loyalty to the pack leader (you). The canine pack leader has a natural right and responsibility to discipline subordinates, if necessary; that's why you can use a leash correction or a commanding, authoritative tone of voice with a dog and not alienate it. Any type of negative reinforcement used on a cat, however, will only cause it to fear and mistrust you. Cats do not learn in the same way as dogs, so don't use the same techniques. You can only get a cat to do something if it sees some advantage to doing so.

A simple summary

✔ Our move from rural to urban and suburban living has helped make the cat the pet of choice.

✔ The cat wins hands down over the dog when it comes to ease of care and ability to adapt to crowded living conditions. Owners with little time or space find the cat to be a much easier pet to take care of than the dog.

✔ Although cats do love and need your attention and affection, they tend to be much less emotionally needy than dogs, whose pack mind-set pre-programs them to need their owners' attentions more frequently.

✔ Cats, on average, tend to cost less to purchase and maintain than other pets, particularly dogs. Cats also tend to do less damage to the home and have fewer trips to the veterinarian. Although smaller pets may be less expensive to own, none of them can come close to the cat's level of intelligence or potential for fun and companionship.

✔ Cats require very little training compared to dogs, making owning one less time-consuming. Basic behavioral requirements such as housetraining and obedience training are normally not an issue for the cat.

Chapter 4

Which Cat Is Right for Me?

NOW THAT YOU HAVE definitely decided to get a pet and know that a cat is the right choice for you, it is time to narrow down the search. Which cat will it be, and where will you find your special cat?

The next few pages will help you decide what type of cat to buy or adopt, where to find it, and how to determine if it is healthy and well adjusted. The information here will get you started with the right cat and help guarantee that few, if any, problems will pop up to interrupt the thrill of being a first-time cat owner.

In this chapter...
✓ Pedigreed or mixed?
✓ Kitten or cat?
✓ Where to find your cat
✓ Choosing one cat from many

ADOPTING A CAT FROM AN ANIMAL SHELTER CAN BE A REWARDING EXPERIENCE

Pedigreed or mixed?

ONE OF THE FIRST DECISIONS *you must make is whether to get a pedigreed (or purebred) cat from a reputable breeder or organization, or a mixed-breed cat from a shelter, private seller, or some other source. For most cat owners, the choice is easy; the vast majority of us have a mixed-breed cat that we got from a shelter or a private person who happened to have some kittens. Is this the best choice for you?*

Pedigreed pussy pluses

Let's talk about pedigreed cats first. As I mentioned in Chapter 2, a pedigreed cat is a domestic cat whose lineage (or pedigree) includes only purebred ancestors and whose breed is accepted for competition by one of the several cat associations. Cats of each individual breed have predictable appearance and **temperament**, although each cat still has its own unique personality. The appearance of a particular breed may appeal to your aesthetic sense; you can buy a cat whose looks you like. And most cats within a breed have very similar temperaments, so buying a pedigreed cat generally removes much of the guesswork about how it will behave. For example, if you choose a Siamese, be prepared for an active, gregarious cat with a loud voice. Choosing a Persian, however, means owning a reserved, docile cat with a quiet voice. This does not mean that all Persians or Siamese are alike behaviorally, but just that they tend to behave more like cats of their own breed than like cats from another breed.

Take a look through a cat breed book and you will see how varied and beautiful the breeds are. This variety and predictability appeals to many cat lovers. Size, coat color and length, and temperament can, to a great degree, be predetermined. What you see is what you get.

■ **The mixed-breed cat** *can be every bit as appealing and lovable as its more illustrious pedigreed cousin.*

DEFINITION

How a cat behaves in a general sense is referred to as its **temperament**. *Cats with different temperaments interact with people or other pets in different ways; some are shy and placid, while others are gregarious and very active. A cat with an undesirable temperament might be extremely fearful of strangers or be very combative with other cats. A cat with a good temperament will be friendly, relaxed around strangers, and not overly fearful.*

■ **Even-tempered and calm,** *the ornamental Persian longhair can usually be guaranteed to make a placid and loving companion.*

Obtaining a pedigreed cat usually means buying one from an established breeder (although some are available in shelters). When you buy from a breeder, many concerns are automatically taken care of; a responsible breeder will usually provide clients with a health guarantee and will have already begun a cat's necessary vaccinations. Responsible breeders also care very deeply about their breed and make sure each cat they sell is a good representative of the breed.

Buying from a breeder also increases the odds that the cat was raised in the best environment possible, with good mothering in a clean, sociable atmosphere. Breeders often allow their kittens access to their homes; this helps acclimate them to people and household settings well before they are sold.

Pedigreed pussy minuses

The biggest disadvantage to choosing a pedigreed cat has to be cost, which can vary from a few hundred to well over a thousand dollars, depending on the breed and the quality of the pet. Most cat owners do not expect to pay that kind of money for a cat, no matter how cute or elegant. Availability is often another issue; often a specific breed of cat is not available locally, which means you either have to wait for months until one does become available or buy one from a breeder located far away. When you buy long-distance, you often only get to see photos of the cat and must deal with shipping – always a traumatic experience for a kitten or adult cat.

Which breed?

If you decide on a pedigreed puss, your next step is to choose the breed you want. The first thing to do, then, is to learn as much as possible about the 40 or so cat breeds. You can do so by reading as many cat magazines as possible, which often publish in-depth breed profiles. Also, consider buying a book that focuses on the differences between the cat breeds.

Once you narrow down your list of breeds to just one or two (which could take a while), your job will be to locate a few reputable breeders, hopefully close enough to your home to drive to. More on that in a moment.

INTERNET

www.fanciers.com

Try the Cat Fanciers web site for useful lists of breeders for every cat breed, both in North America and the rest of the world.

INTERNET

www.breedlist.com

You can learn about the personality profiles of the different cat breeds by logging onto the Fanciers Breeder Referral List web site, which gives comprehensive info on each cat breed.

Mixed-breed kitties

So how about a mixed-breed kitten or cat? There are certainly more than enough of them to go around, because so many unneutered cats have unrestricted access to the outdoors. Choosing to buy or adopt one will probably save a life and will help ease the glut of unwanted cats sentenced to a short, unappreciated life. Mixed-breed kittens and cats are a real bargain, too, costing little or nothing, depending on where you go. Shelters usually ask you to pay for neutering and vaccinations, while private parties found in the newspaper are usually happy to give kittens and cats away.

The disadvantages to choosing a mixed-breed cat are few. Of course, you probably will not know the cat's history and environmental background. If its parents had physiological and/or behavioral problems that can be passed on to their kittens, you may not know that either. You also will not be able to predict what a mixed-breed kitten will look like when it matures or what its temperament will be – again because little or nothing will be known of the parents' hereditary profiles. Additionally, a mixed-breed cat or kitten might have had one or more traumatic experiences before becoming available, which can seriously affect its personality. For instance, if a kitten was mistreated when it was only weeks old or taken from its mother and littermates at too young an age, troublesome personality problems can arise. With most pedigreed cats and kittens, these traumatic events are normally not an issue.

Most shelters know at least something about the cats and kittens they have. They've watched their behavior and can advise you about any quirks your pet might have.

Kitten or cat?

MOST OF YOU WILL WANT A KITTEN, for obvious reasons. A kitten is incredibly cute. You get to see it grow up and have the opportunity to help shape its temperament. Who can resist an adorable, sweet little kitten? Choosing a kitten also enables you to start it off on the right health track. Your veterinarian will get to access its health from an early age and help the kitten steer clear of any nasty diseases and conditions.

Adults have their charms

Don't ignore the charms of a juvenile or adult cat. Cats over the age of 6 months are always available at shelters. Even pedigreed cats can often become available, either from breeders looking to sell off unneeded breeding stock or from owners who can no longer take care of their pets. Many older cats are mixed-breed pets who were abandoned or given up or strays brought into a shelter.

Choosing an older cat can have its advantages. Being fully grown (or close to it), there will be no surprises regarding appearance and size. Also, the cat's temperament is, by and large, already formed, so you know what you are getting right from the start. Plus, you have the opportunity to save the life of a sweet cat who otherwise would most likely be put down or spend the rest of its life in the shelter.

■ **While the charms of a kitten** *are obvious, an immature cat will need more time and attention than an older cat.*

Where to find your cat

SO NOW YOU'RE READY to start looking for a new addition to the family. Where exactly should you look? The answer depends on whether you have decided on a pedigreed or a mixed-breed cat.

Responsible breeders

What is a reputable, responsible breeder? In my opinion, a good breeder should:

1. Always be as interested in you as you are in them. This means they care enough about their cats to ensure they go only to capable, loving people. If a breeder seems to be asking you lots of questions, don't be annoyed; it's a good thing. They are making sure that their beloved cats continue to be treated well and aren't headed into an irresponsible situation. A good breeder will not sell a cat to anyone who intends to let it roam the neighborhood. Most breeders will also require you to have the cat **neutered**, unless it has highly desirable genetic traits and the chance to better the physical and behavioral characteristics of its breed. If a breeder is eager to sell you a cat or kitten without first determining if you are a capable, caring owner, leave and find a more discerning breeder.

> **DEFINITION**
>
> *Any cat that has been* **neutered** *has had its primary reproductive organs removed, preventing it from reproducing. A general term, neutering refers specifically to spaying a female (removal of the ovaries and uterus), or castrating a male (removal of the testes).*

2. Raise cats that conform to the written standard for the physical characteristics of the breed in question. Established by the major cat associations, these standards are set to ensure consistency among the breeds. Breeders who go against these written standards run the risk of ruining the looks and temperament of their breed. Examine the cats closely, paying attention to head shape, coat length and color, eye shape and color, tail length, and overall build. For instance, a Siamese cat should be lithe, muscular, and somewhat long-bodied.

> **DEFINITION**
>
> *A* **pedigree** *is a written record provided to a buyer by the breeder that documents a cat or kitten's family history, showing what level of competition each of its ancestors attained. A kitten or cat with a good pedigree has a large number of ancestors that reached championship status in the show ring.*

3. Properly register their purebred cats with a reputable cat association. Such an organization ensures that the breeder is producing cats that represent the standard of that breed and also keeps records of each cat's **pedigree**.

4. Allow you to examine cats thoroughly so you can check for structural flaws, illnesses, or behavior problems.

5. Keep his or her *cattery* clean and fresh. Any cattery that appears dirty or smells bad should not be considered.

6. Compete regularly in cat shows to keep their breeding skills sharp and up-to-date.

7. Socialize their cats and kittens with other cats and people from an early age, instead of keeping them isolated in cages.

8. Handle the kittens from an early age.

Finding a breeder

So where can one find these wonderful cat breeders? The following are a few sources that might help locate a good breeder near you.

1. **Magazines:** Magazines such as *Cats* and *Cat Fancy* always have sections that list breeders of every popular cat breed. Locate a few near your part of the country and consider calling or visiting.

2. **Web sites:** A search of the Web will reveal a multitude of cat breeders and other resources.

3. **Cat clubs:** Local or national breed clubs make it their business to know who is breeding good-quality cats for their respective breeds. Most of the time, these clubs are organized and operated by caring breeders. Contact one of the national or international cat associations for a list of breed clubs near you.

4. **Cat shows:** The best breeders always attend and compete in cat shows. Check the local newspapers, cat magazines, breed club periodicals, or the Web to find out when a cat show is going to be being held nearby and go check it out.

5. **Veterinarians:** Most caring, competent vets can put you in touch with a reputable cat breeder, so don't hesitate to give him or her a call. He or she will know if the breeder in question has healthy cats, too, which should be at the top of your concerns.

6. **Classified ads:** Competent breeders sometimes advertise in the local newspaper, so don't hesitate to give them a look. Be aware, however, that many fly-by-night outfits also use this venue. Always make sure to visit the cattery and make a thorough investigation before committing to anything.

WARNING SIGNS

When examining any cat or kitten you are interested in obtaining, be sure to look for the following:

- Any discharge from the eyes, ears, nose, penis, vagina, or anus, which could indicate serious illness
- A pronounced limp, which could point to a structural problem
- A greasy or overly dry coat, another indicator of illness, or improper diet
- Any visible parasites
- Polydactyl feet (too many toes, remember?)
- An injured or kinked tail
- A severe underbite or overbite
- A bloated stomach, often indicative of a worm infestation

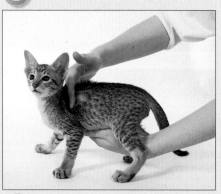

1 Check the ears

2 Check the anus

3 Check the coat

4 Check the mouth

Shelters

Many, many of the cats obtained in North America and much of Europe come from pet shelters. The vast majority of these cats are of the mixed-breed variety, although occasionally a purebred cat or kitten might show up in a shelter. A reputable pet shelter can be of great help to a new cat owner. In addition to providing adult cats and kittens for adoption, a shelter usually provides low-cost neutering services (often a required condition of adoption), pet counseling, and classes on diet, health care, and training. A good shelter will have a considerate, informed staff ready to help you at every step.

> **DEFINITION**
>
> **Euthanasia** is a procedure performed by a veterinarian in which an animal is painlessly killed by means of a lethal injection. Old, terminally ill, or severely injured pets are often euthanized, as are unwanted pets, even though they are in perfect health.

Choosing to rescue an unwanted pet from a shelter is a very nice thing to do. Every year, caring shelter personnel are forced to perform *euthanasia* on millions of cats that cannot find a home in time. Due to space limitations, many shelters have a time limit on how long an animal can stay at the facility before being euthanized; some do so after only 3 days. This death sentence rarely applies to purebred cats and kittens, whose numbers are low and demand high.

So, when deciding on what type of feline to get, please strongly consider adopting a mixed-breed cat or kitten from a shelter. Saving one life may not seem like much, but it's a start.

Choosing a good shelter

So how do you go about finding a reputable shelter? First, let me say that there are two main types of shelters: shelters that set a time limit on each pet's life, and "no-kill" shelters that keep an animal until it finds a home. No-kill shelters have been increasing in number (thankfully) but are still not in the majority because there are simply too many unwanted pets – a result of owners refusing to neuter cats who are then left outdoors, unsupervised.

Whether a shelter is a "kill" or "no-kill" usually has little if any bearing on how well it is run; which you choose is up to you. Many people feel more comfortable with a no-kill shelter, however, since there is no guilt pressure. You do not end up adopting a cat due to pity alone, and your choice of pet can therefore be a more objective one.

Finding a shelter near you

The first thing you can do is check out the nearest Humane Society shelter, or any municipally run shelter. These are usually run in an efficient manner, with well-trained staff and excellent conditions. Normally large operations, these shelters always offer a variety of helpful info and will often assign someone to your adoption to help you make a wise choice. Find these shelters either through the Yellow Pages or by speaking to your veterinarian. Vets often offer their services at a low cost to shelters, making them an excellent inside source of information.

There are probably a number of privately run shelters in your area, as well. These will also be listed in the Yellow Pages. Although private groups are rarely funded as well as the bigger municipal shelters, they do a great job most of the time. Most no-kill shelters are privately run and operate on money taken in from adoptions, as well as charitable donations and special community fund-raising events.

Visit a few shelters before making any adoption decisions, just to see how they are run and what kind of cats are available. Doing so will give you a chance to compare facilities; some will be well run and spotless, while others may be less so. Always choose a shelter that is clean, with healthy-looking animals and a helpful, caring staff. The shelter of your choice should make neutering mandatory for any pet being adopted and should be reasonably priced. In addition, the screening process you are put through should be thorough, to ensure you are capable of taking care of a cat or kitten. By being somewhat discriminating, a shelter helps keep an animal from ending up back at the shelter, looking for another family to go home with.

Classified ads

You may decide to look for a cat or kitten in the classifieds, where private individuals interested in selling or giving away cats or kittens place ads. Often an ad will have been placed by a well-meaning private party whose cat "accidentally" delivered a litter of kittens. When this happens, the kittens are usually given away for free.

Beware of ads placed by profit-hungry individuals looking to make a fast buck in the pet business. These "backyard breeders" often breed purebred or mixed-breed animals in their homes in an attempt to cash in. Beware of these people, as they know little about breeding, often keep their cats in deplorable conditions, and have little concern for the animals in question.

If you decide to locate a cat or kitten through the classifieds, I advise you to only consider those ads that charge nothing or, at most, charge a modest fee to be used to have the pet neutered. Doing so will help you avoid the hucksters out there who do more to harm cats than help. If you do adopt a cat or kitten this way, take it to your veterinarian immediately, before it even gets to your home. This way, you can make sure it is healthy and does not have any infectious conditions that could harm another pet in the home – or you.

Private individuals

If you know someone in the neighborhood who has kittens up for adoption, it might be worth your while to check it out. Despite the fact that the owner showed less than stellar common sense in allowing his or her cat to get pregnant in the first place, the kittens are, after all, innocent and deserve decent loving homes. Realize that the owner probably won't have had the mother or kittens examined by a veterinarian and that the birthing conditions might have been less than ideal, with the mother not receiving much, if any, prenatal care.

If the owner is attempting to sell the kittens, he or she might be a backyard breeder – someone out to make a fast buck at the expense of some innocent animals. It's best not to encourage these types, despite the irresistible plight of the kittens. If the little ones are up for adoption, though, take a look. You might end up finding a pearl.

■ **Although neighborhood kittens** *will probably have received little or no professional care, they may still be worth considering when you are looking for a new cat.*

Just make sure to take the kitten directly to your veterinarian for vaccinations and a thorough examination before bringing it home.

Strays

At one time or another, most of us have been in a position to adopt a stray cat hanging around the house. You know the story: The straggly little thing without identification tags that keeps showing up, using your kid's sandbox for a toilet. For a few days you ignore it. Then you put out some water. Then you leave a little dry food out. Before you know it, the cat adopts you and ends up being part of the family. I have done this, as have many of you, I'm sure. Strays can make great pets. When you save a cat from the streets, it seems to understand this and somehow appreciates you more than other pets might.

Health and behavioral problems with strays

As I said, stray cats can make great pets, but they sometimes come with a number of health and behavior problems. Most will be infested with external and internal parasites, including fleas, ticks, and numerous types of worms. In addition, strays usually have not received any vaccinations and can carry a host of infectious diseases. These deadly diseases can all be spread from cat to cat through bites, saliva, or even by sharing food or mutual grooming. Taking in a stray without bringing it right to your veterinarian can, therefore, mean a death sentence for any cats you may already have at home.

Strays might also have been injured by vehicles or by other animals at some time. Breaks, sprains, abscesses, eye disorders, internal injuries, or other structural problems can result, which can end up costing you plenty to treat. In addition, many strays become very cautious around people due to the hardships of the street. Often they remain this way for the rest of their lives, perhaps warming up to only a few people – you being one.

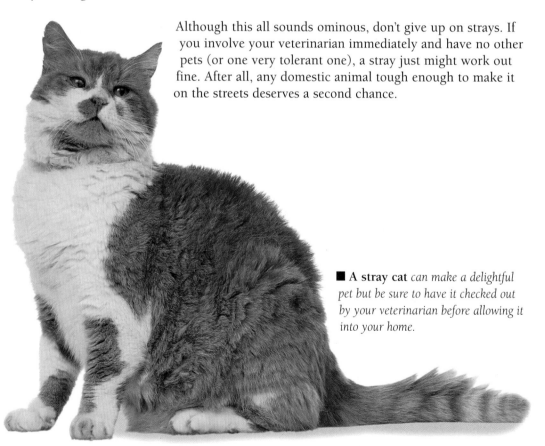

Although this all sounds ominous, don't give up on strays. If you involve your veterinarian immediately and have no other pets (or one very tolerant one), a stray just might work out fine. After all, any domestic animal tough enough to make it on the streets deserves a second chance.

■ **A stray cat** *can make a delightful pet but be sure to have it checked out by your veterinarian before allowing it into your home.*

Choosing one cat from many

ONCE YOU HAVE FOUND *an agreeable place to get your kitten or cat, you will have to choose one special pet out of many. Shelters especially will have many sweet faces staring back at you; how on earth can anyone pick just one? I'll take them all! No. Let's get hold of ourselves and determine a way to choose one from many.*

Health

When you're looking at a kitten or cat, look first at its general appearance. Does its coat look clean and free of mats? Does it have any scabs, scars, or missing hair? Any of these could point to ill health or parasitic infection. Look also for any unusual discharges or signs of diarrhea. A cat or kitten who is not using a clean litter box might also be ill, so watch for that.

Pick up the cat or kitten and examine its body. Any lumps you find could indicate a tumor or an injury. A bloated belly on a kitten can mean a case of worms. Are its ribs sticking out? This could point to malnutrition or a digestive problem. Being very small for its age could also point to malnutrition or some other medical problem.

Also watch the animal walk. Any limping or an otherwise unusual gait? Look for malformed legs, spine, jaw, or tail. Make sure to also look into the animal's mouth to check for missing teeth, abscesses, or any other unusual oral problems. You want to see pink gums and nicely formed teeth.

> ### Trivia...
> *Cats have been kept in homes for thousands of years, and differences in cat populations and local climates naturally created certain breeds over time. But it's only in the last hundred years or so that we've begun to selectively breed cats for various physical characteristics.*

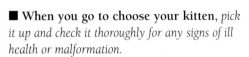

■ **When you go to choose your kitten,** *pick it up and check it thoroughly for any signs of ill health or malformation.*

If an adult cat seems cautious or nervous around you, do not attempt to examine its mouth, as it might panic and bite. Cat bites tend to be extremely infectious.

NEUTER OR NOT

The drive to breed is a strong one among all unneutered cats. By the time a male or a female cat is 6 to 8 months old, it will begin showing an instinctive need to find a mate and will also become less playful and more competitive toward cats of its own gender.

Less-than-lovely behaviors

For owners who have not had their cats neutered, a bevy of unwanted behaviors can pop up. Males will want to get outside and roam the neighborhood in search of females and to claim and defend what they perceive to be their territory. In doing so, they will almost certainly get into fights with other males, and run the risk of getting injured by a vehicle or infected with one of many diseases spread from cat to cat. If kept indoors, an unneutered male will spray urine all over the home and most likely become quite vocal in his attempt to tell you he wants out.

Unneutered females allowed to venture outside will almost certainly become pregnant over and over and may also get into fights with other cats, both male and female. Like a male, she, too, could expose herself to injury or infection, possibly leading to death. If kept in the home, she will cry and perhaps mark with urine and leave spots of blood – all in all, a very unhappy owner-pet relationship.

■ **A tom cat** (*unneutered male*) *tends to roam over a large area, fighting for possession of its territory and the right to mate with any females in sight.*

Do it early

Does all that sound like something you would want to deal with? I didn't think so. But guess what? The solution is a fairly straightforward one; simply have your male cat castrated or your female spayed by the sixth or seventh month of its life. Doing so will prevent the undesirable behaviors from ever happening, or minimize them if they have already begun. Unless the cat or kitten you obtain is a prized pedigreed animal capable of winning championships in the show ring, you really have no reason not to neuter.

In addition to ending unwanted behaviors, neutering will help extend the life of your new pet. Your neutered cat will have no chance of developing ovarian, uterine, or testicular cancer, and the risk of mammary gland cancer is significantly reduced.

Perhaps the best reason to have your new pet neutered is to help solve the fearsome problem of feline over-population. Take a look at how many cats are in shelters in your area, then multiply that by a few thousand in order to get a feel for the crisis. Literally millions of cats and kitten are put to death each year because owners refuse to neuter their pets. Do us all a favor and have your beloved pet neutered, for the good of the species.

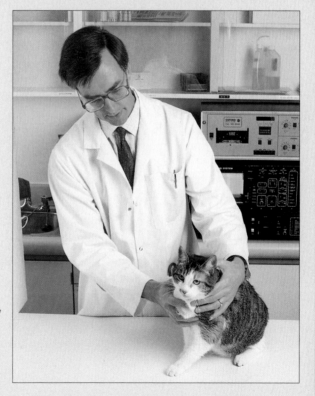

■ **A female cat can be spayed** *any time from the age of 6 months to prevent pregnancy. The operation will be performed by a qualified veterinarian under general anesthetic.*

Age

How old a cat or kitten is can play a part in your choice. For instance, a kitten younger than 8 weeks old should not yet be separated from its mother and littermates, because the 6- to 8-week period is a critical time for cats to learn important social skills. Kittens adopted before the eighth week often develop antisocial behaviors and varying levels of fear aggression. Though nearly irresistible, a 3- or 4-week-old kitten should not be away from its mother and littermates for at least another month. Good breeders know this and will never allow a customer to take a kitten home before the eighth week, usually making them wait until the tenth or twelfth week to ensure the best socialization possible. If the owner of a litter of kittens wants to unload them at too young an age, consider finding another source for your cat.

■ **This 5-week-old kitten** *needs to stay with its mother for at least 3 more weeks. Never take a kitten home before it is mature enough to leave its mother as it will not be properly socialized.*

On the other end of the spectrum, the age of an adult cat for sale or adoption can also be an issue. You may not want a cat that is very old, not only because of health issues (which affect old cats just as they do old humans), but because you may only have a few short years to share with the cat. Some people love the gentle, settled personalities of older cats, but they're not for everyone. If you're choosing an adult cat, you may want to look at juveniles under a year old, as they tend to learn new routines more easily than older cats. Plus, you will be assured of having many happy years together. If you simply fall in love with an old cat, though, and feel you can deal with the realities of the situation, consider giving it a loving home for however long it will be with you. Taking home an older cat will make you a very special cat angel.

Temperament

No one wants to adopt an antisocial, nervous, or excessively aggressive cat or kitten. We would all prefer a friendly, confident cat or kitten at ease with its surroundings, right? You can help ensure this by carefully observing the cat or kitten while it is around other felines. It should be calm, inquisitive, and relaxed around you and others. A kitten should have a desire to play with other kittens and show little if any fear. If it huddles in a corner by itself or is constantly fighting or bullying others, it may not be the best choice.

When examining kittens, try throwing a balled-up piece of newspaper toward them. The kittens who show interest and want to play with it are probably your best choices.

Avoid a kitten who is afraid of the ball, or who bullies others in an attempt to monopolize the ball. Fearful or dominant kittens often turn out to be problem pets. Also try clapping your hands or scratching your nails along the floor. The kittens who show mild interest usually make good pets, while those showing fear or no interest at all often do not.

If you are considering buying a purebred kitten or cat, make sure to read up on the various breeds before looking at any kittens. Each breed has unique behavior patterns. An adult Norwegian Forest Cat will not act like an adult Abyssinian, even though most kittens are pretty similar in their behavior.

A simple summary

✔ You have many choices about what kind of cat to get. You can decide on a pedigreed cat or go with a mixed-breed pet. The decision really depends on your own personal needs and wants, and on what you can afford.

✔ Although most people want a kitten, adopting a juvenile or an adult cat has its advantages. You get to see the developed size and personality of the cat right from the start. You also know about the cat's health and won't be surprised by any health problems that can develop as a kitten matures into an adult.

✔ You can find the perfect cat or kitten in many different places, including a responsible breeder, a shelter, a private individual, or even from the street.

✔ Choosing one cat or kitten from many is hard, but not impossible. The pet's overall health, as well as its age and temperament, are the main factors to consider when you're making this choice.

✔ Neuter your new cat by the time it is 6 or 7 months old. Doing so will improve its health, keep it safe, and prevent the needless destruction of millions of unfortunate animals each year. Unless your cat is a champion purebred animal, it is best to have it neutered.

Part Two

CORRECT NUTRITION IS ESSENTIAL

CAT BASICS

NOW THAT I HAVE ABSOLUTELY convinced you that a cat is the right pet, I want to help ease you into actual cat ownership. Once you have decided on what type of cat to get (and where to get  it from), you will need to prepare your home for its arrival. You'll need to go shopping, and to make your home a safe place for a kitty.

Easing your new buddy into your home and teaching it some basic rules comes next, as does how to care for it and keep it healthy. Beyond *learning* all about basic cat care, you will also need to learn ways to stimulate your cat's mind and body, to keep it *happy* and well adjusted.

Let's move on now, and get into the nitty-gritty of cats. By the time you finish this part, you will nearly be an *expert*!

Chapter 5

The New Arrival

Congratulations! You and the perfect cat have found one another, and you are now ready to take your feline friend home to start a meaningful, long-lasting relationship. But wait: Is everything ready at the old homestead? You are going to need some essential supplies and you also need to prepare your home so that there's nothing your new cat can destroy, and so that nothing will harm your new friend.

That's what this chapter is all about. I'll give you advice on just what supplies are needed to make your home as cat-friendly as possible so the welcome home is painless and easy. I'll also tell you how to set up your home to make it safe for the little critter.

In this chapter...
✓ The essential stuff
✓ Creating a safe environment

YOUR CAT WILL SOON MAKE ITSELF AT HOME!

The essential stuff

EVERYONE, PETS AND HUMANS *alike,*
needs certain essential supplies to be happy
and comfortable. For me it's a good book, a
comfy chair, and a cup of hot tea. For your
new cat, the comfy chair is probably
important, but there's a lot more. The
following are items I consider essential
to the happiness and well-being of any
domestic feline, be it a 10-week-old
fur ball or a wizened senior.
Although you will almost certainly
add to this list over time, for now
it's a good starting point.

CREATURE COMFORTS

Litter box

Usually made of plastic, the litter box you buy for your cat
should be about 3 to 4 inches high to prevent your pet from
pawing **litter** out of the box and onto the floor. A litter box
with lower sides might be in order for a young kitten or an
older cat, however, to make sure it has no trouble getting in
and out.

The box can be open with no cover,
although many cats seem to prefer a
closed box, which affords a bit more
privacy. A closed litter box will come with a
removable plastic top that's about a foot
high. It clips to the lower tray and detaches
quickly, allowing easy clean-up.

■ **Cats are intensely private**
creatures and most will prefer to carry
out their toileting in a covered litter box.

A PROPER BURIAL

As you probably know, most cats (both wild and domestic) long ago developed the wonderful habit of burying their wastes. Ever wonder why? Are they just being considerate roommates or compulsive neat freaks? Yes to both, but there is more to it than that.

Cats in the wild developed the behavior millions of years ago for an important reason. By burying their waste, they could hide evidence of their presence from the local predators – whose keen noses would otherwise easily track a cat down simply from the trail of waste material left on the ground. To avoid being caught (and possibly eaten) by those predators, the cat simply buries its waste.

Burying waste is also a way for cats in the wild to avoid territorial disputes with others of their own species. If a cat left its waste out in the open, it would be telling other cats in the area, "Hey, this place is all mine," which definitely invites confrontation. And with confrontation comes the possibility of injury – something that could mean death for a wild cat. (Cats do not have friendly, helpful veterinarians out in the forests and jungles yet.)

Thankfully, domestic cats have retained this clever behavior. They bury their urine and feces, which helps keep odor down and allows us to keep them indoors in a safe, cozy environment. What a break; no getting up early to walk your tabby!

Waste burial is not a completely instinctive feline behavior. While still with their mom, very young kittens learn to perfect their waste-burying skills by watching their mother do it. Kittens taken away from their mothers at too young an age (before the seventh or eighth week) often do not perfect their burying skills, causing owners to often have long-term house-soiling problems with their cats. There's another good reason never to take a kitten from its mother and littermates before the eighth week of life!

■ **Although cats are clean** *by nature, the young kitten has to learn how to bury its waste. Toilet-training will be much easier if the kittens can learn from their mother.*

Litter

Before you buy your first bag of litter, be sure to talk to the person you got the cat from to find out what brand of litter the pet is used to. Then, if possible, simply continue to use the same brand at home. This will help your cat understand exactly what the litter box is for in your home. Abruptly switching from one brand of cat litter to another (especially with kittens) can often cause a cat or kitten to stop using its litter box, so, to be safe, stick to the same brand your cat knows.

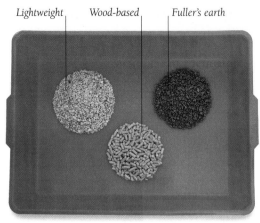

Lightweight   Wood-based   Fuller's earth

DIFFERENT TYPES OF CAT LITTER

A litter box should be filled with a brand of litter that does a good job of absorbing and hiding waste and that your cat likes. This last point is really important, because if you like the features of a litter and your cat doesn't, the cat will refuse to use the litter box. It's that simple.

Litter scooper

Some litters are made of clay, while others use different absorbent substances to do the job. Many brands of cat litter available today are designed to collect urine and feces into small clumps that can then be scooped out easily with a long-handled metal or plastic **scooper**, available at all pet supply shops. Using a clumping litter and a scooper enables you to get all the soiled material out of the box immediately, which keeps the box much cleaner and fresher.

Whether you use clumping litter or the kind that doesn't clump, your cat or kitten's litter box should be scooped clean of all waste materials at least once a day to keep it as free of odors as possible. This will help you to avoid house-soiling problems in the future, because most cats will stop using a litter box once it has become too dirty. When scooping the waste out, be sure to search out and remove all clumped litter, as well as any feces.

Even scooping out your cat or kitten's litter box every day, you should still think about completely replacing the litter about once a week if you use regular litter, and once every 2 weeks if

DEFINITION

*A **scooper**, a long-handled device that looks like a slotted plastic shovel, is designed to scoop out clumps of litter that have absorbed cat waste. The slots let the clean, unused litter filter back into the litter box, while effectively capturing the waste clumps, which can then be discarded. Be sure to buy a scoop that will not absorb odors or rust.*

you use clumping litter. Remember that if your cat thinks the litter box is too dirty to use, there will always be a potted plant filled with nice unscented soil as an attractive alternative! Before placing new litter into the litter box, be sure to clean it thoroughly with a mild soap and water. This will disinfect it and remove any lingering odors.

Try putting down a thin layer of baking soda into the litter box first, followed by the litter. The baking soda will help absorb unpleasant odors and make the box smell sweeter to both of you.

Cat food

You will need to have some cat food available from the moment your little friend comes home. I will discuss good nutrition in depth in Chapter 9; right now I just want to make sure you have the right food available and have a good idea of when and how much to feed.

Any cat or kitten you bring home should be eating solid food and will be if it is at least 7 or 8 weeks old. The best idea is to buy a few weeks' supply of whatever the cat has already been eating. By continuing to feed this food, you will help avoid any digestive upsets that can occur whenever any animal is suddenly switched over to a new brand of food. Once your cat has settled in, you can then gradually switch it over to whatever type of food you have decided is best.

The food you will eventually be feeding your cat might be dry kibble, canned food, or even a home-cooked diet, depending on what you believe is most convenient and healthy. The different foods will be discussed in detail in Chapter 9, so be patient. Right now, just be sure to have at least a 2-week supply of whatever the cat was eating already. As long as it is a nutritious food designed specifically for cats, it should be fine for now.

■ **Prepared foods** *are easy to obtain but whether you feed your cat canned or dry food, make sure it is specifically designed for the feline digestion.*

Never feed your kitten or cat any type of food not designed and formulated specifically for cats.

Cats have very specific nutritional needs. For instance, dog food does not contain enough protein for a cat, nor does it have *taurine*, a nutrient essential to a cat's health. Be smart and feed food designed with a feline in mind!

The cat's dishes

You will also need to have a dish for your cat's food and a small bowl for water. The food dish needn't be huge, as even the largest cat won't eat all that much in one meal. Anything about 5 to 6 inches in diameter should do, provided it has high enough edges to prevent food from spilling out. Don't use a dish much larger than this, as you might absentmindedly begin filling it to its capacity each feeding time, ultimately leading to a pudgy pet. The water bowl should be a bit larger and deeper, to ensure that a good supply of water is always on hand.

A small dog's self-waterer works well, too. It's easy to fill and clean and you don't have to fill it up as often as a regular bowl. Plus, some cats have a habit of pawing their water and spilling it. Since the self-waterer holds more water, it withstands more pawing and spilling.

Both bowls should be ceramic, glass, stainless steel, or some other material that is dishwasher safe. They should not be absorbent or capable of rusting. Also, make sure not to use any ceramic dish or bowl that has been glazed with a lead-base glaze, as this can cause lead-poisoning. If a dish is being sold as a decorative item, it may have lead in the glaze. If it's being sold as a plain old dish for people to use, it's probably fine for your cat.

Avoid plastic cat dishes – they can absorb and harbor bacteria. Some cats also develop acne on their chin if they eat from a plastic dish, because they are allergic to plastic.

DEFINITION

An essential amino acid, your cat needs **taurine** *to properly form protein in its body. As it is not naturally formed within a cat's system, the cat's diet must supply the cat with taurine each day of its life. Only animal proteins can supply your cat with taurine, which makes it impossible for a cat to be a vegetarian. Without taurine, cats can develop heart disease, as well as disorders of the nervous and reproductive systems. A taurine deficiency can also lead to blindness, stunted growth, and even death.*

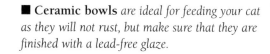

■ **Ceramic bowls** *are ideal for feeding your cat as they will not rust, but make sure that they are finished with a lead-free glaze.*

Scratching posts

Cats need to scratch every day. Scratching helps them shed the outer sheath of their claws, and so is an essential part of their grooming ritual. Cats also stretch their spine as they scratch, and they use the behavior to mark their territory. Scratching is an instinctive and important behavior, and if you don't supply your cat or kitten with a scratching post (or two), it will use your sofa, bedpost, door, or armchair.

To satisfy your pet's need to scratch, be sure to buy one or two scratching posts at your local pet supply store. Post are usually covered with something rough, such as carpeting or wound rope. The post might be high enough so that your cat can anchor its front paws on top and get a good stretch, so pass by those puny 1-foot posts and go for something tall.

The scratching post should be located close to where your cat or kitten likes to sleep or nap, because right after waking is a feline's favorite time to scratch and stretch. If you have more than one cat, several scratching posts are mandatory to prevent competitive, territorial scratching all over the house.

■ **All cats need to scratch** *from time to time to keep their claws healthy and to mark territory. Provide your pet with a scratching post to prevent damage to your furniture.*

The kitty condo

Pet supply stores also sell cat furniture called kitty condos or cat trees. These are 4- to 6-foot-high, multilevel, carpeted structures that most cats and kittens love to play and sleep on. Most are designed to double as a scratching post, with the plush carpet coverings providing the perfect texture for scratching. Kitty condos usually include a semiclosed box-like structure that cats like to sleep in, as well as a comfy upper level that acts as a perfect observation point, enabling your pet to survey its kingdom.

Toys

Your new cat will need to have some fun toys around the home so it can exercise its natural instincts for hunting and chasing.

Toys are not optional for a cat — every cat needs things to play with to keep its mind and body exercised.

INTERNET

www.21cats.org

This is a great site for information on just about everything to do with cats, including what kind of supplies and toys are best and why your kitty needs them.

Supply your pet with toys made from rubber or plastic or any material that won't easily tear or break into edible pieces that might choke your cat. Furry mouse toys, small balls with bells inside, teaser wands with feathers attached to the end of a long string, or whatever your pet finds amusing will do. Some cats even like chasing after a wadded-up sheet of newspaper. Pet supply stores also have wind-up or battery-operated toys that will amuse and stimulate your pet for hours, so don't hesitate to check them out.

Do remember, though, that some toys are only safe when you play with them together. Toys such as feathers, with parts your cat can pull off and swallow, are best put away when you're not around.

■ **Stimulate and exercise your cat** *with a selection of toys. Toys should be made from tough, durable material that can take a lot of battering.*

Grooming supplies

Although most cats do a great job of keeping themselves neat and clean, they still need your help. (How to groom your cat will be covered in detail in Chapter 8. For now, let's just make sure we have the right equipment on hand.) You'll need to keep a good comb and brush handy. Some longhaired breeds (especially Persians) will need daily grooming, because their downy undercoat gets easily tangled and matted. Also, even if you have a shorthaired cat, it's a great idea to brush it every day, to accustom the cat to being picked up and handled. Cats brushed regularly from a young age usually come to love it. Brushing and combing regularly will also help minimize the formation of *hairballs* – a real health problem for cats. Getting loose hair off your cat or kitten will also help keep your carpets and furniture a bit less hairy.

For a shorthaired cat, choose a soft, short-pronged slicker brush, which will do a great job of removing hair and gently scratching and tickling your cat. For a longhaired cat, pick a brush that more closely resembles those used by people who have long hair.

A comb is a necessity for longhaired cats and should be used only after the pet has been brushed well. The comb will separate the hairs nicely, ensuring that no tangles or mats form. If you have a cat with exceptionally long, thick hair

> **DEFINITION**
>
> *A **hairball** is a solid mass of cat hair that can form in a cat's stomach or intestines over time as a result of the pet's daily grooming. When a cat licks itself clean, it swallows some hair, which sometimes does not pass through and out of the cat. A large enough hairball can cause intestinal blockages that can only be relieved by surgery.*

METAL COMBS   SLICKER BRUSHES

(such as a Persian or Norwegian Forest Cat), consider buying both a wide-tooth comb and a fine-tooth comb. Use the wide-tooth comb first, then finish with the fine-tooth comb.

A sharp pair of scissors might be needed for longhaired cats, who sometimes get impossibly knotted mats of hair in their coats. These must be cut out, because leaving them in can eventually cause the cat a lot of pain. You most likely already have a pair of scissors that will work. Just take care not to use a gigantic pair, as these could injure your pet and take too much hair off.

Nail clippers

Your cat's claws grow just as your nails do and will sometimes need trimming. If left too long, they can damage furniture and your skin. They can get caught in carpeting as the cat walks across the room. Nails left really long can curl back into the cat's pads and be very painful. Buying good-quality nail clippers from your local pet supply store is, therefore, a necessity.

Take care not to buy nail clippers designed for dogs, as they will not properly fit your cat's claws and could injure it. Only buy clippers made for clipping a cat or kitten's nails.

Collar and ID

Even if you keep your cat indoors all the time (bravo for you!), consider a collar with an identification tag; sometimes cats sneak out of an open door or window and get lost. If you let your cat out of the house at all, even just in the backyard while you're around, a collar with an ID tag is an absolute must. Cats can become lost or injured out there in the cruel world.

■ **An identity tag** *should always be worn by your cat. It should contain your name and address or telephone number so that a wandering cat can be safely returned to you.*

Buy a stretchable collar – one that will not choke the cat if it gets caught on a branch or fence. Some are even designed to break away if they get caught up, ensuring that the pet will not be choked. Onto this collar you should attach a plastic identification tag with the cat's name, your address and name, and your telephone number clearly printed, so that any good Samaritan who finds your pet can get in touch with you. Any pet supply shop can have an identification tag made for your pet in a few days.

First-aid kit

Unfortunately, your cat will most likely get sick or injured sometime in its life. To deal with these undesirable events, you will need to have a pet first-aid kit handy. Having such a kit could save your cat's life one day, as your veterinarian's clinic might not be close by or could be closed at an inopportune time. Right now I will just tell you what supplies to have on hand; in Chapter 14 I will give you some advice on basic first-aid techniques.

Your kitty first-aid kit should include:
- Adhesive tape
- Antibacterial scrub
- Cotton swabs
- Disinfecting solution
- Gauze pads
- Mineral oil
- One or two rolls of gauze
- One or two small towels
- Rectal thermometer
- Rubbing alcohol
- Small blanket
- Small flashlight
- Syrup of ipecac
- Tweezers

RECTAL THERMOMETER

DISINFECTANT   MINERAL OIL

■ **First-aid equipment** *should always be on hand to treat any unexpected injuries to your pet.*

Never give your cat or kitten aspirin or ibuprofen, as they are extremely toxic to felines and can easily kill your pet. Never give any medications to your cat or kitten without first speaking to your veterinarian!

Cat carrier

Every cat owner should have a sturdy cat carrier on hand. They are a must when you are transporting your pet. Cats usually stay calmer inside a warm cozy carrier, and they are much safer, too. Use the carrier to transport your cat to and from the veterinarian, the shelter or breeder, or from house to house.

You can find a decent, affordable cat carrier in your local pet supply store. Make sure it is large enough to house your cat comfortably. It might also be a good idea to keep a cushy pad, towel, or blanket inside to make it warmer and more comfy.

■ **A secure carrier,** *made from wire or wicker, is ideal for transporting your cat to and from the vet or when moving house.*

Creating a safe environment

BEFORE YOUR CAT COMES HOME, *you need to go through your house from stem to stern and make sure everything is safe. Cats and kittens are very curious little critters; combine this with small size and their ability to leap, and you've got an animal who can get into almost any area of your home. Many of these areas may seem safe to us but can be downright lethal to a feline because of its small size. For instance, an innocent little houseplant such as a dieffenbachia can be fatal to a nibbling cat.*

The next few sections I will point out special areas, objects, and situations that you will need to move, remove, or change before kitty comes home in order to prevent a potentially fatal accident from occurring. But you should also do your own survey of your kingdom from a cat's eye view. Get down on the floor and look around. What would you chew on and get into if you were a kitten?

Windows and doors

If you regularly leave a door or window to the outside open during the day, now is the time to change that habit. Absent-mindedly creating access to the outside will only lead to heartbreak.

It takes a cat several weeks to figure out where home is, and a new cat that gets out may never find its way back to you. An escaped cat might also wander off and get killed by a car or neighborhood dog or be adopted by a well-meaning cat lover. Check

every possible escape route a new cat or kitten might find in your home, putting special emphasis on areas that are high up, low down, and out of your normal field of vision. Remember, cats operate in a three-dimensional world. Make sure all windows have sturdy screens in place. The same goes for all doors; keep them closed unless a secure screen door is in place. Also, be sure to instruct every member of the family, especially young children, to close promptly all windows and doors.

■ **Confine your new cat** *to the safety of your home. Make sure that all doors and windows are kept shut to prevent your pet from straying.*

Whenever you or a family member leaves the home through an outside door, always be sure to first look down and behind you, in case a quiet little feline is afoot. Not doing so could enable your cat or kitten to slip out of the home, possibly for the last time.

Power cords and outlets

Try to minimize or hide all the power cords and wires in your home to prevent your cat from chewing on them and being electrocuted. Place wires under carpets when possible or tack them beneath moldings along the floor. If this is not possible, spray a taste repellent such as Bitter Apple on the wires, or wipe them down with a vinegar and water solution to make them bitter-tasting. Additionally, install baby guard wall socket plugs into all your unused electric wall sockets. Doing so will prevent a curious little paw from reaching in and getting a shocking surprise.

Household toxins

Your home is filled with chemicals that can hurt or kill your new pet. Think not? Think again. Take a look under your kitchen sink, in the cupboard, or in your garage or utility room. See any bleach, insecticides, cleaners, solvents, lubricating oils, or antifreeze? Maybe some laundry detergent or tarnish remover? All are deadly to a cat.

A cat who has ingested a toxic substance may go into shock or experience seizures, convulsions, and loss of muscular control, followed by respiratory failure, paralysis, and death. Some less-toxic substances may render the cat sleepy or lethargic or irritable and hyperactive. Many toxins will cause the cat to vomit and/or drool, with diarrhea and excess urination also possible. Not a very good scenario.

Your cat does not know how lethal certain household substances can be and must rely on you to keep them out of its environment. Some toxins (such as antifreeze, certain fertilizers, and cough syrup) may actually taste good to a cat, and, therefore, are especially dangerous. If potentially lethal substances are left out in the open, your cat will eventually find them and investigate. Kittens and young cats are especially prone to poisoning due to their incredibly curious minds. You can never be too careful!

■ **Excessive salivation,** *or drooling, may be a reaction to poisonous toxins. Check whether your cat has swallowed any toxic substances.*

COMMON HOUSEHOLD TOXINS

The first step in preventing your cat from being poisoned is to know what common household substances can harm it. These include:

- Acetaminophen
- Acids of any type
- Alcohol
- Antifreeze
- Aspirin or ibuprofen
- Chlorine bleach
- Drain cleaner
- Fertilizer
- Gasoline or diesel fuel
- Household cleaners such as Windex, Lysol, Mr Clean, and others

- Insecticides
- Motor oil
- Paint
- Prescription drugs
- Solvents, such as paint thinner, rust remover, and tarnish remover
- Rat poison

ASPIRIN

An ounce of prevention

Prevention by removal is the only effective way to dissuade your cat from eating toxic substances; just one lick of some poisons could be fatal. So it is up to you to remove all toxins from the cat's world. Get all of these substances out of your cat's environment and behind securely locked cupboards, preferably located high up in the garage. Remember that cats are really curious and are adept at getting into impossible places.

If your cat has access to the outdoors, you must be careful about putting fertilizer down on gardens and lawns, as the cat will spend a good amount of time digging and frolicking all over these areas. Rather than choosing a chemical fertilizer, consider using an organic alternative such as manure, especially for the garden.

Clean up all oil spills, particularly those on the driveway, in the garage, or on the street. Contact with oil can make your cat ill. Above all, make sure that no antifreeze is left on the floor, driveway, or street, as it is highly toxic and can kill if even a tiny bit is ingested. Antifreeze has a taste that cats love, so beware.

Keep all over-the-counter and prescription drugs stored away safely. Many cats can open medicine cabinets, so consider not keeping household cleaners under the kitchen or bathroom sinks, either, as many cats can easily open these with a flick of a paw.

■ **Many common household substances** *are extremely toxic to your cat. Keep all bleaches and other harmful cleaning material well out of reach from your curious cat.*

Install childproof locks on all cupboards and drawers that contain any toxic substances or edibles you don't want your cat to get into. All that's needed is a drill and a screwdriver; they install easily and could save your pet's life. You can find these childproof locks at any good hardware store.

IN CASE OF POISONING

Be sure to have an emergency telephone number for your vet handy, as well as the listing for a 24-hour clinic. Also, in the US, you can call the National Animal Poison Information Center at 1-800-548-2423 for expert advice on what to do if your cat has ingested a toxic substance. If all else fails, try 911; someone there may be able to help. Whatever you do, get your cat to a veterinarian as quickly as you can.

If your cat has ingested a poisonous substance, you may need to act quickly to save its life. The common treatment is to induce vomiting, unless the poison consumed is of a corrosive nature, such as battery acid, fertilizer, or drain cleaner. Allowing these to come back up will further damage the cat's esophagus and oral cavity. Also avoid inducing vomiting if the cat is having convulsions or is losing consciousness.

To induce vomiting, administer 2 or 3 teaspoons of syrup of ipecac. If this is not available, get as much heavily salted water into the cat as possible. After it has vomited, get it to drink as much water or milk as possible. Force-feed it with a turkey baster if necessary. Then get it to the veterinarian as soon as possible.

■ **If your cat has eaten a toxic substance,** *you may be advised by the vet to give it syrup of ipecac to induce vomiting.*

Deadly plants

Many types of house and garden plants are toxic to cats. Any ivy, philodendron, daffodils, or azaleas around your home? All are poisonous to a cat. To make matters worse, most cats like to occasionally munch on plants. Even plants in an outdoor garden can often fall prey to the salad-seeking feline. Unfortunately, this annoying behavior can be very dangerous for your cat.

TOXIC PLANTS

This list is by no means complete. Ask your veterinarian or check at the plant nursery before you bring any plant home.

- Azalea
- Bean plants
- Cactus
- Crocus
- Daffodil
- Dieffenbachia
- Hemlock
- Hydrangea
- Ivy
- Lily
- Marijuana
- Mistletoe
- Mushroom
- Narcissus
- Nightshade
- Oleander
- Philodendron
- Poinsettia
- Potato leaves
- Rhododendron
- Tobacco
- Tomato leaves
- Walnuts
- Yew

DIEFFENBACHIA

The simple solution is to avoid buying any plants known to be toxic to cats. If your cat has access to the outdoors, be sure to avoid planting toxic shrubbery or garden plants as well. Unfortunately, you won't be able to stop your outdoor cat from going over to the neighbor's yard. You will have to decide if allowing it this privilege is important enough to risk poisoning.

What about the safe plants?

Locate whatever nontoxic houseplants you have off of the floor, either in tall stands or from hanging mounts. Plant pedestals should be high and as narrow as the plant's draining dish, to give the cat no footing whatsoever. Never keep any plants on the floor or on shelves with easy cat access.

Trivia...

In the wild, cats eat vegetarian animals and generally consume the prey's stomach and its contents. These contents usually consist of partially digested vegetable matter, which, when eaten by a cat, can provide it with vitamins and minerals not necessarily found elsewhere.

Cover the soil of the plant with marbles or rocks to discourage digging. Wipe down the plant leaves with a dilute soap and water mixture; it won't hurt the plant, and it will taste terrible to the cat. You can also buy a veterinarian-approved taste deterrent and apply it to the plant.

Also, try placing double-sided adhesive tape around the area where you keep your plants; cats hate walking on sticky surfaces. Try aluminum foil strips as well, because cats hate those, too. If you can catch the cat in the act of chewing on a plant, spray the cat with water from a plant sprayer bottle.

A little cat salad

While discouraging your kitty from going near your prized houseplants, you should provide it with some young grass seedlings to chew on. Grow them yourself from grass seed, or purchase the plants at your local pet supply store. Place the permitted plant as far away as possible from your houseplants, so your cat doesn't get confused about what's allowed and what isn't. When given an alternative like this, most cats will forget about the houseplants entirely.

Finally, try to keep your cat's environment as stimulating as possible to prevent boredom – one of the main causes of improper behavior. Lots of toys and objects to investigate, as well as plenty of play time with you, should keep the cat's nose out of your houseplants.

A simple summary

✔ You will need to buy some essential supplies before you bring your cat home.

✔ Buy the litter and cat food your cat is already using, at least for a few weeks. This will help ease the transition for your cat.

✔ Before your new feline friend comes home, make sure to go over your home from top to bottom, in an effort to make it as safe and secure as possible. By removing any potential threats to your new pet's health and safety, you will be able to enjoy a worry-free cat experience.

✔ Pay special attention to toxic chemicals and plants around your home.

Chapter 6

Welcome to My Place!

A NEW HOME CAN BE DOWNRIGHT INTIMIDATING to a cat, particularly if there are small children and other pets around. My aim in this chapter is to make the transition to your house as easy and painless as possible for your new pal.

In this chapter...

✓ Bringing kitty home

✓ The first few hours

✓ Showing your new cat the ropes

✓ Introducing children

✓ Cat meets cat

✓ Setting up a timetable

✓ Indoors or out?

✓ The first visit to the veterinarian

LET YOUR CAT EXPLORE ITS NEW HOME

Bringing kitty home

LEAVING THE ONLY ENVIRONMENT *your new cat or kitten has ever known can be a traumatic experience, although most cats seem to deal with separation much better than dogs. A cat will adapt to its new environment quite quickly and soon forget about its siblings and mother – unless it is a kitten under 7 weeks of age, in which case separation could prove to be more difficult. But I don't have to worry about that with you, because you know better now!*

The right day

When you finally bring your new friend home, try to choose a day on which very little will be happening in your home, so you don't overload the cat's senses. Taking the day off from work would be perfect, so that your pet will have someone to interact with, and so you will be able to relax and give the cat your full attention.

Driving Miss Kitty

Be sure to transport the cat in a carrier with a towel or small blanket inside. This is a lot safer for you, because a cat loose in the car can cause an accident. It's also better for the cat: Being in a fast-moving vehicle can often be quite traumatic for a pet, because so much is happening just outside the windows. Traffic sounds and an ever-changing visual barrage could worry it unnecessarily.

If possible, have a friend do the driving, so that you can concentrate on your new friend without worrying about the traffic.

Also, it is better to keep your cat in a warm, cozy little box by your side or at your feet. Resist the temptation to keep the box in your lap, since an accident could send it flying into the dashboard, possibly injuring the little fur ball before it ever gets home.

Trivia...

Airlines have specific rules concerning what types of cat carriers are acceptable for use. Size and construction are the primary concerns. If the carrier is to be brought on board with you, it must fit beneath the seat in front of you with the cat in it. You will not be allowed to keep the cat (in or out of the carrier) on your lap during the flight, since it could escape and cause major problems on board. If the cat is to be transported in the cargo area (something I don't recommend), the carrier must be made of a rigid, secure material and should contain a water bottle for the cat's use.

The first few hours

BRING THE CAT, in its carrier, into your home, but don't open the carrier yet. First, check that all the windows and doors are securely closed and make sure everything is calm and quiet, so the cat or kitten doesn't experience chaos right from the start. The key is to be laid back and relaxed, with no crazy or unexpected activity. In other words, it's not a great idea to have a refrigerator delivered or plan a birthday party on the same day you bring your cat home!

Keep it calm

If you have another pet in the home, put it in another room with the door closed. Don't worry; I will explain all about introducing the old to the new in the very next section. For now, take the resident pet out of the equation. The new cat or kitten will certainly sense its presence anyway, just from its scent, which will serve as a good start to their introduction.

Bring the cat or kitten into a quiet part of the home and open the carrier, allowing it to come out on its own. Do not physically remove the cat yourself. Don't worry if your new pal does not come out right away. All cats eventually emerge and begin to investigate their new home with great interest. When the cat does come out, don't interfere unless it's to prevent injury.

■ **When you get** *your cat home, open the door to the cat carrier and leave your new pet to venture out in its own time. Do not try to remove the cat yourself.*

A simple offer

A good way to help ease the cat or kitten into the home is to offer it a treat or two. Doing so will make a great first impression. Just imagine moving into a new home and finding a delicious meal waiting for you! Your cat feels the same. Don't worry if it doesn't eat right away; just offering food will be comfort enough. In addition to the food and water, you might consider having a few toys out.

If the cat is at ease and appears confident, try playing with it a bit, perhaps with a ball, a feather toy, or a crumpled sheet of newspaper. This will really break the ice and leave the cat or kitten with a good first impression of you and your home.

Showing your new cat the ropes

WHEN YOU MOVE INTO A NEW NEIGHBORHOOD, you may feel a bit disconnected from all the goings-on until you have gotten around and familiarized yourself with everything. After you have met the neighbors, found the local market and shopping areas, and gotten a feel for the way things work, you relax and begin to enjoy the newness of it all. Having a local friend helps tremendously in cutting through all the confusion and strangeness; he or she can act as a guide, pointing you toward the good stuff.

Guess what? You are that friend for your new cat or kitten. You can make the first few hours much easier by volunteering to show your new friend the ropes. After your cat has had a chance to come out and sniff around a bit, you should casually and playfully give your kitty the guided tour of your home – its "territory" for many years to come.

"Must-see" spots

Start with the most important spots in the home. I'd suggest pointing out the litter box first. Knowing where this key piece of equipment is located will start the cat or kitten off on the right foot; if you're really lucky, the cat may even decide to use the box the first time it sees it. Make sure that the box is located in a part of the home that's easy to get to.

■ **Have a litter box** *ready for your new cat. Position it in a quiet, convenient location, and with any luck your pet should take to it straight away.*

Make sure everyone in the home remembers to keep the door open to the room where the litter box is located, because your cat must have 24-hour access.

The next "must-see" feline point of interest has got to be the feeding area. Most owners locate the food dish and water bowl in the kitchen, although other areas in the home can work well, too. Just be sure that the chosen area can be easily cleaned if food or water spills. Also, don't pick a spot that is a high-traffic area, as this would be annoying and stressful to the pet. Can you imagine having to eat dinner in the middle of a busy local street? Don't put the food near the litter box either; would you want to eat next to the toilet? Lead the cat or kitten right up to the dish and bowl (which should both have something in them), and encourage it to eat or drink. Nothing makes one feel more at home than a good meal, I always say.

A place to scratch

Next, show the new family member where the scratching post is. As I've already mentioned, make sure you've put it close to where you intend the cat or kitten to sleep, because most cats like to stretch out and get in a good scratch first thing in the morning. Because a scratching post is also a territory marker, it must be in a territory worth marking, as well. So a scratching post in the basement or the laundry room will likely go unused.

It's not vital that you get the cat to scratch right away, although you can show the cat what the post is for by scratching your own nails across the rope or carpet surface a few times, just to give it the idea.

If your household is a large one, or if you have more than one cat, I would strongly suggest that you have at least two scratching posts located in different spots, to satisfy the marking demands of both pets. If each cat has its own scratching post located at opposite ends of the home, territorial disputes will be kept to a minimum.

If you've bought a cat tree or condo for your new feline, take the cat over to it and see what happens. It might not be impressed, or it could take to it right away. To spark its interest, try placing a choice treat on each of the condo's levels, or tempt the kitty onto it by using a teaser toy. If the cat or kitten is comfortable with you picking it up, try placing it on top of the structure, usually a carpeted tray with a comfy cat cushion within. In no time at all, your new pal should make this piece of furniture its favorite.

■ **It is a good idea** *to show your new cat its scratching post, since the cat will use it as a territory marker. Place it near to its sleeping area.*

Look at all your stuff!

Be sure to introduce your new kitty to all of its new toys – a particularly happy experience, especially for kittens used to playing with rambunctious littermates. Have a ball or two, a few feather teasers, a furry mouse, and perhaps even a wind-up or battery-operated toy on hand. Old stand-by toys such as a crumpled-up piece of paper or a cardboard box with a few treats thrown in will also be enjoyed.

Apart from showing your new cat or kitten all the key objects that hold importance to it, be sure to simply give it a room-to-room tour, as you would to any new housemate. Let the critter see, sniff, paw, and climb on anything it finds curious, provided it's safe for cats and you don't mind. Just be sure not to encourage it to get interested in any plants, wires, or anything else that could be dangerous. Through it all, allow the cat or kitten to decide where it wants to go and try to avoid picking it up too many times. After all, this is an exciting and slightly overwhelming time for your new cat; try to let it get the feel of its new digs in its own time and manner.

■ **Bond with your new pet** *and make it feel truly welcome in its new home by showing it some new toys, such as a feather teaser.*

KEEP KITTY INSIDE

I am not in favor of owners allowing their cats unrestricted access to the outdoors, for reasons I'll discuss a little later in this chapter. Even if you disagree with me, however, please do not let your cat go outside at this stage. Everything will feel a bit strange for it right now, and letting it out straight away might result in it panicking and running away. Also, the odds of it finding its way back home are very low; research has shown that cats need about 4 weeks to understand where they are in a new "territory." So if you must let your cat outside, wait a few weeks until the kitty has a better idea of the sights, smells, and sounds of home.

Introducing children

CHILDREN JUST LOVE CATS AND KITTENS. How could they not? What could be better than having a walking, meowing, playful little creature ambling about the home? Forget the teddy bear – there's a new cat in town!

What can go wrong?

Unfortunately, problems can often arise between cats and kids, especially toddlers, who are at the age in which all things fascinating must be investigated and handled. Trouble is, many youngsters handle a bit too roughly at first. Many a cat–child relationship has been ruined early on because the child pulled on the pet's hair or tail or roughly picked the pet up when it didn't want to be handled.

Cats and kittens do not normally have the same levels of patience that dogs or other family pets might. They won't tolerate being manhandled, teased, pinched, poked, or prodded. If a child mishandles a cat or kitten, chances are that pet might be cautious around children for a very long time. Remember, cats have excellent memories and can often hold grudges against anyone they feel has hurt or frightened them.

The good news is that, with the right advance preparation, you can prevent this from happening. Your children can experience the same feelings of friendship and affection that you do, provided they abide by certain rules when interacting with the cat or kitten.

■ **Children naturally love kittens** *but they must be taught to handle them gently and carefully. It's very easy for a child to mistreat a young cat without realizing it.*

First, the talk

First, sit down and have a talk with the kids before the cat or kitten arrives. Tell them about how sweet and pretty it is and how soft its fur is to the touch. Then tell them how small and delicate it is (especially if it's a kitten), and that they have to treat it with gentle hands. Remind your kids that, to a cat, they are giants.

Also, suggest that they not chase the cat or kitten the way they might chase a dog, because cats don't like being chased and it makes them very scared – the way the kids might feel when they're watching a scary movie. Instead, it's better to let the cat come to them. When it does, they can pet it gently to feel how soft its fur is.

Also tell your children that, if they pet the cat or kitten in just the right, gentle way, they might get to hear a very special sound, one that cats and kittens make only when they are very happy. If they can get the pet to purr, it means they have made a new friend who will love them like no other, as long as they are always gentle with it.

It's a good idea to have your children offer the new cat or kitten a small, tasty treat every now and then to help convince the pet that these small humans are good to be around.

Also, encourage the kids to toss a ping-pong ball or mouse toy around for the cat or kitten, or get the pet to chase a teaser toy around for a while. Either of these techniques will work to convince the cat that the kids are safe, fun, and rewarding, both emotionally and nutritionally!

■ **Encouraging your child** *to play with your new pets will help them to make friends and be relaxed around each other.*

Cat meets cat

CATS ARE TERRITORIAL ANIMALS, *and they don't always take kindly to having a new cat invading their territory. Therefore, bring a new cat into your resident cat's territory very gradually. Let them get to know one another by scent first, before you allow a face-to-face (or face-to-fang) meeting.*

Introductions by scent

Keep the new cat in a separate room with the door closed, at least for a day or two. Your resident cat will know that a new animal is in the house but will not be able to confront it directly. Let the new cat lie on an old towel or play with a new toy, and then give it to the resident cat to sniff and swat at. Give the new cat something the old cat has been in contact with as well. This way, they can become familiar with one another's scent.

Getting to know one another

After 2 or 3 days of separation, place the new cat in a cat carrier, then open the door to the room and let the resident cat come over in its own time and meet the new addition. Do not open the carrier. Just let them sniff and investigate through the bars for five minutes or so. They may show some territorial aggression or fear. Chances are, though, with the opportunity to physically interact removed from the equation, they will simply sniff each other out at this stage.

First contact

Let them keep meeting like this for a few minutes at a time, at least six times a day for a few days. When they seem fairly comfortable and curious, begin letting the cats interact for short periods of time outside the carrier. Make sure you oversee the meeting, and use caution – you do not want to be scratched or bitten. Don't shut the cats up in one room when they meet; instead, give both cats the opportunity to retreat to a different area of the home, if need be, to avoid a fight. You'll know when they seem to be settling down with one another and it's safe to give both cats free range of the house.

A little bit of hissing and wrestling is normal the first few weeks as the cats work out their place in the feline hierarchy of your house.

Make sure to give plenty of attention to both, so they don't have to compete for your love, and use separate food dishes so they don't have to compete for food. They'll soon work the territory issue out between themselves.

Setting up a timetable

CATS TEND TO GET INTO A ROUTINE OF SORTS. *They like doing things at roughly the same time each day. Eating, eliminating, sleeping, playing, and other activities come at regular intervals that the cat grows accustomed to. They get comfortable with a timetable of sorts and don't always appreciate unrehearsed or unexpected surprises. Throw things off schedule and your cat will likely feel a little stressed, sometimes resulting in some undesirable behaviors. Realize that a predictable environment is a safe one, from a feline's point of view.*

Save the surprises

This doesn't mean that you can't throw in a few surprises every now and then. You certainly can, provided that they don't stress the cat out or pose it any kind of physical threat. In fact, new experiences can help entertain and teach your pet. For the first few months, though, try to keep things predictable and reliable, to give the cat a feeling of confidence in its new surroundings.

Routine activities

Some good ideas about setting a basic daily timetable for your new cat or kitten include:

1. Feeding your cat at about the same times every day and in the same place. This will help build a food drive in the pet, which can later be used as a tool when you're teaching it new behaviors.

2. Scheduling a daily play time for you and your cat or kitten. By doing so, you will help teach the cat or kitten to channel those "kitten crazies" into certain times of the day. We all like to have something to look forward to; why should your feline be any different?

3. Grooming your cat or kitten at the same time each day to help the pet learn to accept and tolerate what might not necessarily be its favorite activity.

■ **Establishing a routine** *for your cat, such as grooming it regularly, will help it to settle down and feel at home.*

4 Maintaining the same basic rules for your cat every day. If it is not allowed on the table, make no exceptions. This kind of consistency will help build a respectful, trusting relationship between the two of you.

5 Attempting to wake up and go to sleep around the same time each day. This predictability in your schedule will help your little fur ball set its own.

After a few months, you will notice that the cat or kitten has begun to develop routine behaviors all its own. As long as they are not in any way harmful or annoying to you or anyone else, go with them. Your cat or kitten will enjoy napping on the carpet in the early afternoon sun each day, staring at the goldfish every evening before dinner, or any one of a thousand habitual behaviors that make it happy. We have them, too, so why shouldn't cats?

Indoors or out?

ONE OF THE MOST *important decisions you will have to make is whether or not to allow your cat outdoors. This decision used to be a simpler one, fraught with fewer dangers and less dire consequences. In the past, when the majority of cat owners lived in rural areas, letting the family cat out for the day wasn't such a big deal – apart from the occasional coyote, neighbor's dog, or another combative cat, not many mortal threats loomed large in the cat's life outside the home.*

Outdoor dangers

Today, everything is different. The majority of cat owners now live in urban or suburban environments rife with all manner of dangers. Fast-moving cars and trucks, as well as a denser concentration of other cats, now pose grave threats to a cat's life. Contrary to what some people believe, cats do not have nine lives, and they cannot take care of themselves in any situation. In the past year alone,

■ **Cats who venture outdoors** *are more likely to catch an infectious disease or suffer serious injury than those who live within the confines of the house.*

I have seen at least half a dozen dead cats in and along a number of heavily trafficked roads in my suburban neighborhood. When faced with a vehicle moving at more than 60 miles an hour, a cat is usually going to lose the race.

Because of the heavier density of outdoor cats in urban and suburban environments, feline diseases have been spreading like wildfire. If you doubt that, just ask your vet.

The following is just a partial list of some potentially fatal feline infectious diseases that have become much more prevalent in the past few decades:

- Chlamydia psittaci
- Feline calicivirus
- Feline herpes
- Feline immunodeficiency virus (FIV)
- Feline infectious anemia
- Feline infectious peritonitis (FIP)
- Feline leukemia
- Feline panleukopenia
- Feline viral rhinotracheitis (FVR)

Sound serious? They are, and they claim the lives of thousands of cats every year. The sad thing is that most of these deaths could have been avoided if the owners had simply kept their cats indoors and gotten them properly vaccinated.

The health difference

Indoor-only cats live on average about 10 years longer than indoor–outdoor cats. In addition to having a much lower incidence of infectious diseases, they suffer less from parasites and poisonings and have a lower instance of joint-related disorders, particularly arthritis. Indoor cats rarely, if ever, get fleas and ticks and worms – parasites that are just waiting to prey on all outdoor cats. Additionally, indoor-only felines rarely get into fights with other

■ **Keeping your cat indoors** *may sound cruel, but indoor cats tend to have longer and healthier lives than cats that are allowed to roam freely in the great outdoors.*

cats or dogs, resulting in fewer injuries and abscesses. And they have a very low incidence of pregnancy, another advantage indoor–outdoor cats cannot claim. Healthier, safer, indoor cats rack up far less in veterinary costs, as well.

The behavior difference

Want more? Okay. Cats allowed to spend a great deal of time outdoors tend to become somewhat less sociable toward people and much less tolerant of other animals, especially other cats. The reason is simple: They have to develop a more cautious nature if they are to survive outside. My question to you is this: Why have a domestic pet if it is only going to become more and more like its wild counterparts?

If you provide your cat or kitten with a stimulating, diverse home atmosphere right from the start, it will have no need to go outdoors. In fact, cats kept indoors from kittenhood rarely want to venture out, despite the occasional window or door being left open. They develop a love for their own territory, namely the confines of your home. Outdoors is the territory of other cats, dogs, cars, and people; why would they want to go out there and compete for such a huge place?

It is only when a cat is allowed out routinely that it becomes addicted to the lure of the hunt and the search for a mate.

■ **If you provide your cats** *with enough stimulation, they will not miss being outdoors. Indeed, many cats prefer to stay inside, and will not attempt to go outside, even when given the opportunity.*

Cats are not wild animals

Some people say it's cruel to keep a cat indoors all the time; they feel that it denies the cat the ability to express its true self. We must remember, however, that the domestic feline is not a wild animal, despite the fact that it can stalk, leap, and mate, much like its wild cousins. The cat has been domesticated, and it is not a wild animal.

With that domesticity comes the understanding that these pets have been behaviorally changed to better fit into our homes and lives, and that these changes, though not as dramatic as those applied to the dog, nonetheless make life outdoors a risky proposition at best for today's domestic cat.

Why let a cat out?

People who support letting cats outside need to think long and hard, then, about their real motivations for letting domestic felines outside and into harm's way. Are they just too busy to play with their cat indoors? I say it is more cruel to let a cat out, knowing that in doing so, you may be condemning it to a shorter and less healthy life.

A safe space outside

If you absolutely can't bear the thought of your kitty going through life without feeling the wind in her fur, there are some safer options available. First, consider screening in a porch or deck, then allowing your cat access to it through a small cat door. Or, you can build a small cat run on the side of your home, fenced in with chicken wire, also accessed from your home by a small cat door.

If you try this, be sure to enclose the top of the run as well, to prevent your agile climber/leaper from escaping. Many pet supply stores sell prefabricated cat runs that take only minutes to assemble and install.

For apartment dwellers who have a hallway, you can consider opening your front door and letting the cat wander out to investigate.

You can even play a quick game of fetch out in the hallway, using a favorite toy or a crumpled sheet of paper. Just be careful not to allow the cat access to a flight of stairs that leads outside, or to an area too large for you to easily retrieve the cat if necessary.

Trying one of these alternatives will give your cat the chance to stretch its legs and experience life outside of the home, while still being safe and under your care.

The first visit to the veterinarian

NEXT TO YOU, perhaps the most important person in your cat or kitten's life is the veterinarian. Besides giving vaccinations and treating injuries, he or she is often called upon to play medical detective with pets who aren't feeling well but may not be exhibiting symptoms that clearly point to a specific disorder. The veterinarian can give expert nutritional advice and can even help with behavioral problems, particularly those directly related to one or more health issues. In other words, it pays to have a great veterinarian on your side.

Start off right

Immediately after getting your kitten or cat, be sure to schedule a visit to the veterinarian of your choice. Why? Simple. First, you want to start off on the right track and establish a good working relationship between your new pet and the veterinarian. The sooner he or she gets to know your cat, the easier it will be for the vet to spot something out of the ordinary.

Second, you will want to make sure that your new feline is in good health, for its own good as well as the good of any other pets you might have who could contract a disorder from the new pet if the problem goes unchecked. Parasites such as fleas, ticks, or worms, or an infectious disease such as feline panleukopenia or feline infectious anemia could be passed on to other pets. Your vet can prevent this by detecting one or more of these conditions and treating them (if possible) before they have a chance to infect other pets.

■ **It is important to have** *your vet give your new cat a thorough checkup to identify any potential health problems.*

INTERNET

www.ivillage.com/pets/
features/petpourri/
articles/0,4437,
17000,00.html

This long address brings you to an excellent article about how to choose a veterinarian who can become your partner in caring for your cat.

What will the vet check?

During your initial visit to the veterinarian, he or she will also give your new pet whatever vaccinations are necessary in order to build its immunity to dangerous diseases such as rabies and feline calicivirus. The cat's weight, pulse, and rate of respiration will be measured – all important factors in determining its state of health. The veterinarian will listen to the cat or kitten's heart and lungs and check for any unusual discharges from the eyes, ears, nose, anus, and vagina or penis, which could also indicate illness. The pet's gums, teeth, and ears will be examined, as will its entire body, to check for any unusual growths, injuries, or *abscesses.* Even your cat's coat will be examined, as an excessively dry or greasy coat can point to illness.

A fecal sample might also be taken on the initial visit to check for internal parasites. The veterinarian will probably ask you to bring a sample with you, because extracting one from a cat or kitten during the visit can often be traumatic. Some vets might also take blood and urine samples, which, when analyzed, can be a strong indicator of the pet's overall health.

As you can see, the initial visit to the veterinarian is vital to your new pet. While you're at the vet's, don't hesitate to ask about diet, feline behavior, and even what toys or household items are safe or unsafe for the cat or kitten to interact with.

Trivia...

A structural problem such as hip dysplasia could be detected by the veterinarian, prompting you perhaps to bring the cat or kitten back to the breeder or shelter before you've both had a chance to bond too closely. Hip dysplasia is a deformity in the hip joint, preventing the head of the femur from properly fitting into the socket of the pelvis. Cats suffering from hip dysplasia are subject to pain, limited mobility and range of motion, and premature onset of arthritis. The unstable joint can, however, be repaired through surgery, although the procedure can be expensive. Hip dysplasia is an inherited disorder and can only be avoided by diligent breeding practices.

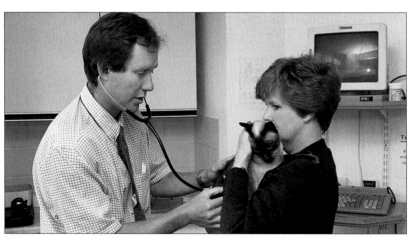

■ **Your cat's respiration** *can be checked by your veterinarian. This will give the vet an indication of the cat's general condition.*

A simple summary

✔ Consider taking the day off when you bring your new cat or kitten home, so you'll have plenty of time to spend with the new family member. Your cat might be a bit tentative at first about its new digs.

✔ Be sure to transport the cat in a sturdy carrier, and keep things relatively quiet and stress-free at first to make the transition easier.

✔ For the first few hours at home, keep distractions and noise to a minimum. Move any resident pets into another part of the house, so as not to overwhelm the new cat or kitten. Let the pet investigate, and consider giving it a treat or two, to let it know that the new home is a good place to be.

✔ Make sure you give your new feline a good tour of your home on the first day. Show it where the litter box and feeding areas are and also where the scratching post or kitty condo is.

✔ If you have children, talk to them about the new arrival before the cat actually comes home. They should understand that the new cat or kitten can't play rough or be mistreated.

✔ Set a loose timetable to help your pet adjust to life at your house. Cats are creatures of habit and routine; by providing it with a reliable schedule of events, you will help it make the transition from its old home to yours.

✔ Allowing your new feline to go outdoors will expose it to a number of dangers. Keeping your cat indoors will add years to its life and keep it happier and healthier.

✔ An initial visit to the veterinarian is essential. In addition to evaluating your new kitty's current health, the veterinarian can provide you with a wealth of information on a variety of topics, including, diet, behavior, and environment.

Chapter 7

Is Everybody Happy?

YOUR NEW CAT HAS SETTLED NICELY INTO YOUR HOME, and now it's time to fine-tune the day-to-day relationship a bit. In this chapter, I am going to show you how to address a number of key issues that can profoundly affect the relationship you are in the process of building with your new cat or kitten. Just like a marriage, the cat–owner relationship is an evolving, ongoing process – one that should get better and better as the years go by.

In this chapter...
- ✓ Litter box etiquette
- ✓ Boundary training
- ✓ Table manners
- ✓ Going for a ride
- ✓ Are you talking to me?
- ✓ Coming when called

YOU WILL NEED TO BUILD A RELATIONSHIP WITH YOUR CAT

Litter box etiquette

IN CHAPTER 5, *I discussed buying a litter box. Now I'd like to go into the subject a bit more deeply, to make sure everything is arranged to avoid any problems. Inappropriate elimination is the number-one reason cats end up in shelters. Whether or not a cat or kitten is properly using its litter box can have a profound effect on its relationship with you, so let's make sure everything is going perfectly.*

As I mentioned before, most cats will come into your home knowing how to use a litter box, since they have learned this behavior from their mother and littermates. That's a real plus, as far as pets go. Hopefully, your new feline is currently using the litter box regularly, with no accidents.

■ **Cats are naturally clean** *and most will happily use a litter box provided that it is always kept in the same place and cleaned regularly.*

Trivia...

If you have a dog, the litter box must be located in a spot that the pooch cannot get to. Know why? It's because dogs, for some ugly reason, like to consume cat feces. Yuck! It's nasty but true. To get around this, you should locate the litter box high up, on top of a cabinet or table too high for the dog to get to. Or put it in a room with a door that can be propped open about 3 or 4 inches – wide enough for a cat, but too narrow for most dogs to squeeze through (except a tiny little Chihuahua, or one of those little wiener dogs).

The right spot

The first thing you should do to ensure reliable litter box use is to keep the litter box in the same location all the time. Remember that cats are creatures of habit, and they expect things to be the same from day to day. If you move the litter box from room to room or floor to floor, you're asking for trouble. Moving the box will just confuse the cat, who might decide to eliminate where the box used to be, even though it isn't located there any more. Think about it: How would you like it if I moved your toilet all over the house? It would be pretty annoying, wouldn't it?

Make sure you put the litter box in a quiet, low-traffic area. If the spot is too busy, your cat may refuse to use the box. You wouldn't appreciate using the facilities in the middle of a crowded room, would you? Once you have found a good place for the box, leave it there!

Keep it clean!

No cat or kitten will reliably use a dirty box, so scoop every day, and change the litter once a week. There's no point in trying to cover up the smell, because cats, with their super-sensitive noses, will never be fooled. And they have to get right down level with the litter, so keep the box clean!

The number-one reason why a cat will refuse to use its litter box is that it smells bad. Always remember to keep the litter box as clean as possible!

One more point regarding the litter box: If you have two cats, I strongly recommend buying a second box and putting it in a different room. Often the resident cat will initially object to the presence of a new feline and will lay claim to "its" litter box, forcing the new pet to eliminate outside the box. Or, the resident cat will refuse to use the old box once the new cat has begun to. Having two boxes – one for each cat – will solve those problems. Remember: Two cats, two litter boxes.

■ **If you have two or more cats,** *it is probably best to provide each with a separate litter box, preferably in different rooms. Most cats will object to sharing a box and may choose to eliminate elsewhere.*

Boundary training

MOST CAT OWNERS HAVE *some areas in their home that they want to be off-limits to their cats. I know I do. I do not want my cat jumping up onto the dinner table while I am eating, leaping up onto a table with a vase of flowers on it, or going anywhere near my houseplants (nontoxic though they may be).*

You need to set the rules right from the start, in order to avoid confusion and conflict in the future. One way to help do this is to give the cat well-defined boundaries. Impossible you say? Nothing is impossible!

Start with a squirt

First, be sure to start boundary training when the cat is still young. A 5-year-old cat will not learn nearly as fast as a 3-month-old kitten, so start boundary training the day your little puss comes home.

Next, decide where you do not want your cat to go. The dinner table, the bookcase, the kitchen counters, or wherever else you decide (remember it still is your home, at least legally) can be off-limits.

■ **Use a plant sprayer** *to squirt your cat if you see it jumping up on to any forbidden surfaces. Simply fire a jet of water at its rump – this will deter the cat from trespassing in future.*

Then, get yourself a plant sprayer bottle or water pistol and keep it on hand for quick use whenever the cat goes where it's not allowed.

If kitty jumps up, immediately give it a quick little squirt of water (on the rump, not the face, please!). The cat will quickly get the idea: Table equals water; water bad!

The squirt of water will work well for any forbidden areas in your home; just spray the cat with a jet of water when it crosses whatever boundaries you have set. On the corner table with the crystal vase? Squirt! Near the cutting board in the kitchen? Squirt! Balancing on the bookcase? Squirt! You get the idea, as will the cat after a few short weeks.

INTERNET

www.wicatclub.com

For a great assortment of articles on feline behavior and training, check out this site from Cats International.

Sticky bits and other deterrents

To teach the cat about other boundaries in the home, and to make sure the rules are enforced when you are not around, try putting double-sided sticky tape around the off-limits objects or areas. Cats hate walking on it, and the moment they do, they will usually back off. Just be sure to put down two rows of the stuff, to make sure the cat won't just step daintily over the tape. Also, do not use the tape on finely finished wood, as it may mark the surface. Strips of aluminum foil can also be used to establish a boundary line for a cat, as walking on them is unpleasant.

■ **Aluminum foil** *can be placed around any areas that you wish to keep off-limits to your cat. Cats hate the feel of it under their feet.*

Most pet stores will also sell a commercial cat repellent designed to turn the cat away from any treated areas. Before using one, however, check with your veterinarian, who should be able to determine if the repellent is nontoxic. Never use a toxic substance to repel your cat!

If you don't want the cat in certain rooms of the home, simply keep those doors shut tightly. To make up for any frustration your cat might feel from being kept out of certain areas, be sure to make the acceptable areas as fun and interesting as possible, by making toys, scratching posts, a kitty condo, or even a small bag of catnip available.

Never, ever strike your cat or kitten, for any reason. Physical force never teaches a cat anything except to fear the attacker. If you want your cat to love and trust you, remember never to hit it.

■ **Interesting toys** *will stimulate your feline and prevent boredom and frustration. This should help to keep your cat from demanding entry to forbidden areas of your home.*

119

Table manners

CERTAIN BASIC RULES OF ETIQUETTE *should be followed at dinnertime. If they're not, your dinner (or that of your pet) could become an obnoxious experience. A pet not accustomed to how things are done in your home might end up begging, stealing food from another pet (or you), or even getting into a fight over a tasty morsel in someone else's dish. Dinnertime should be an enjoyable, relaxing time for all, and I'll tell you how to make it so.*

No begging

First, make it clear to your new cat or kitten that begging at the table is simply not acceptable behavior. This should be discouraged not only because of the nuisance it can become, but because too many calories of rich table food can quickly make your pet dangerously pudgy. Also, give the cat a quick squirt of water with a plant sprayer bottle or water pistol whenever it jumps up onto the table.

To discourage your new cat or kitten from begging, never feed it from the table. This is the single most important thing you can do to discourage begging. Simply make it unprofitable.

No stealing

Next, make sure the new cat does not bother or interrupt the meals of any other cat in the home, who might not take too kindly to the new kid on the block sticking its little nose into the wrong food dish. Of course, this means each cat in the house must have its own food dish. Usually the resident cat will

■ **Begging is unacceptable** *behavior in a cat, and must be discouraged at all costs. Make sure that you never feed your pet from the table.*

make it very clear to the new pet how important it is to stay clear of its food (a swat or a hiss will generally do the trick). If your new feline is successfully stealing food from the resident cat, however, put an immediate stop to it by separating the two pets during feeding time and maintaining the separation until both are finished eating. By doing so, you will ensure that both are receiving the correct amount of food each day, and that no conflicts or bad feelings erupt between them. It's difficult enough to get a resident cat to accept a perfectly behaved new cat or kitten, let alone one who steals food. By keeping your eye on this, you will be helping to keep the peace.

If you have a dog in the home, it becomes even more important for you to keep the new feline away from its dish during dinnertime. Even a cat-loving dog can become quite protective of its food; the new cat or kitten could get bitten badly if it sticks its nose in the wrong place.

Prevent this by feeding the cat and the dog in different areas. The dog can eat in the kitchen while the cat eats in the laundry room. Or, you can locate the cat's dish high up, where the dog cannot reach. Consider staggering feeding times as well; whichever pet is liable to try stealing food from the other should eat first, so that its hunger is satisfied by the time the other pet begins eating.

Whatever method you use, realize that dinnertime is very important to most animals and should not be interrupted or made stressful. Making sure that the new cat or kitten gets into an acceptable feeding routine will go a long way toward keeping the peace in your home.

■ **Provide a feeding dish** *for each cat. Otherwise, you may find one cat is stealing food from the other, leaving the other poor puss undernourished. Fighting may also break out between the two.*

Going for a ride

YOUR NEW CAT OR KITTEN *will eventually need to learn how to tolerate car rides. Trips to the veterinarian, to a friend or relative's home, or to some other destination occasionally come up, making it necessary for your feline to feel at ease while in transit.*

This shouldn't be a big deal for most cats, but often is because of a simple mistake made by many cat owners: Allowing the cat to be loose in the car. This can create a vulnerable feeling for many felines, who, when loose in a car, feel as if they are in a fishbowl, surrounded by glass on all sides. If the cat or kitten panics, it could cause you to lose control of the car. Not a good idea. That's why a cat must always be in a cat carrier in the car.

Cat, meet carrier

Most cats like to be in snuggly little spots, so if you simply leave the carrier out all the time with a towel inside, the cat may take to sleeping in it regularly. You can even occasionally feed your cat inside the carrier. Doing so will help condition the pet to tolerate or even like this handy device.

To get your cat further accustomed to being in its cat carrier, consider regularly showing it a tasty treat, then placing the tidbit into the carrier with the door wide open (or even off).

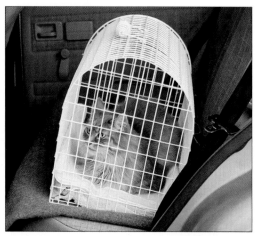

■ **Take your cat** *for a ride in the car on a regular basis to get it used to the experience.*

Your new pet has probably already ridden in a car at least once for its trip to your home. You've probably taken your cat to the vet in a car, as well. Cats are smart critters, and if a car ride always means a trip to the vet, they'll quickly figure it out and resist the idea of getting in the car. That's why you should take your cat for a ride at least once or twice a month. Simply place the pet inside its cat carrier, then place the carrier in the car and go for a short drive around the neighborhood. Visit a friend or relative's home, or go fill up the gas tank. By doing so, you will be teaching your feline that the car is not a scary place to be.

Are you talking to me?

SOME CATS DO NOT LEARN *to respond to their names. I believe this happens because their owners don't bother to teach them. Most cat owners do not tell their cats to do much of anything, and so rarely combine the pet's name with an activity and a resulting reward – which is what happens in dog training.*

The cat's name

I think it's a good idea to teach your cat to recognize its name. Doing so will increase its intelligence and awareness and will help lay the foundation for any further training you might want to do. For instance, if you ever want to teach your cat to come when called or to fetch a ball (yes, cats can learn these things, and much more!), having it recognize and respond to its name will be a great first step. Also, if you cannot seem to find your cat in or around the home, having it recognize and respond to its name means the cat will seek you out instead.

■ **Reward your cat** *with a tidbit if she comes when you call her. She will soon associate treats with hearing her name.*

123

Teaching your cat its name

Teaching your cat to recognize and respond to its name is easy. All you need do is say its name and then closely follow the sound with a pleasant experience. This will teach the cat to expect something good each time its name is mentioned. The pleasant experience can be an affectionate stroke, a tasty treat, or even a quick play session with the pet's favorite toy.

Conditioning your cat

Because cats normally respond when they think something good is on the way (those narcissistic little devils!), you will be creating a **conditioned response** in the pet; it will soon begin associating its name with the pleasant experience, so that eventually just saying its name will work to get the pet to pay attention to you. It will hear its name and anticipate the good stuff.

Each time you stroke or cuddle your cat or kitten, make sure you say its name softly several times. Also, right before giving your cat a meal or a treat, say its name a few times. It will slowly but surely begin associating its name with attention and treats, which is just what you want. Eventually (say after about 2 or 3 months of this), simply saying its name will evoke a response. Odds are that your feline will perk up and begin to pay close attention to you the moment that magic name is mentioned.

DEFINITION

You have all probably heard about the experiment that the scientist Ivan Pavlov did long ago with dogs: right before feeding them, Pavlov would always ring a bell. Eventually, just the ringing of the bell caused the dogs to salivate, whether or not food was given afterward. This is a perfect example of a **conditioned response**; *the dogs didn't even think, they just reacted. It's like when we see the traffic light turn green. We don't even think about pushing down on the gas pedal, we just go. That's a conditioned response.*

■ **Before you put down** *your cat's food, say its name a few times. By conditioning it in this way, your cat will soon learn to come whenever you call it.*

Coming when called

ONCE YOU HAVE TAUGHT *your cat or kitten to respond to its name, it's only a short step away from learning to come to you when called. Why not? Many cats already do it without their owners even realizing it. Have you ever seen a person go out on the back deck and tap on the top of a cat food can with a fork in an attempt to get his or her cat to come in for its dinner? That's a perfect example of a cat coming to its owner when called.*

The same often happens with an indoor cat who hears the electric can opener start up. Assuming that it's a can of cat food being opened, the cat rushes into the kitchen for its supper. Another perfect example of a cat coming on command.

Why teach a cat to come?

What possible reason could you have for teaching this very "dog-like" behavior to your cat? First, like any other learned behavior, it stimulates the cat's mind, which is always a good thing. Second, it creates a closer tie between you and your pet; when you call out to your cat, you know it will be thinking of you. Third, it allows you to find your feline if it has disappeared. This can be especially valuable to owners who allow their cats to go outdoors.

■ **Teach your cat** *to come on command. It is not a difficult trick to teach and you will strengthen the bond between you and your pet. It will also stimulate your cat in the process.*

TEACHING THE COMMAND

Here's how to teach your cat to come when called:

1. First, make sure that you feed your feline at regular times, instead of *free-feeding* it. This will help you better predict exactly when it will be hungry, a necessary ingredient in teaching it to come. Feeding your cat at exact times each day will establish a hunger drive in the cat, which you will then be able to use for training purposes.

2. Next, buy a toy clicker gadget from a local toy store – the kind you had when you were a kid. When you push down on the metal tab, it makes a loud click.

3. Now, right before you put the cat or kitten's food down, call it by name or by making whatever sound you desire (many owners just say "kitty-kitty-kitty...")

As soon as the pet appears, click the clicker four or five times, then place the food down. Repeat this procedure every time you feed the cat or kitten for one month.

4. Finally, try this: At a time just before your cat's normal dinnertime, with a tasty treat in one hand and your clicker in the other, call the cat, using whatever verbal cue you have been using at dinnertime. Make sure you are not in the cat's regular feeding area when you do this, so you can really check how well the cat has learned the behavior. If you have done your training well, the cat should come to you (provided it can hear you).

5. When your cat does come, immediately click the clicker a few times and give it a treat. The clicker is used as an easily heard way of telling the cat "Yes, you have done it right!" Its sudden, percussive sound works better than your voice, as it is much less familiar and more noticeable.

DEFINITION

*Keeping food in your cat's dish all the time is known as **free-feeding**. Though convenient, this form of feeding tends to lower a cat's food drive and is not the most healthy way to feed a cat. Bored cats will nibble all day, taking in far more calories than they need and eventually becoming obese. Cats, like people, should be a little bit hungry when they sit down to a meal.*

Once you have your cat coming to you on command, try calling it at different times of the day and from different locations.

Just be sure to always reward the pet with a treat, since cats, unlike dogs, won't always come to you out of affection or because you want them to (can you imagine?). Basically, they have to be bribed!

A simple summary

✔ Locate litter boxes in a quiet place, keep them clean, and keep Fido away from them.

✔ Teaching your new cat or kitten where it can and cannot go in and around your home will help keep future conflicts to a minimum. Make sure that you are always consistent: If the cat is not allowed on the dinner table on Tuesday, don't let it up there on Thursday!

✔ Everyone in the family, humans and animals included, needs to respect whatever eating etiquette you have established. Do not under any circumstances reward begging, and don't let one pet invade the eating space of another.

✔ Be sure to occasionally take your cat for rides in the car, to ensure that it is ready for a trip when necessary. Always use a well-constructed cat carrier when doing so, to keep the pet calm and to prevent you from being distracted while driving.

✔ Teaching your cat to recognize and respond to its name will increase its awareness, strengthen the bond between the two of you, and enable you to get its attention when necessary.

✔ Training your cat to come to you when called is a great way to stimulate its mind and body, as well as a fail-safe way of locating your pet when it is nowhere to be found.

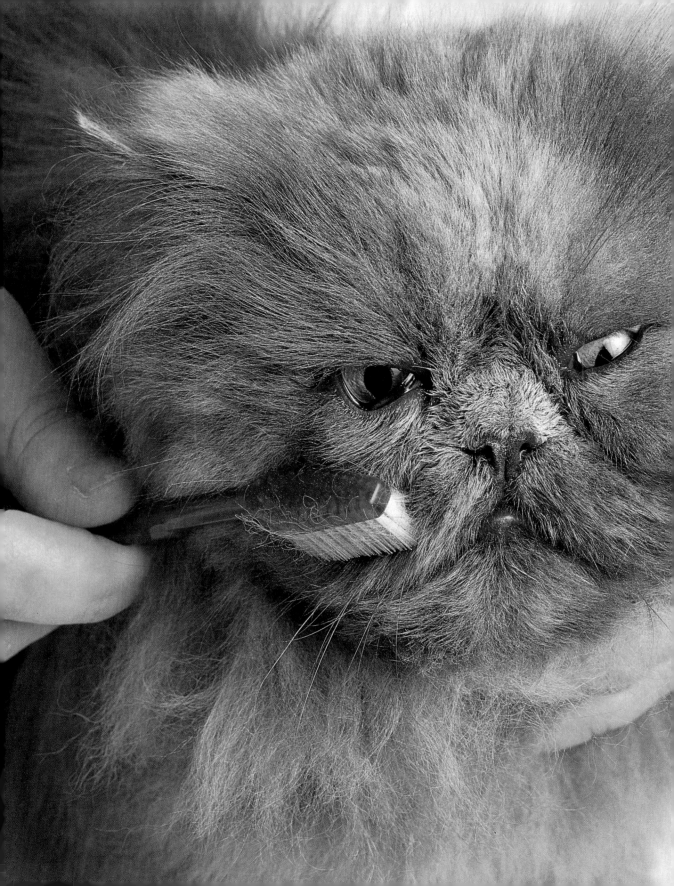

Chapter 8

You Look Marvelous!

ONCE YOU GET PAST THE FIRST DAY, you and your cat have a whole lifetime together. You will need to keep your cat well groomed and ensure that it stays as healthy as possible for as long as possible. And that means developing a good partnership with your veterinarian. This chapter discusses how to keep your cat or kitten looking great, by covering all aspects of grooming, from brushing and combing to bathing, nail care, and even cleaning and inspecting your feline's teeth.

In this chapter...

✓ Brushing and combing

✓ The feline manicure

✓ The dreaded bath

✓ Cleaning ears

✓ Playing cat dentist

CLEANING AND GROOMING MAY REQUIRE A DEGREE OF COOPERATION

Brushing and combing

YES IT'S TRUE *that cats keep themselves very clean. In fact, they spend hours each day grooming themselves all over. Your cat still needs a helping hand from you, though, to maintain that fabulous "I just came out of the salon" look that all felines crave.*

You should teach your cat or kitten to accept being brushed and combed regularly right from the start. It's easier to do this with a kitten, because they tend to learn faster and tolerate new behaviors better than adult cats. Grown-up felines need to stay clean and good-looking, too, though, so don't hesitate to start grooming your feline, even if it is over a year old.

■ **Accustom your cat** *to being groomed from an early age. Kittens are more tolerant to new experiences than the adult cat.*

The benefits of brushing

Brushing your cat helps remove excess hairs from the coat – hairs that could end up being swallowed by the cat as it grooms. These swallowed hairs can collect in the cat's stomach or intestines, eventually forming hairballs. Though normally passed or regurgitated by the pet, sometimes hairballs can create dangerous intestinal blockages that require veterinary care.

Regular grooming will also help desensitize your cat to being handled and touched – a problem with some cats, especially adults, who prefer to decide for themselves when they will surrender to a human. A cat that tolerates handling is much easier to treat medically.

Another benefit of regularly grooming your cat is that there will be less cat hair all over your house. It will reduce the chance of anyone having an allergic reaction, too.

*A **mat** is a dense, hopelessly tangled mass of hair that can form in a cat's coat. Mats closely resemble dreadlocks, which also cannot be combed or brushed out.*

The longhaired cat

For a longhaired cat or kitten, you need a good short-bristled cat brush and a fine-tooth comb (both available in any good pet supply store). Some cats can become wary of the comb, because this is the tool that usually finds *mats* in the pet's hair. That is why you should start combing out your longhaired cat's hair before any mats or tangles form. By doing so, your pet will have no reason to fear the comb.

Begin combing the pet lightly each and every day, for just a minute or so, even if it doesn't particularly need grooming. You can have the cat in your lap or on top of a table or even on the top tier of the kitty condo. Just make sure the cat can get a good grip on whatever surface you put it on. A slippery surface could cause the pet to become stressed, making grooming a scary and difficult procedure. While slowly and lightly combing your feline's back and sides, talk to it in a pleasant voice and praise it for being so good. You can even give it a small treat or two to really make the process a happy one. Over a week or so, build up the time spent combing until you can easily cover the entire coat. Be sure to go easy, especially around sensitive areas such as the feet, head, and tail.

A longhaired kitten may not yet have its full coat, but the hair will probably be long enough to get a comb through anyway, so do not hesitate to give it a go.

Next, get your cat or kitten used to light brushing all over its body, in much the same way you did with combing. Brush only for a minute or so, and always praise and talk in a quiet, pleasant voice. Give the cat a treat or two to reinforce the activity.

After your cat is accustomed to being lightly combed and brushed, it should be ready to tolerate more vigorous combing – the kind needed to remove mats and tangles. If you encounter any, gently tease and comb them out, taking care to avoid pulling the cat's skin. Some mats and tangles can take a while to get out; just be patient. If a mat or tangle is simply impossible to remove, you will need to cut part or all of it out with a sharp pair of scissors. Always cut away the least amount of hair necessary to get the mat out, and never let the scissors touch the skin. Take an extra moment or two to look between the toes of your longhaired cat, as this can be an area where mats abound. If you find any, gently snip them out.

Do not attempt to cut out any mats or tangles from your cat's body if you have any apprehension about it, because you might slip and hurt your cat. Also, don't try to remove mats and tangles from a cat who puts up a fight, as you will almost certainly both get hurt.

If either of these situations apply to you, have a professional groomer take care of your cat. He or she will do a great job, while saving you the stress of having to fight your uncooperative feline.

The shorthaired cat

A shorthaired cat will need far less brushing than a longhaired cat needs. A slicker brush will work well to remove excess hair, and a comb is still a good idea for sensitive areas around the face, ears, feet, and tail.

Put your shorthaired cat on a raised surface on the floor. Then simply give its short coat a quick, vigorous brushing, making sure to include the area between the cat's shoulder blades – a spot most cats find difficult to clean. Be sure to praise and reward it throughout the procedure.

When brushing, you may try brushing against the "grain," or lie, of your cat's coat first, then with it. In doing this, you will remove the most loose hairs possible. It will also momentarily expose your cat's skin, enabling you to check for sores, scabs, parasites, and rashes.

■ **Cats with fine, short hair** *are much easier to groom than longhaired felines. Simply brush vigorously all over the cat's body with a bristle brush to remove dust and dead hair from the coat.*

The feline manicure

EVEN CATS WITH SCRATCHING POSTS *will usually need to have their nails trimmed at least once a month so that they do not become overgrown. Very long nails can get caught in your carpet, furniture, and clothes, injuring your cat and damaging your valuable property. A cat's nails can even grow so long that they curl back into its pads. Ouch!*

I strongly suggest that you do not force an adult cat to have its nails trimmed. With those sharp claws, you could be seriously hurt. Instead, let a professional groomer do the job for you. A professional will be more used to handling a reluctant puss, and will know how to avoid those talons!

Trivia...

Unless you get them accustomed to it at a very young age, handling the feet tends to be a stressful experience for most cats. Feet are essential to a cat's survival. If its feet were injured, a cat in the wild would be unable to hunt, climb, or defend itself. This protective instinct has been passed on to domestic cats, making them quite particular about having their feet touched or manipulated. Starting this procedure while the cat is still young is the best way to minimize this protective instinct.

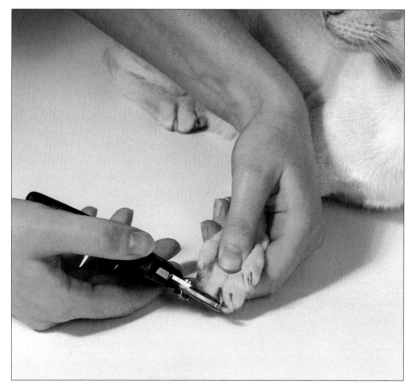

■ **Trimming the claws** *is a vital part of your pet's grooming ritual. Cats that are kept indoors need a regular manicure to prevent their claws from becoming overgrown. Your groomer or veterinarian will carry out this procedure if necessary.*

133

Getting used to a trim

Try the following steps to help condition your kitten (preferably) or cat to accept having its nails trimmed:

1 Each day, while petting and stroking your cat, briefly and gently touch its feet, one at a time. Very gently squeeze on its toes to extend the nails out of their protective sheaths, just for a second or two. While doing so, praise the pet lavishly. Afterward, give it a tasty treat.

2 After a week of brief, gentle handling, begin exposing the cat's nails long enough for you to see them clearly. If your cat's nails are white, the tips will appear almost transparent. This is the part that can be clipped. The section of nail with the pink center should never be cut. Called the *quick*, this part of the nail's interior has a vein running through it. If you cut the quick, you'll hurt the cat, and the nail will bleed.

> **DEFINITION**
>
> The **quick** is the vein that runs through the nails of the cat. The quick ends about one-eighth to one-fourth of an inch from the end of each nail. When trimming the cat's nails, it is essential not to cut the quick.

3 Next, while gently massaging your cat's feet and exposing its nails for a very short period, begin to briefly touch the nails with the tip of your nail clipper (available in any good pet supply store). Don't trim anything yet; this exercise is simply to desensitize the cat to the feel of the metal clipper on its nails. Continue doing this for several days before moving on. After each session, always praise and reward the cat.

4 Once your cat has become accustomed to having its nails briefly touched by the clippers, you can go ahead and clip one or two nails. You do not want ever to cut the quick! On white nails the quick will be visible, but on black nails you will not be able to see it. Only trim the very tip of the nail (about one-sixteenth of an inch) and you'll be fine. This is important! You must avoid pain and bleeding at all cost if you are to continue trimming your feline's nails regularly. When in doubt, always trim off less nail. Realize that, at this point, you have to build up your own skills and confidence, so be sure to take your time and trim only a few nails at first. Trim a nail or two each day until you've done all four paws. As always, praise and reward the cat after each session.

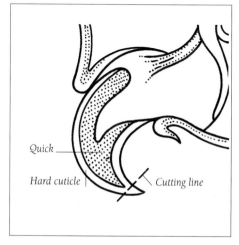

Quick

Hard cuticle

Cutting line

WHERE TO TRIM THE CLAWS

(5) You should be ready now to trim a paw at a time, or even all four paws at once. Be confident and reasonably fast, because taking a lot of time will make the cat nervous. Kitty will also sense your hesitation and become even more wary. So be sure and quick about it. And never take off more than one-sixteenth of an inch! Do as many paws as you can before your cat lets you know it's had enough.

If this nail-trimming procedure makes you or your cat too nervous, don't continue. Let a professional groomer do it instead. This will enable you to remain a trustworthy person in your pet's eyes.

The dreaded bath

MOST CATS DO NOT NEED TO BE BATHED. Remember, they are very clean animals who do a great job of keeping clean all by themselves. Try getting a Labrador retriever to do that! However, some cats will need a bath now and then for various reasons. A show cat will need to be bathed before each show, particularly if it is a longhaired breed. A cat allowed outside regularly (not my recommendation) will sometimes get too dirty for it to be able to clean itself fully. An indoor cat may get into something, such as paint or cooking oil, that you don't want it clean off on its own. Or a cat might become infested with external parasites such as fleas, ticks, or mites and need a special medicated bath.

For whatever reason, the time will probably come when you have to give your little fur ball a bath. Unfortunately, as with nail trimming, most cats don't want to be bathed. They just don't like water all that much and won't tolerate being thrown into the tub (unlike your dirty Labrador).

So how can you get the cat clean? As with nail trimming, desensitizing your cat to the procedure is usually the way to go. This means starting as early as possible – the younger the better.

Getting a 12-week-old kitten to tolerate being bathed is a much less daunting prospect than doing so with a 5-year-old rescue cat, believe me (I have the scars to prove this!). Don't worry, though; if you do have an older cat, it can still be conditioned to accept a bath gracefully, provided that you exercise some patience and smart conduct.

HOW TO BATHE A CAT

Here is how to go about getting your cat or kitten conditioned to being bathed:

1. Place a rubber mat in your kitchen sink. This will give the cat something to grip onto and prevent it from slipping around on the porcelain or steel surface. Have a bowl of warm water right nearby on the counter.

2. Place your cat on the mat in the dry sink. Praise it and give it a small treat. Then place a few handfuls of water onto its back and massage it into the coat. Do not put the cat under the faucet or the sprayer in the kitchen sink. Just use your hands to wet it. Keep the pet in the sink for another minute, then remove it, dry it off lightly with a towel, and offer another treat. Do this once a day for 3 days.

3. Now you can try the real deal. Follow the same steps as before, only this time wet the cat down thoroughly, making sure to get the warm water well into the coat. Don't pour water on the cat's head, though, and don't make it stand in water. Instead, use a moistened wash cloth, which will help prevent the cat from panicking and trying to bolt. Offer a treat at this point, although most cats won't be interested. It's the thought that counts, though.

4. After wetting the cat thoroughly, work a small amount of a veterinarian-approved shampoo into the coat. Be nonchalant and upbeat about it – and quick. Once you have worked the shampoo in, rinse the cat completely, using either a plastic jug or a hose attached to the faucet. If the cat has a long coat, consider following the shampoo up with a conditioner. Just be sure to rinse all of the shampoo and conditioner out of the pet's coat.

5. Dry the cat off thoroughly. Do not use a hair dryer, as this could scare or injure the cat.

Be sure to continue the rinse-only procedure at least once each month, to get your cat used to it. Then, give the cat a bath only when necessary.

If your cat or kitten puts up a great fuss over being bathed, consider calling it quits and letting a professional groomer take over. It's just not worth ruining your relationship with your pet over a bath, and one or both of you could get hurt.

Cleaning ears

KEEPING YOUR CAT'S EARS CLEAN *and parasite-free is vital to its comfort and well-being, especially for outdoor cats, who can become infested with ticks, fleas, and mites, and who will become dirtier than any indoor feline could. Signs that your cat might need its ears cleaned include persistent head shaking or scratching, holding its head to the side, or even persistent meowing. If you see any of these signs, carefully examine each ear to check for parasites, dirt, or infection. Indoor cats may also need a gentle ear cleaning from time to time, simply because it's hard for them to clean inside their ears.*

Basic cleaning

Begin by placing the cat on your lap and gently stroking it, all the while talking to it quietly. Gradually begin stroking and rubbing its head. Then look into each ear, checking for dirt, parasites, or any type of discharge, which could be an indication of infection.

If the ears appear dirty, take a cotton swab dipped in mineral oil and gently swab the visible inner areas of each ear, taking care not to stick the swab down into the ear canal. Be quick and casual about it. If your cat is uncomfortable and squirms, consider doing only one ear at a time; come back an hour later to do the other ear.

If you find parasites or signs of infection in your pet's ears, or if the ear cleaning seems to hurt the cat, take it to your veterinarian, who will know how to effectively deal with the situation. If your cat or kitten simply will not put up with having its ears cleaned by you, have your veterinarian or professional groomer deal with it to save your relationship with the pet and to prevent injury to yourself.

If you have more than one cat, they may groom one another's ears. Yet another advantage of having more than one!

■ **Scratching may indicate** *that your puss is suffering from parasites. Check ears regularly for signs of infection or irritation.*

A DAILY INSPECTION

Most loving cat owners handle their cats quite a bit each day while playing or grooming. Your cat probably likes being touched by you, so why not take advantage of this? While grooming, massaging, or stroking your pet, pay attention to its physical condition. Is its coat dry and brittle, greasy, or lustrous? Does it have any odd growths or sores? How about parasites? By inspecting your cat or kitten closely each and every day, you will be able to catch a number of developing problems before they have a chance to become serious.

During your daily inspection, be sure to examine:

1 The cat's coat, which should be lustrous and shiny, not oily, dry, or brittle. Check also for bare patches and for parasites. Check that the skin is pink and healthy-looking, not dry and flaky. Any rashes should be shown to your vet.

2 The cat's body, which should be free of lumps, abscesses, sores, or swelling. Check also for a swollen abdomen or bladder (located between the stomach and groin), either of which could point to problems ranging from worm infestation to kidney stones to cancer or intestinal blockages.

3 The cat's orifices, which should not have any discharges – a sure sign that your cat has an infection.

4 The cat's legs, which should move freely without causing the pet pain.

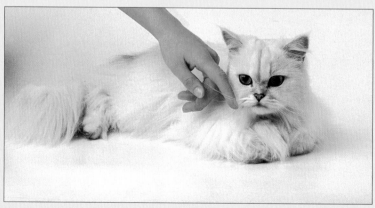

■ **As you pet your cat,** *check for any signs of ill-health. The feel of your cat's coat will give you a good indication of its general condition.*

Playing cat dentist

YOU NEED TO BE AWARE *of the condition of your cat's teeth, because tooth decay affects cats, too. And without healthy teeth, life for a carnivore isn't much fun. Plaque build-up on your cat's teeth can result in tooth loss and gum disease, as well as bad breath. If allowed to progress without treatment, these dental conditions can make your pet's life miserable.*

Open wide

You can help prevent tooth loss or gum problems, simply by inspecting your pet's teeth and gums regularly. It's best to start when the cat is still young, because adult felines might not take too kindly to having their precious teeth probed. To do so, you will obviously need to open the cat's mouth. Here's how to do that:

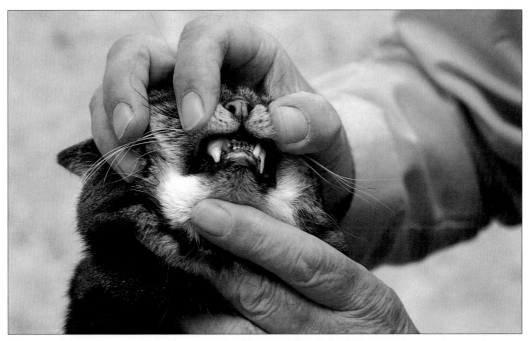

■ **Gum disease** *is a common infection in the feline world, and should be treated promptly. Mouth disorders can prevent the cat from eating properly and may make grooming difficult.*

1. Place the cat in your lap or next to you and stroke it slowly, encouraging it to relax. Then, casually place your hand atop the cat or kitten's head, positioning the thumb and middle finger of the hand right at the corners of the pet's mouth. Hook these two fingers into the mouth slightly so that the tips of your fingers are close to the pet's molars.

2. Tilt the pet's head back until its nose points up. This will effectively open the cat's mouth, allowing you to inspect the teeth and gums. Do so quickly, all the while talking quietly to the cat. Look for food build-up; loose, discolored, or chipped teeth; bleeding; inflamed or discolored gums; or anything else out of the ordinary. If you see anything suspect, be sure to take the cat to the veterinarian as soon as possible for a thorough oral examination.

If your cat vigorously resists having its mouth opened and examined, back off and don't continue, as it could seriously injure you with a bite or a flurry of scratches. If you suspect problems in your pet's mouth but it will not allow you get a closer look, see your vet right away.

The annual cleaning

Many veterinarians now recommend that cat owners bring their cats in once a year for an ultrasonic dental cleaning. Doing so will help guarantee that your cat has healthy teeth and gums for many years. And that will enable your cat to eat well and feel great.

The only drawback to having this cleaning done is that the great majority of veterinarians put the cat under general anesthesia. For a healthy adult cat, this shouldn't pose a problem. For the very old or very young feline, however, using general anesthesia poses some risks. If your pet's teeth or gums are very dirty or diseased, the risk might be worth it; if not, consider passing on the procedure.

Brushing a cat's teeth

If your cat or kitten tolerates having its teeth and gums inspected, you should actually be able to brush its teeth, using a specially formulated nonfoaming cat toothpaste favored to the feline taste. Sold with a small toothbrush (often a soft rubber one that fits over your fingertip), the cooperative kitty can have its teeth brushed several times each month, to help keep plaque to a minimum.

INTERNET

www.PetEducation.com /cats.htm

This site, from Doctors Foster & Smith, has lots of great articles on preventive care for cats. The good doctors will also be happy to sell you all kinds of dental care and other products through their online catalog.

You can also wipe your cat's teeth clean using just a gauze pad wrapped around your finger. The scaling action of the gauze may be all your cat needs. If you do opt for toothpaste, please do not use your own. Toothpaste for humans is designed to be rinsed out of the mouth, and cats cannot spit and rinse.

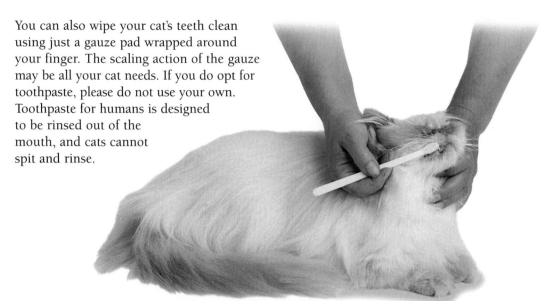

■ **Use a small soft toothbrush** *and a specially formulated feline toothpaste to clean your cat's teeth. Brush gently to prevent tartar buildup and gum disease.*

A simple summary

✔ Condition your cat to regular grooming at an early age and it won't be a struggle later.

✔ Brushing and combing helps rid your cat of excess hair that might otherwise form harmful hairballs.

✔ Even cats with scratching posts need to have their nails trimmed at least once a month.

✔ Most cats do not need to be bathed regularly, but a bath now and then may be required. If you can't get your cat to accept a bath from you, let a professional groomer do it.

✔ Keeping your cat's ears clean and parasite-free is vital to its comfort and well-being. Regular gentle cleaning with a cotton swab will do the trick.

✔ Cats can also get cavities and gum disease. Regular inspections of your cat's mouth will let you know when it's time for a trip to the cat dentist.

Chapter 9

What's for Dinner?

FEW PREDATORS CAN BOAST of being as triumphant as the cat. Blessed with a large brain, an athletic body, and the superb ability to silently stalk prey, both wild and domestic cats are more than a match for the unsuspecting animal unlucky enough to be called dinner. The mouse is the perfect cat food. All other cat foods, whether dry or canned, commercial or homemade, try to replicate the perfect nutrition present in the mouse. In this chapter I'm not going to suggest that you feed your cat mice, but I will make some recommendations about what, how, and when to feed your new pal. Nutrition is a key part of your cat's health, so pay attention!

In this chapter...
✓ The basics of feline nutrition
✓ What kinds of food are out there?
✓ Feeding kittens
✓ Feeding adult cats

The basics of feline nutrition

WHAT YOU FEED YOUR CAT OR KITTEN *will have a direct influence on its overall health and happiness. Poorly fed cats can suffer from a variety of health problems, from retarded growth or immune disorders to internal disorders and even behavioral problems. A cat fed a nutritious diet will live a longer, better life than one fed poor-quality food and will have far fewer health problems. Making sure your cat or kitten is fed properly will help it avoid skin and coat disorders, bladder problems, digestive maladies, and even certain forms of cancer – proven to thrive when a poor diet has reduced the efficiency of an animal's immune system. In other words, it's vital that you feed your new cat properly!*

Pass the protein, please

Cats are **obligate carnivores,** and do best on a high-protein diet, with that protein coming predominantly from meat. The amount of protein cats need (about 30 to 35 percent of the total diet) is much higher than what humans need and higher even than what dogs need.

Cats' protein needs are also quite complex. Many of the proteins that we are able to synthesize from other foods, cats must have directly in their diets. Taurine is a good example, but it is not the only example.

Because of their protein needs, cats cannot survive and thrive on a vegetarian diet or on a diet of dog food.

And the other good stuff

Cats also need a fair amount of fat in their diets (about 8 to 10 percent), as well as carbohydrates (around 30 to 40 percent, somewhat lower than for humans). Vitamins, necessary for the regulation of many internal processes, are also crucial to a cat's well-being, as they are to all other living things. All of these nutrients must be present in your cat's diet if it is to thrive.

Trivia...

Unlike humans, cats manufacture vitamin C (ascorbic acid) within their own bodies. This adaptation is vital to cats, because little or no vitamin C is contained in the types of foods they eat. Cats can also survive on less water than many other animals. Wild cats get much of their water from the live prey they catch and consume. Since most cat species evolved in arid climates, they also have the ability to retain water by concentrating their urine output, a useful function accomplished by the kidneys.

DEFINITION

Obligate carnivores *are animals that are obliged to eat meat. Cats must get their vitamin A, arginine, niacin, vitamin D, and taurine directly from animal sources. They cannot live without these nutrients in their diet.*

What kinds of food are out there?

THE CAT FOOD CHOICES *available to you in the supermarket and pet supply stores are wide and varied, and most provide adequate nutrition for your pet. Most owners rely on these commercially available cat foods as the main source of nutrition for their pets. Some cat owners are choosing to supplement these commercial diets with some fresh foods, or even go all the way and prepare the cat's food themselves. Although it can be time-consuming and expensive, homemade food does have its advantages. Let's take a look at the options now.*

Dry foods

The most widely used type of pet food today, dry cat food is convenient and economical. With a very low water content, it has a fairly long shelf life and will stay fresher longer in your cat's bowl. Dry food is also slightly more abrasive than other foods, and may help clean your pet's teeth to some degree. In my opinion, however, this claim has been exaggerated by the pet food companies.

Research does not show much of a decrease in tooth decay among cats raised on dry food.

Dry pet food can be divided into two categories: supermarket brands and premium brands (usually only available at pet supply stores and veterinarians' offices). Supermarket brands tend to be less expensive. They also have less meat and more preservatives, coloring agents, and taste enhancers, and can also have measurable levels of pesticide residue and residual amounts of antibiotics and hormones used in raising the meat that goes into the mixture. Bargain brands may contain low-quality meat and meat by-products not approved for human consumption by the United States Department of Agriculture (USDA). The term "meat by-products" can legally include beaks, feathers, bones, heads, organs, skin, and even fecal material (yuck!). It is even perfectly legal

■ **Crunchy and nutritious,** *dry food is a popular option for your feline. It is also easy to prepare and will stay fresh for longer than canned food.*

in some cases for dog and cat food companies to use diseased or dying animals in their foods! However, most of the big name-brand dry foods, which are more expensive, currently produce a quality product that will promote good health in your cat.

When choosing any brand of cat food, make sure you read the list of ingredients first. Choose a food that uses only real meat instead of meat by-products. Also look for a food that uses natural preservatives like vitamin E and lineolic acid, instead of less-nutritious chemicals.

Premium dry foods have more meat – which is part of what makes them expensive. They are also manufactured in smaller batches and are normally made with better ingredients than the supermarket brands, including better meat, fresher grains, fewer preservatives, and all the necessary vitamins and minerals. Because many of these premium dry foods have little or no preservatives, their shelf life is shorter than the foods you can buy in the supermarket. Percentages of protein, fat, carbohydrates, and other ingredients are carefully adjusted in these foods to match the unique needs of your cat, regardless of age.

I recommend premium brands over supermarket brands, even though you have to pay more, because with cat food you pretty much get what you pay for. You will see the difference in the quality of your cat's skin and coat, and even in its behavior, when you feed a better brand of cat food.

WHAT TO LOOK FOR

No matter what brand of dry food you choose, make sure it has:

- Meat as the primary, or first ingredient
- The proper nutrient balance for the age of your pet
- A freshness date somewhere on the package
- The manufacturer's guarantee that the product is nutritionally complete, as tested in AAFCO (Association of American Feed Control Officials) feeding trials
- Whole, cooked grains instead of grain "fractions" such as peanut hulls, empty grain husks, or even sawdust
- As few artificial ingredients and preservatives as possible.

Canned food

Canned cat food can provide good nutrition for your cat and, as an added bonus, has a very long shelf life. Available in a wide variety of quality levels, it can be fed alone or as a supplement to dry food. Canned cat food should have meat as its primary ingredient; some have more cereal than meat, requiring the manufacturers to list cereal as the primary ingredient. Avoid canned foods with grain as the first ingredient.

Canned food tends to contain about 50 to 70 percent water.

The high water content in canned food has its good and bad sides. The good side is that these percentages closely resemble food in the wild, and as such will supply your cat with more moisture than will dry food. This can help prevent kidney disease caused by a lack of water in the pet's diet. The extra water can also make elimination more regular. On the bad side, the high water content makes canned food more expensive and less nutritious pound for pound. You end up paying for water instead of food.

As with dry pet foods, the quality of canned food varies. Cheap supermarket canned foods have the same drawbacks as cheap dry foods: poor meat sources and a high percentage of poor-quality grains, preservatives, and other undesirable ingredients. Pet supply stores carry higher-quality brands of canned food at a higher price. As a rule, try to avoid canned food that costs less than a dollar for a 12-ounce can.

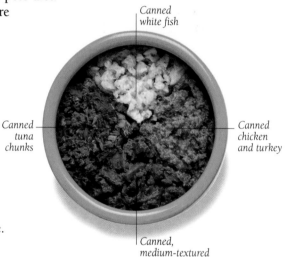

Canned white fish

Canned tuna chunks

Canned chicken and turkey

Canned, medium-textured lamb chunks

In addition to being a good source of nutrition on its own, canned food can be used as a supplement to dry food, increasing its palatability and water content. Many owners simply feed their cats both.

Semi-moist food

Lighter and easy to store, these semi-moist, mock ground meat foods are very palatable to most cats. They are expensive, however, and often contain a lot of preservatives, artificial colorings, binders, and sugar – ingredients that give the food its meat-like texture. Though capable of providing nutrition, semi-moist food is, in my opinion, the least desirable of all the commercially available foods. Simply put, avoid these foods.

Homemade food

Many cat owners are beginning to appreciate the benefits of preparing their pets' food right at home, in their own kitchens. Using fresh, raw, or lightly cooked meats, cooked vegetables, and important vitamin and mineral supplements, many owners with time on their hands prepare meals for their cats that taste good and are superior to commercial foods in several ways. In addition to being fresh, home-cooked cat food is free of artificial ingredients, pesticides, hormones, antibiotics, and preservatives. The meat used is generally only lightly cooked or raw, ensuring that it contains the highest possible amounts of amino and fatty acids, protein, vitamins, and minerals.

The meat used in home-cooked pet food need not be cooked, provided it is fresh; the digestive tract of the cat is designed to digest raw meat more efficiently than our own, due to stronger digestive acids and enzymes. If using raw meat still disturbs you, though, lightly cooking the meat won't be a problem.

The drawbacks to home-cooking are few, but should be mentioned. First, muscle meat is not enough. You have to prepare a complete balanced diet, and that takes some work and skill – as well as several supplements that can be difficult to find. Second, it is time-consuming. You have to spend nearly as much time preparing food for your cat or kitten as for yourself. Even preparing larger batches of cat food and freezing for use later on takes time, both in preparation and in thawing and re-heating. You have to shop more often, too. But if you feel you can do it, it's great nutrition for your cat.

■ **Home-cooked food** *will be a welcome treat for your pet and make a change from prepared foods.*

INTERNET

www.holisticat.com/ rawdiet.html

For more information on how to put together a properly balanced and healthy homemade diet for your cat, as well as some sample recipes, check out this site from Holisticat.

Do not embark on a homemade diet without first reading up on what goes into a balanced diet for a cat. There are many web sites and books available that can tell you more.

Feeding kittens

KITTENS NEED TO TAKE IN PROPORTIONALLY
*more food each day than adult cats do, because of their
rapid rate of growth. Little ones need more protein, fat,
and calories than adult cats do. So for your
little guy, you should choose a food
specifically formulated for the needs of
a kitten. Because kittens grow so very
quickly, nutritional deficiencies at this
stage will create problems all their lives.
So please, use a food
specifically formulated for a
kitten's special needs, as using
an adult food could result in
severe health problems,
including retarded growth and
stunted mental development.
Don't skimp on your kitten's diet.*

■ **Feed your kitten** *with food specially
formulated for the young cat. Kittens have different
nutritional requirements from the adult cat.*

Which kitten food?

Dry or canned will do, provided the food meets the nutritional needs of a kitten.
I recommend you discuss your choice of food with the breeder or shelter where you got
your kitten, or with your trusted veterinarian. During the first week or so, you can
continue feeding your kitten the same food it was eating before you brought it home.

*When switching a cat or kitten from one type of food to another,
it is very important to do so gradually, over at least a 10-day period.*

If you change diets abruptly, it can cause diarrhea. To switch your kitten
over, remove about 10 percent of the old food each day, replacing it with 10
percent of the new food. Your kitten will be eating the new food entirely by
the tenth day. If the pet shows any digestive upset during the switchover, reverse
the process so it is again eating a higher percentage of the old food. Don't hesitate
to take as long as 3 weeks or more, if necessary, to switch diets.

How many meals?

A kitten up to the age of 6 months should eat at least twice each day, due to its rapid growth during this period. In fact, kittens younger than 4 months of age should probably be fed three times a day, because of their tremendous need for nutrients. Kittens, on average, need about two to three times more food per pound of body weight than adult cats do.

Some owners simply leave food down for their kittens, and you can certainly do this with dry food (wet food will quickly smell bad and spoil). Many owners need to do so, as they are often not home during the day to provide that second or third meal. The only drawback to leaving food down (or free-feeding) is that some cats can become overweight from it, while others can become finicky, because food is always available. Use your best judgement; if you see that your kitten is growing nicely, and is neither finicky nor food-obsessive, then simply stick with the status quo.

CALORIE GUIDELINES

The following are approximate daily caloric requirements for adult cats and for kittens. They are general guidelines, though. Your cat may need less or more, depending on its age, health, and activity level.

For adult cats

Under 10 lbs:	30 to 40 calories per pound of body weight
Over 10 lbs:	25 to 35 calories per pound of body weight

For kittens

Under 4 months:	90 to 125 calories per pound of body weight
4 to 6 months:	55 to 70 calories per pound of body weight
6 to 9 months:	40 to 50 calories per pound of body weight

The following are general guidelines for determining the caloric value of the food you are feeding to your cat.

Dry:	approximately 400 calories per cup
Semi-moist:	approximately 250 calories per cup
Canned:	approximately 150 calories per cup
Homemade:	varies widely according to formula

Feeding adult cats

CONSIDER FEEDING *an adult cat twice a day, at regular times. Doing so will help your cat develop a good appetite. This is a healthier way for your cat to eat and will help prevent finickiness. A cat with some interest in food is also easier to train. Measured, regular meals will enable you to control how much your cat eats, which is important for maintaining optimal weight. You will also know a lot sooner if your cat has lost its appetite – often an indicator of illness.*

■ **Feed your cat** *regular, measured meals. This will allow you to to keep a watch on its weight and prevent over- or undereating.*

How much?

Every cat is different and needs a different amount of food. A laid-back cat on the chubby side should be fed less than an active, slim cat who runs circles around your home all day. Start out by feeding the amount the manufacturer recommends, then watch how it affects your cat's activity level and weight. Adjust your cat's food intake to maintain its optimum body weight and condition.

TWO IMPORTANT RULES

1 **Make sure clean water is always available for your cat or kitten.** Water is necessary to all of your cat's bodily functions; without it, life could not exist. Your cat will drink when it needs to, but only if the water is clean. So don't forget to change it often!

2 **Always make sure that your cat or kitten's food dish and water bowl are clean.** Cats tend to be quite particular regarding hygiene. Every day, wash all your cat's dishes with soap and water, and rinse them thoroughly. You wouldn't want to eat or drink from dirty dishes, and neither does your cat.

Do not feed too much; the slim model is best for most cats. A good general rule is that you should be able to easily feel your cat's ribs, but not see them. The feeding guide on the can or bag is only an estimate and may need to be increased or decreased depending on how your cat looks. After only a few weeks, you should become familiar enough with your cat's appearance and eating habits to be able to adjust food amounts.

Adults only

Adult cats need less protein than kittens do, but still require more than dogs or humans. Be sure to feed an adult cat a food specifically designed for cats.

Do not feed your adult cat kitten food, as the additional protein could overwork the kidneys. The additional calories of kitten food could also eventually cause your adult cat to become overweight.

Some simple guidelines

Cats have developed a reputation for being finicky that is not necessarily deserved. Your cat's eating habits usually develop as a direct result of how you feed it. The more variety a cat is offered, the more likely it will develop finicky eating habits. The best advice is to find a quality complete and balanced cat food that your cat likes and stick with it. After all, you don't want to give cats a bad reputation, do you?

■ **Find a balanced diet**
that your cat likes and stick to it. Constantly changing your cat's food will encourage it to become a fussy eater.

Here are a few more guidelines on feeding your adult cat:

● Feed your cat at the same time and in the same place each day
● The average 7- to 9-pound cat, with normal activity, requires about one 8-ounce measuring cup of dry food per day
● Cats exposed to the outdoors will burn more calories each day and will also require more nutrients during cold weather
● Use the feeding instructions printed on your cat food as a guide, but monitor your cat's body condition to avoid overfeeding

A simple summary

✔ Cats have specific nutritional needs and cannot thrive on a vegetarian diet or a diet designed for dogs or humans.

✔ Feeding your feline a quality food is one of the keys to keeping it in great shape. A poor diet will result in a dull, dry coat; itchy, flaky skin; and even emotional and behavioral problems.

✔ With cat food you pretty much get what you pay for. Look for brands that have more meat and less grains and fillers.

✔ A homemade diet can be very nutritious for your cat, but you must do your homework first to make sure you are feeding your cat a complete and balanced diet.

✔ Make sure your cat always has clean feeding dishes and access to clean water.

✔ Kittens are growing so rapidly that they have very high nutritional demands. Your kitten will not develop properly without a high-quality diet made just for kittens. Adult cats, however, don't need the extra protein in kitten food.

✔ Feeding an adult cat two measured meals a day is best for the cat's health and well-being. Adjust the amount you feed your cat based on the cat's physical condition. A good general rule is that you should be able to easily feel your cat's ribs but not see them.

Chapter 10

That Extra Edge

So you've read the rest of part two thoroughly and now you know all about providing your cat or kitten with the essentials. Your furry pal is eating well, looking great, and feeling just fine, thanks to you and your veterinarian. What else is there to do? Plenty! Once you have ensured its good health through proper diet, grooming, and health care, you need to concentrate on keeping your cat physically and mentally fit. This chapter will show you how to stimulate your feline friend's body and mind and provide it with a sense of purpose. By doing so, you will help guarantee its happiness for years to come.

In this chapter...
- ✓ Exercising kitty
- ✓ Enriching your cat's environment
- ✓ Feline massage

CATS NEED EXERCISE TO STAY FIT AND HEALTHY

Exercising kitty

HUMANS AREN'T THE ONLY ONES *who need exercise. Your cat needs it, too, to stay healthy and happy. A cat who never gets any exercise will put on weight – always bad for the health. The sedentary cat will also tend to become bored. Think about it: Cats in the wild lead a dynamic, active life. They never become obese (a common condition among housecats) and have an almost limitless supply of stimuli. In addition to hunting and killing prey, courting, and reproducing, most wild cats have to be on the lookout for competitors out to beat them to a meal and predators out to eat them. Can you imagine how fit you would be if something out there wanted to eat you?*

Exercise a cat?

But wait a minute. Most cats sleep away much of the day, only coming to life late at night for a half-hour of insane cavorting, usually when you are trying to sleep. They just don't seem like the type of animals who would willingly join you for aerobics.

Well, you are right, in a way. Even in the wild cats nap about 16 hours a day. And how does a leopard hunt? Not by chasing its prey for miles over the savanna. No, it hunts by waiting, stalking, and pouncing. It uses a tremendously fast burst of strength and speed instead of a long, drawn-out aerobic effort. By hunting in this way, cats are able to conserve energy very efficiently. The result is that cats just aren't programmed to exert themselves for long periods of time.

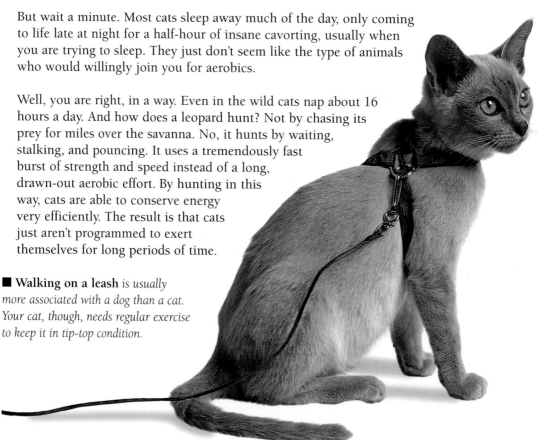

■ **Walking on a leash** *is usually more associated with a dog than a cat. Your cat, though, needs regular exercise to keep it in tip-top condition.*

So how do you motivate your cat to get going? The answer is two fold. First, you can use a prime motivator – food. Any cat with an average or better food drive will be willing to learn and perform a new activity in exchange for a tasty treat offered at the right time. Second, you can take advantage of your cat's instinct to stalk and pounce on small, fast-moving objects. Ever tease a cat with a toy mouse suspended from the end of a wand? Every cat I have ever known, when presented with this kind of stimulus, has pounced on the furry little toy, or at least tried to swat at it a few times. By stimulating your cat with toys in this way, you can get it moving. Most cats and kittens will go after a ball or a furry toy tossed across the room. Chances are, yours will, too.

■ **Motivate your cat** *with a game of ball. Most felines will enjoy patting and pushing a small ball around with their paws.*

Will exercise for food

To use food as an exercise motivator, you need to put your cat on a regular feeding schedule. Why? So that you can better predict when your cat will be hungry. Your pet will begin to anticipate feeding time, instead of simply wandering over to its bowl every so often to pick half-heartedly at food that's always available. If you bring food out only at precise times, your cat will respond more actively to any treats offered. Its excited anticipation is what will help you to get the cat moving. A small bit of cheese or a dollop of meat-flavored baby food on the end of a spoon is all that will be needed in most cases.

Hunting for treats

Once you have your cat or kitten eating at specific times each day, it will begin to think about food more and will be highly motivated to go after a tasty tidbit it might find lurking around your home. To get your cat up and hunting, place some bits of food around the house. Use small treats that won't make a mess, perhaps a piece of dry cat food or a small piece of hard cheese. Do this right before you leave for work or school in the morning. Don't worry; your cat's great sense of smell will eventually alert it to the tasty tidbit's presence and location. Try leaving one beside a bookshelf, one beneath the television, or one behind the sofa. Because your cat's world tends to be more three-dimensional than yours, consider leaving a treat atop the refrigerator, or wherever your feline likes to perch up high to survey its kingdom.

INTERNET

www.healthypet.com

Check out the American Animal Hospital Association Healthy Pet home page for all sorts of useful information on your cat's health, including tips on feline exercise.

Do not put treats for your cat in a place where someone might slip on them. Also, don't leave any in areas close to trouble spots, such as a potted plant, a garbage pail, or a piece of fine furniture. And never encourage your pet to go near any areas containing toxic substances.

Come to me

In Chapter 7, I explained how to teach your cat to come to you when called. You can use this trained behavior to get your pet running to you whenever you call its name. Just like the cats that rush into the kitchen upon hearing the electric can opener, your cat will get off its furry rump and come to you when it hears its name – a perfect way to exercise your cat or kitten.

After you have successfully taught your cat to come to you, try calling out its name any time, always rewarding it with a choice treat when it does come. Unlike dogs, cats will rarely perform a learned behavior just to please you; they are much more self-centered.

■ **Use treats to reward** *your cat whenever it comes to its name. If you fail to reward your cat, it will soon start to ignore you, and you will have lost an opportunity to give it some easy exercise.*

You must always reward your cat or kitten with a tasty tidbit whenever it comes running to you. Not doing so will quickly sour the pet on the whole notion of rushing around the home at your beck and call. Positive reinforcement must occur every time!

Stair master

Get your cat or kitten to climb a flight or more of stairs several times each week by occasionally relocating her food dish at dinner time. Place her meal at the top or bottom of a flight of stairs, depending on your home's layout. If the cat has trouble locating the dish, try moving it up just a few steps at first, eventually placing it as far away as possible.

Chasing toys

Because of their predatory instincts, cats love to chase erratically moving objects. You can take advantage of this and get your cat moving by enticing it with various toys, including the following:

- Teaser wands
- Mouse toys
- Balled-up paper
- Wind-up toys
- Toys suspended from a string
- Balls
- Suspended feathers

The object is to keep your cat moving for at least 10 minutes. Have these sessions several times each day for best results. If you stick with it, your cat will have fun and get into great shape!

■ **Your cat will love** *to play with a piece of string dangled from on high. Simple objects such as this will amuse your playful puss no end.*

You will be amazed at the variety of cat toys available at your local pet supply store, but cats I have owned have loved to play with empty thread spools, crumpled-up sheets of paper, ping-pong balls, and the plastic ring pried from the neck of a juice bottle.

Cats often love the simplest toys. Don't spend lots of money on them when you don't have to!

Two cats are better than one

Although cats in the wild are basically loners, most housecats do appreciate the company of other cats. In fact, as near as we can tell, your cat sees you as another cat – just a really big one with the thumbs needed to open the cat food can.

A great way to keep cats active while you are away from home is to have two, not one, right from the beginning, preferably siblings or kittens of the same age. They will play with one another and keep each other company all day long, burning calories and keeping their minds active.

Unlike dogs, two cats really aren't much harder to care for than one. Cost isn't a major consideration either; food doesn't cost all that much for two 10-pound pets, does it? The extra money spent on a second litter box and one extra visit to the vet will be money well spent.

Walk your cat

No, you are not hallucinating. Your cat can learn to walk on a leash and harness, if you start out early. It's a good way to get the cat outside without subjecting it to the dangers of cars, cat fights, or infectious diseases contracted through physical contact with other cats. A cat will never walk on a leash the way a dog does, but you can meander around together outside, enjoying the sights and smells.

Teaching an adult cat to walk on a leash and harness can be difficult, however, as it could panic easily. Don't try this with a cat over 4 or 5 months of age unless it is extremely outgoing and confident.

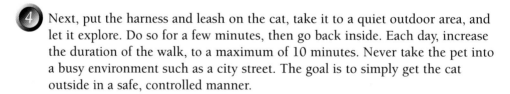

Here's how to train a cat to walk on a leash:

① Buy a *cat harness* from your local pet supply shop. It must fit properly, or your cat will escape. The employees at the store can help with this. (Don't use a collar and leash designed for a small dog – only a harness will work with a cat.)

② Place the harness on the cat inside the house, while rewarding it with small treats. Slowly increase the time the harness is on until the cat can wear it without worry or discomfort. This may take several days.

③ Then, clip a very light leash to the harness, the type made for a tiny toy dog breed. Let your cat walk around the house for a few minutes, dragging the leash. Then, pick up the end of the leash and follow the cat around the home. Let the cat guide you, and periodically reward it with a treat.

> **DEFINITION**
>
> A **cat harness** is a bridle of sorts, usually made of sturdy nylon cord. Part of it fits around the cat's midsection, while another part goes around the pet's neck. The two sections are connected atop the cat's back by a third piece, on which is attached a metal ring. To this can be connected a leash. The harness spreads the tension of the leash out, so that the pet doesn't feel controlled as much or pulled around by the neck.

④ Next, put the harness and leash on the cat, take it to a quiet outdoor area, and let it explore. Do so for a few minutes, then go back inside. Each day, increase the duration of the walk, to a maximum of 10 minutes. Never take the pet into a busy environment such as a city street. The goal is to simply get the cat outside in a safe, controlled manner.

Walking outside on a leash is not a suitable exercise for all cats, however. A nervous and timid cat will not find it a rewarding activity. If your cat is young, outgoing, and well-adjusted, though, a daily walk around the yard will be an enriching, calorie-burning experience for your puss.

Enriching your cat's environment

DECADES AGO, *zoo animals had little to do but pace and eat. The boredom and inactivity resulted in a host of physical and behavioral problems, including weight disorders, unpredictable aggression, antisocial behavior, poor parenting skills, and even sterility. Kept in barred cages, wolves, lions, bears, and apes became listless and troubled.*

Trivia...

Keepers of bottle-nosed dolphins in water parks worldwide often teach complex behaviors to their charges to keep them mentally active. Intensely intelligent and communicative, these incredible creatures often learn a behavior, then teach it to other dolphins without any prompting from their keepers!

Today, zookeepers know better. They create interesting habitats and activities for their animals. Polar bears usually have a pool stocked with live trout to stimulate their hunting skills. Leopards have tall trees to climb and eat in. Wolves follow invisible scent trails laid down by zookeepers to stimulate their sense of smell. These additions excite the animals and give them purpose.

The problem of bored cats

Domestic cats need to feel that way, too. Unfortunately, most of them spend their days in homes that are lonely and boring. While left alone, their instincts to hunt, explore, play, and socialize are rarely engaged. Instead, most cats spend their days eating, sleeping, and getting into trouble. They often obsess about food – sometimes the only stimulus available to them while their owners are at work.

If zookeepers can invent ways to stimulate captive animals, you can do the same for your cat. By encouraging new activities and enriching the home environment, you can make your cat happier, healthier, and more confident.

The following are some easy-to-implement behavioral and environmental enrichments designed to relieve boredom and stimulate your cat's mind, resulting in a happier, calmer, healthier cat. Use your intimate knowledge of your cat's personality when deciding which enrichment devices to use. For instance, if you know your pet hates being around other cats, avoid any activities that require it to do so. If your cat or kitten is a real acrobat, use enrichment devices that encourage it to leap, jump, and climb. Don't force your shy cat to socialize with the neighbors, but do encourage it to chase a teaser toy if it likes doing so. Be inventive and supportive, and always strive to make your cat's life as interesting and fun as possible.

INTERNET

www.awionline.org

Log on to the Animal Welfare Institute's web site for information on zoo enrichment programs and how animal welfare groups are trying to make zoo life as pleasant as possible for the captive animals.

Be social

Socialize your cat from kittenhood on to provide it with a wide spectrum of experience and to minimize antisocial behavior later on. Try to involve other people in your cat's life. Have a neighbor or friend come over during the day while you are at work. Let them offer the cat a few treats and spend some quality playtime, so the cat learns that you are not the only pleasant person in the world.

If at all possible, involve other animals in your cat's life. Although most cats will accept another pet only if they have grown up together, some will tolerate other cats if the visitor poses no threat (in your cat's mind) to its territory. The best solution is to get two kittens instead of one, and let them bond right from the start. The partnership they develop will help keep both mentally stimulated for years to come

■ **Two are better than one:** *Consider getting two kittens – they will provide company and amusement for one another well into old age. If you have two cats, they will not need human company so much.*

Fun toys

Provide toys for your cat. Chewing on or playing with the appropriate item will help pass the time. Just be sure the toy cannot be swallowed or ripped into pieces small enough to choke on. You can find cat toys in any good pet supply store or online at any of the major pet sites. Also, try leaving a few catnip-filled mice or crocheted balls in various places around the home. These will excite your cat and give her something to look forward to each day. Make sure to move them around the home so the process doesn't become predictable.

■ **Catnip-filled toys** *can be hidden around the house for your cat to find. Replace them frequently, however, as they do lose their scent.*

Think about investing in a few wind-up or battery-operated toys, available at any good pet supply shop. Many of these can be extremely exciting and motivating to even the most staid cat; the toys move around the floor in an erratic fashion, much the way a fleeing mouse might. Buy a few, and, at random times during the day, turn them on and watch your cat turn into a real tiger!

If you really want to excite your cat, buy a small plastic toy train set. Set it up in a corner of your home and turn it on a few times each day. Your cat will switch into predator mode and pounce on the fleeing choo-choo. Make sure to turn it on only a few times each day, for only a few minutes at a time, so that the cat does not become bored with the activity.

Radio and television

A radio or television can be a real comfort to a cat. Leave one on in a room with the door closed to give the impression that someone is home. Pet supply stores and web sites also sell videos made especially to amuse cats, showing life-size images of birds and squirrels cavorting around. These can be extremely stimulating to your cat.

Hide some food

Food hidden inside a ball will stimulate most cats. Zookeepers smear peanut butter over the inside surface of an old tire, then give it to a bear, who will spend hours licking it. Do the same for your

INTERNET

www.cattv.com/Videos forCats.htm

Check out this web site for videos featuring cavorting squirrels, chirping birds, and squeaking mice – all designed to capture the attention of your TV-watching feline.

pet. Many pet supply stores sell durable rubber balls and other small toys that are hollow inside. Place kibble, cheese, or a small amount of canned food inside, then leave the ball out before you go to work.

Egg tartare

A raw pigeon or quail egg still in the shell can be very stimulating to a cat. Left in a pet's dish, many do not at first know what to do but will soon figure it out. Fear not; your pet's powerful digestive system can handle it raw. At first, you may need to prick a pinhole into the egg to release enough scent for the cat to show interest.

Changing dinner

Changing the time of feeding or the location of your cat's food dish will stimulate its senses and get its mind working. Every so often, move the dish to a different location and watch what happens at feeding time. Also, every now and then feed the cat an hour later or earlier.

Something's fishy

Placing a small aquarium in your home will really get your cat's predatory juices going. A 10- or 20-gallon tank with eight or ten small fish is all you need; your cat will watch them with hunger and fascination. Just make sure that the top of the tank is securely closed off from probing paws. The pet supply shop employee you buy the tank from will help show you how to cat-proof the tank. Your cat will watch the fish swimming about with desire and wonder!

Someplace to climb

Kitty trees and condos are great additions to your home. These carpeted, multi-tiered play structures can provide your cat with a place to rest, explore, eat, scratch, or perch. You can also buy perches that clip onto windowsills, to make them even more accommodating to your cat.

If you are handy with tools, you might try building your own kitty condo.

■ **A fish aquarium** *will provide endless entertainment for your predatory puss. But, do make sure that the fish are in no danger from probing paws.*

The base should be an enclosed wooden box large enough and heavy enough to safely support the rest of the structure. Bolted to this can be a 2-inch-thick wooden dowel, 2 to 4 feet high, with a wooden platform bolted atop it. This platform can be made of light plywood and should be smaller than the base. The entire structure should be covered in a durable indoor/outdoor carpet. Consider carpeting each piece of the condo before assembly.

For the birds

A window with a good view is a bit like cat TV. Make sure there's an interesting program on by placing a bird feeder near your window. The birds will quickly learn that the cat can't get to them and will gather round and put on a good show.

On the trail

Scent or food trails left in your home can stimulate your cat's sense of smell and keep it busy for hours. Leave a trail of tiny treats through the home, or simply rub a piece of aromatic cheese onto several nonabsorbent pieces of furniture, leading to a small treat.

A good trick

Trick training can expand the minds of cats. Teaching your cat to sit or come for a treat will get it's mind working and widen its repertoire of behaviors. To learn how to teach your cat more tricks, see Chapter 17.

In the box

Cats love cardboard boxes. A simple enrichment tool, most cats will enjoy crawling in and out of one. Simply get a box from the supermarket and put it on the floor, either empty or with some shredded or crumpled newspaper in it, then toss a few tasty treats into it. Don't leave the box out all the time, though, or it will lose its charm. Instead, take it out only three or four times a week, for an hour or so each time. To really get your cat going, turn on a battery-operated cat toy, place it in the box, and watch your cat go completely nuts!

■ **Provide a cardboard box** *for your cats' amusement. Most felines will love a game of hide-and-seek with their companion.*

Feline massage

RECOGNIZED BY VETERINARIANS as an excellent form of pet therapy, a regular regime of massage can be highly beneficial to a cat. Massage provides a feeling of intense well-being and helps relax tense muscles. It also improves strength, coordination, and circulation, and restores flexibility to stiff joints. Massaging your cat regularly will also make grooming and trips to the vet much easier. Above all, it can increase the bond between you and your cat. And besides, it just feels good!

Massage can also be good for you. Studies have shown that cat owners who massage their felines for even a short period of time lower their blood pressure significantly. Hospital patients, when provided with a cat to massage and pet, almost always improve faster than patients not afforded the pleasure.

Have I convinced you to begin massaging your cat or kitten? Good. Then, here's how to go about it.

Massaging your cat

1. First, it's always better to start handling and massaging your feline when it is still a kitten. Most adult cats will allow their owners to stroke and massage them, though, so it's never too late. Start lightly massaging specific areas on your pet's body while it is lying in your lap or beside you on the couch, in a relaxed state. Be sure not to use heavy pressure; just press lightly with two or three fingers, using circular motions.

2. Start with the pet's neck, and slowly move down each side of its spine, perhaps switching to a thumb and forefinger, with your thumb on one side of the spine, and your forefinger on the other. During the massage, be sure to speak quietly to the cat or kitten to relax it.

3. Continue moving down the cat's body. Avoid the rump, however, as most cats dislike being handled in this sensitive spot. Then work slowly down each leg, gently rubbing down to each paw.

4. Then, place your cat or kitten on its side and gently rub its belly with your fingertips, using circular motions. (Not all cats enjoy this, so don't force the issue if your cat resists.) While doing so, you can also stroke the cat or kitten's head gently, while talking in a relaxed voice. After you finish, offer your pet a delicious treat.

Remember to limit the time of the massage to only a minute or so when you first start, especially with an adult cat. If you go about it slowly, your cat should begin looking forward to the sessions with great anticipation!

Never force a cat or kitten to accept a massage if it doesn't seem open to it. If a pat on the head is all it will stand still for, that's fine.

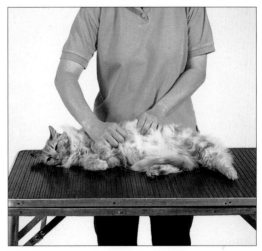

■ **Massage can be a therapeutic experience,** *but don't expect your cat to lie still for a long period, especially when you first start.*

A simple summary

✔ Finding ways to exercise your cat or kitten will help improve its general health, keep it slim and trim, and help relieve boredom – often a problem with "latch-key" felines who have little to do during the day except sleep and eat.

✔ By enriching your cat or kitten's environment, you will help expand and stimulate its mind and body. Doing so will add purpose to your feline's life, help keep it fit, and uplift its spirits.

✔ Enrichment devices are easy to buy or make. By including a few in your cat's life each day, you will be tapping into its instincts and activating its senses.

✔ Massaging your cat or kitten regularly will help it enjoy being touched, relax both of you, increase your pet's circulation, and soothe its muscles. Scheduling a daily massage will strengthen the bond between you and give you both something to look forward to.

PART THREE

NEVER LET YOUR CAT STEAL FOOD

PROBLEMS IN PARADISE

SOONER OR LATER SOMETHING LESS THAN perfect is going to happen to your beloved cat, either physically or behaviorally. If it can happen to us, it will happen to them. My job is to *prepare* you for those bumps in the road as best I can so you and your feline buddy will suffer as little  as possible. I'll talk here about the physical and behavioral problems that can arise with cats, with an emphasis on how to *avoid* what can be avoided.

A friend of mind once told me that the only problem with pets is that their lives are shorter than ours. She has a point. We can't avoid the inevitable. So I'll also talk about ways to *cope* when your cat reaches the end of its life.

Chapter 11

An Ounce of Prevention

A N IMPORTANT PART OF owning a cat is making sure that it stays
healthy and happy. How should you go about doing this? Most
people wait for their cat to get sick before they think about health care.
I think this is a wasteful and dangerous way to ensure good health.
After all, what if a little problem goes undetected until it turns into
a killer disease? Not much can be done at that point. Wouldn't it be
smarter to avoid some illnesses altogether by simply instituting some
preventive steps? I think so, don't you?

In this chapter...
- ✔ Your veterinarian's role
- ✔ Vaccinations
- ✔ Why cats get sick
- ✔ Why cats get injured
- ✔ The best way to keep your cat healthy

REGULAR TRIPS TO THE VETERINARIAN ARE ESSENTIAL TO MAINTAIN THE HEALTH OF YOUR CAT

Your veterinarian's role

NEVER UNDERESTIMATE THE *importance of your veterinarian in keeping your cat healthy and happy. From administering vaccines to catching cancerous growths to parasite control to answering your innumerable questions, your veterinarian should be, next to you, the most important person in your cat's life.*

An annual exam

In Chapter 6, I recommended that you take your new cat or kitten to see a qualified veterinarian as soon as possible, to evaluate its overall health and to get you on the right rack caring for your new friend. To take full advantage of your veterinarian's talents, you should now consider seeing him or her at least once each year, to maintain your cat's good health and to catch any potentially serious illnesses before they become an issue.

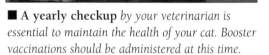

■ **A yearly checkup** *by your veterinarian is essential to maintain the health of your cat. Booster vaccinations should be administered at this time.*

Most cat owners bring their cat in for an initial visit but never think of going to the vet again unless their cat gets sick. If you do this, your cat will be missing out on needed vaccinations, and, more importantly, the trained eye of a caring professional who might spot a serious condition in the early stages – something you wouldn't necessarily catch in time. Even if your feline friend seems to be in the best condition, be sure to visit your veterinarian at least once each year to ensure your cat receives the best attention.

The visit should include:

- Any vaccinations you and the vet feel are needed.
- An examination of the cat's body, from nose to tail, to search for any lumps, growths, abscesses, parasites, or anything else out of the ordinary. He or she will also palpate, or manipulate the cat's body, to assess the health of the pet's internal organs.
- Weighing the cat and taking its temperature.
- Listening to its heart and breathing.
- Inspecting the cat's teeth and gums, ears, anus, and vagina or penis.
- Checking the elasticity of the cat's skin – an indicator of how well hydrated the pet is. Poor elasticity often points to dehydration.

Ask the vet

Your vet can also be relied upon for great advice on cat behavior, diet, environmental issues (particularly regarding toxic substances), how to bathe a cat or clip its nails, and even information on acquiring a new pet.

Finally, rely on your vet to keep accurate records of every interaction he or she has had with your cat. Doing so could be a big help in diagnosing a chronic condition that might otherwise be difficult to spot. Accurate records kept over a long period, when analyzed, can reveal a pattern not easily seen in one or two visits.

Vaccinations

CATS, LIKE HUMANS, SHOULD BE protected by vaccinations against a number of serious and potentially fatal infectious diseases. Vaccinations guard your cat against viruses or other diseases that can make it sick or even threaten its life. It is imperative that you have your cat or kitten properly vaccinated.

The basics of vaccinations

A vaccination is an injection given to your cat that contains a deactivated, or killed, form of a disease, often a *virus*.

Once injected, the vaccine is recognized as an invader by the pet's immune system, which immediately begins manufacturing proteins called antibodies, designed to destroy that specific type of invader. Once made, these antibodies remain in the cat's system, guarding against future infections.

> **DEFINITION**
>
> A **virus** *is a microscopic organism that contains genetic information but cannot reproduce itself. To replicate, a virus must invade another cell, insert its own DNA into the unfortunate host, then take over that cell's reproductive machinery.*

There are a number of deadly contagious diseases that infect, sicken, and kill thousands of cats and kittens every year, particularly felines allowed to go outdoors and those spending time in shelters and catteries. The good news is that you can effectively protect your cat or kitten from most of these killers simply by allowing your veterinarian to vaccinate your furry friend at the appropriate time.

It gets complicated

Once upon a time, veterinarians routinely vaccinated cats every year against a wide variety of illnesses. But it's not that simple anymore. Some vaccines have been known to cause problems, including skin cancers at the site of the vaccination. And others simply haven't been proven to effectively convey immunity against disease.

Moving away from the "one protocol fits all" idea of feline vaccinations, a report released late in 2000 by the American Association of Feline Practitioners and Academy of Feline Medicine Advisory Panel on Feline Vaccinations says each cat's vaccination needs should be evaluated individually, based on the cat's age, health, and circumstances. In other words, you and your veterinarian need to sit down every year and discuss your cat's circumstances and then decide how best to proceed with your cat's vaccinations.

Another common practice that the report discourages is the use of polyvalent vaccines (that is, a single shot that contains the vaccine for more than one illness), other than those containing combinations of FPV, FHV-1, and FCV (more on these in a moment), because these combination vaccines "may force practitioners to administer vaccine antigens not needed by the patient." In addition, the panel concluded that "as the number of antigens in a vaccine increases, so too does the probability of associated adverse events."

The report also made some specific recommendations for vaccines, which I will summarize for you in the following sections.

Rabies

Rabies is a deadly virus that affects warm-blooded animals, including humans. Usually transmitted through saliva when an affected animal bites its victim, rabies can also enter the body through deep scratch wounds or even, in some cases, through inhalation. Once in the victim's system, the rabies virus multiplies and eventually enters the nervous system, traveling to the spinal cord and brain. The victim may hallucinate, see imaginary objects, or have seizures. A rabid animal may attack other animals or even its owner. Once infected, any animal who hasn't been vaccinated against rabies will eventually die.

The new report highly recommends the rabies vaccine for all cats. Vaccine manufacturers are required by the USDA to establish a minimum duration of immunity for rabies vaccines, and there are products available that are labeled for use every year and every three years. However, the frequency and type of rabies vaccination is often governed by state and local laws.

Never ever handle a wild raccoon, skunk, opossum, fox, bat, or other warm-blooded species, particularly if it appears to be sick or injured. If it's infected with the rabies virus, a bite could be extremely serious.

Feline panleukopenia (FPV)

Also known as feline distemper or feline parvovirus, feline panleukopenia is a potent virus that can lie dormant in the environment for many months before infecting an unvaccinated cat or kitten. Indoor cats are vulnerable because owners can unwittingly carry the virus in on their shoes or clothing.

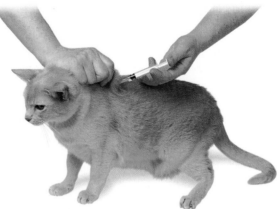

The report highly recommends this vaccine for all cats. A booster should be administered one year after the first vaccination, then no more than every

■ **It is possible to vaccinate** *your cat against FPV. This is highly recommended since the virus can be transmitted via human footwear to felines.*

three years. Interestingly, research so far indicates that immunity is sustained for at least 7 years after vaccination. However, the research is not definitive, and the panel recommends a 3-year interval for now – even though the labels on the current vaccines suggest annual revaccination.

Feline infectious peritonitis (FIP)

Next to panleukopenia, FIP is the biggest cause of death by infectious disease in cats, mainly infecting kittens and young cats. No vaccine existed until 1990. But there is still a lot of controversy about whether the vaccine that is currently available actually provides protection from this disease. Since the vaccine has not yet been proven beneficial, the panel does not recommend routinely administering this vaccine. If you keep your cat indoors exclusively and never bring another cat into the home, there is no danger of contracting this disease.

Feline leukemia virus (FeLV)

Highly contagious and deadly, this virus can be passed from cat to cat by saliva, urine, feces, or blood. Drinking from the same bowl or playing with an infected cat can place a healthy cat at risk. A few cats infected with FeLV do not actually become ill but remain carriers of the virus for the rest of their lives.

"The decision to vaccinate an individual cat against FeLV infection should be based on the cat's age and its risk of exposure," says the report. Vaccination is recommended for cats at risk, such as those allowed to roam outdoors, cats in shelters, and cats that live in households with many other cats or where new cats are introduced

INTERNET

www.vetcentric.com

Log on here for answers to nearly any medical question that you might have about your cat.

frequently. However, it is not recommended for cats that have little or no risk of being exposed to other infected cats. FeLV vaccines also do not induce protection against the disease in all cats, so preventing exposure to infected cats is still the best way to prevent FeLV. If vaccination is deemed appropriate, annual revaccination is recommended.

Feline immunodeficiency virus (FIV)

A *retrovirus*, FIV is similar to HIV (human immunodeficiency virus) in that it attacks the body's immune system, eventually making the patient unable to deal with common infections. The disease is spread by contact with contaminated saliva, usually from the bite of an infected cat – another reason why cats should live indoors. There is currently no vaccine to protect against this disease.

> **DEFINITION**
>
> A **retrovirus** *differs from a standard virus in one special way: Instead of injecting DNA into a host cell in order to take over its reproductive abilities, the retrovirus uses RNA instead. Basically, RNA is a simpler form of DNA. The AIDS virus HIV is a retrovirus, as are several other viruses that target the immune system.*

Feline respiratory disease complex

Most infectious upper respiratory diseases of cats are caused by two contagious viruses: Feline herpesvirus (also known as feline viral rhinotracheitis, or FHV-1), and feline calicivirus, or FCV. Both viruses cause similar symptoms in cats. A third organism, feline chlamydia, also causes upper respiratory infections.

Feline herpesvirus, the most common viral infection in cats, can cause sores to develop on the infected cat's mouth or nostrils; these closely resemble the human cold sore. All three of these diseases cause upper respiratory problems, including sneezing, runny nose, coughing, and eye infections.

Kittens, unvaccinated cats, and cats in multi-cat homes are at greatest risk and can contract one or more of these respiratory infections through contaminated material and from other cats. The diseases are occasionally fatal for kittens, although most cats do recover.

Feline viral rhinotracheitis and feline calicivirus (FHV-1 and FCV) vaccines are highly recommended for all cats, according to the report. A booster should be administered 1 year after the first vaccination, then once every 3 years – although, again, the vaccines currently available are labeled for annual revaccination. Research so far indicates that vaccine protection lasts at least 3 years. However, vaccines can only induce an immune response that lessens the severity of the disease – they do not offer complete immunity. In addition, the FCV vaccines that are currently available probably do not induce protection from all forms of the virus.

When it comes to feline chlamydia, because the disease itself is not severe and most cats can be treated, and because the number of adverse events associated with the use of the vaccine is relatively high, routine vaccination is not recommended.

Other illnesses

Dermatophytosis This fungal skin infection is also sometimes called ringworm. Vaccination has not been demonstrated to prevent infection, or to eliminate the disease-causing organisms from infected cats, so routine vaccination is not recommended. Vaccinations are used primarily to help treat difficult cases.

Bordetella bronchiseptica This is another respiratory infection. The efficacy of this vaccine has not been independently evaluated, and how often to revaccinate has not yet been determined. Routine vaccination is not recommended, but it is reasonable to consider vaccinating cats in environments where the infection is present.

Giardiasis Routine vaccination for this intestinal parasite is not recommended. However, infected cats who were vaccinated had less severe signs of the disease and were contagious for a shorter period of time, so vaccination may be considered where there has been significant exposure to the protozoan that causes the disease.

When to start

When should your cat or kitten be vaccinated? Good question.

Kittens should normally receive their first vaccination by 8 or 9 weeks of age, and follow-up vaccinations every three to 4 weeks until they are 12 weeks old.

Your pet is not fully protected until this complete series of vaccinations has been administered. A booster vaccination is recommended at one year of age.

When the vaccination history of an adult cat rescued from the street or a shelter is not known, I recommend having it vaccinated straight away, even if you suspect someone might have already had the cat vaccinated.

The vaccination won't do any harm to the cat and could, in fact, prevent it from catching something fatal.

■ **Early vaccination** *will protect your young kitten from a whole host of serious, life-threatening diseases.*

CANCER AND VACCINES

Veterinarians have learned that the vaccines we use to successfully protect cats from infectious diseases can occasionally cause a type of cancer known as fibrosarcoma, a malignant tumor often appearing just beneath the skin, sometimes at the site of a vaccination.

The report says: "Although vaccine-associated sarcomas have been reported to develop in association with administration of a variety of vaccines, current data suggests they are more frequently associated with administration of feline leukemia virus vaccines and adjuvanted rabies virus vaccines." (An adjuvant is a substance that is added to increase the efficacy of the vaccine.) Rabies vaccines have been developed that do not use adjuvants, but the report says it has not yet been established that these new vaccines will reduce the likelihood of cats developing vaccine-associated sarcoma.

Not enough is known yet about vaccine-associated sarcoma to make any specific pronouncements, and a task force has been formed to study the problem and come up with some answers. One of the things the task force has done so far is establish standardized injection sites for vaccinations. Be sure to discuss injection sites with your vet. By using standardized injection points on the cat for each vaccine, veterinarians and medical researchers hope to gather statistical data that could lead to an answer to the question: "Do certain vaccinations cause cancer?"

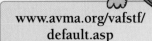

INTERNET

www.avma.org/vafstf/ default.asp

This page has the latest news from the Vaccine-Associated Feline Sarcoma Task Force, a joint effort of the American Association of Feline Practitioners, the American Animal Hospital Association, the American Veterinary Medical Association, and the Veterinary Cancer Society, to investigate vaccine-associated cancers. You'll find a frank discussion of the risks and benefits of vaccinating your cat.

The bottom line

With all that's still not known about vaccinations and all that's changing, sometimes it's hard to know what's right for your cat. Make sure your veterinarian stays current on all reports regarding new feline vaccination techniques. In the U.S., veterinarians can do so by reading all literature generated by the American Association of Feline Practitioners (AAFP). Then discuss your options with him or her, and together you will be able to figure out what's best for your cat.

Dog owners are usually responsible about vaccinating their pets, but all too often cat owners aren't. As a result, more cats than dogs contract rabies.

Why cats get sick

ALTHOUGH MOST CATS will live a relatively healthy life, many will develop illnesses along the way that require more than just rest and love to cure. Some, such as incontinence and parasitic infection, are fairly easy to deal with, while others, such as cancer and heart disease, can be life-threatening, difficult, and often heartbreaking.

Why do cats get sick? There are too many reasons to list here. Generally speaking, a malady can be caused by genetic or *congenital* defects, an infectious agent (such as a virus), or an unfortunate accident (such as poisoning or a car accident).

Infections

Viruses, bacteria, and parasites are perhaps the three most common causes of illness among all animals, including cats and humans. For instance, feline panleukopenia is caused by a virus spread from cat to cat, usually among outdoor cats. Periodontal disease, or disorders of the gums, are often caused by bacteria that form and fester on a cat's gums and teeth. Parasitic dermatitis, a disorder that causes a cat's skin to become red, itchy, and inflamed, affects cats infested with fleas, ticks, mites, or some other type of obnoxious pest trying to grab a free ride.

Fortunately, most infectious diseases can now be prevented through vaccination, good hygiene, and by keeping your cat indoors. Most infections plague cats that are allowed to venture outdoors unrestricted or those unvaccinated pets that come into contact with an infected feline.

■ **Parasitic infestation** *and infectious diseases are more common in cats that are allowed outside. Vaccinate your cat and keep it indoors to prevent unwelcome infections.*

Leave me alone!

Another cause of illness in cats has to do with the nature of their immune systems. Traditionally solitary creatures, cats in the wild tend to establish fairly well-defined territories and only come into contact with other cats during mating season or territorial disputes. Because these wild cats don't have much contact, the spread of disease has always been relatively rare. One cat may get sick, but since that cat doesn't have anything to do with other cats, the illness is not passed on.

Enter the human being. In the past few thousand years, we have significantly manipulated the lifestyle of the cat. Domestic felines now come into contact with one another much more frequently than wild cats do. The domestic cat's immune system has not had quite enough time to keep pace, however; as a result, its immune system is not as efficient at producing antibodies to fight diseases as is our own or that of the very sociable dog – who lives in packs in the wild. So what we have today is an animal with an average immune system living under much more crowded conditions than it has ever been designed to cope with, biologically speaking. In time, the cat's immune system will, of course, evolve and become as efficient as our own. In the meantime, though, communicable diseases are capable of spreading more easily if a cat has not been properly immunized.

> **Trivia...**
> While the lion is probably the only species of wild cat that chooses to live in groups (called prides), studies of domestic cats – house cats, barn cats, and feral cats – have found that they live in an astonishingly wide variety of arrangements, from close-knit groups to loose associations to loners and everything in between.

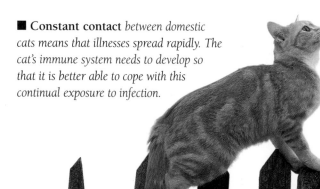

■ **Constant contact** *between domestic cats means that illnesses spread rapidly. The cat's immune system needs to develop so that it is better able to cope with this continual exposure to infection.*

Why cats get injured

CATS ARE INJURED MORE OFTEN *these days than they ever have been. Why? Because so many cats are allowed to roam outdoors freely, often in suburban or urban environments.*

The number of cars on the roads has increased dramatically, along with the number of cats allowed outdoors. In my opinion, this is a recipe for disaster.

Contrary to popular belief, cats are not immortal creatures blessed with supernatural abilities. They are mortal, have only one life each, and can lose that life easily to a car speeding down the street.

Other animals

Other cats and dogs can also injure your outdoor cat. Unneutered male cats are especially susceptible to getting into fights, as they are apt to be much more territorial toward other male cats and will also fight for access to females in heat. A cat can also get hurt by wild animals, including raccoons, coyotes, and even large birds of prey.

Poison

Your cat can also get hurt around your house. Usually these injuries involve poisoning or electrocution. (Chapter 5 explains how to make your home safer for your cat.)

■ **Unneutered male cats** *commonly fight with one another, especially over territory and females. Fighting can be serious and injury to one or both cats often results.*

The three most common causes of serious poisonings in cats are snail bait, rat poison, and ethylene glycol antifreeze. Only a little of these substances can cause life-threatening poisoning. Treatment for poisoning is prolonged and expensive, and it is not always successful. So please do be careful!

The best way to keep your cat healthy

IT'S A SIMPLE LIST, REALLY. And if you've read this far, you already know how to keep your kitty healthy. But to be sure, check out the list below:

1. Feed the cat a nutritious, veterinarian-approved diet that contains all the nutrients necessary for growth, cell replacement, and overall metabolic function. Good stuff in, good stuff out.

2. Make its environment as safe as possible. I know that sounds simplistic, but it's true. How to do this is covered in Chapter 5, so feel free to reread it!

3. Have your cat vaccinated regularly, especially if it goes outside or has regular contact with other animals that do (such as dogs). Too many potentially fatal diseases and disorders can be easily passed from cat to cat for you to ignore this. If, after all I have said, you still decide to let your feline outside, vaccinations become essential.

4. Keep your cat indoors!

5. Keep your cat well-groomed and free of parasites.

6. Exercise your cat's mind and body every day.

7. Be sure to make the cat's environment as stimulating and exciting as possible.

INTERNET

www.catfamily.com

Log on to this site, then click on the Cat Tips button for great safety tips.

■ **A healthy cat** *is one that is stimulated both mentally and physically. Provide plenty of toys for your cat, and try to play with it every day.*

No chocolate!

Chocolate is poisonous to cats because it contains a substance called theobromine, a naturally occurring compound. Theobromine causes different reactions in different cats: Those with health problems, especially epilepsy, are more affected by theobromine than are healthy cats. Theobromine can cause cardiac irregularity, especially if the cat becomes excited, and this can kill a cat. Theobromine also irritates the gastrointestinal tract and in some cats can cause internal bleeding that can be fatal.

Caffeine, tobacco, aspirin, Tylenol, daffodils, nutmeg, and a lot of other things that are relatively harmless to you can kill your cat. Never assume because something is safe for humans that it is safe for cats.

A simple summary

✓ Maintaining your cat or kitten's health requires you to develop a good working relationship with your veterinarian, who is perhaps the second most important person in the pet's life – after you.

✓ Deciding on and implementing a proper course of vaccinations is the key to maintaining good feline health. Work with your veterinarian to decide which vaccines are right for your cat.

✓ Bacterial or viral infections, parasites, and hereditary and congenital defects are the main reasons domestic cats get sick.

✓ A cat's immune system is not as robust as ours, so it's our job to keep them away from wild animals and other cats that could make them ill.

✓ Cars and household accidents are the main reasons that cats get injured.

✓ The best way to keep your cat healthy is to feed it well, keep it safe, and give it lots of exercise and love.

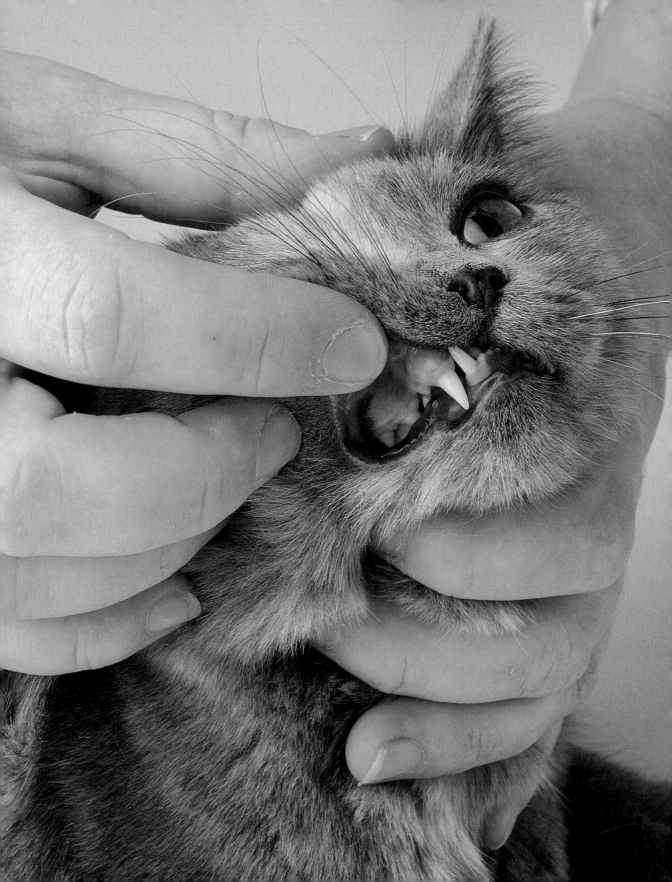

Chapter 12

Cat Maladies and Treatments

CATS CAN GET all kinds of illnesses and disorders. This chapter will explain how they affect your cat, as well as their causes and treatments.

In this chapter...

- ✓ Infections, infestations, and allergies
- ✓ Skin and coat disorders
- ✓ Digestive disorders
- ✓ Heart disease
- ✓ Respiratory disorders
- ✓ Musculoskeletal disorders
- ✓ Nervous disorders
- ✓ Hormonal and metabolic disorders
- ✓ Urinary disorders
- ✓ Eye and ear disorders
- ✓ Dental problems
- ✓ Cancer

CONSULT YOUR VETERINARIAN WHENEVER YOUR CAT SHOWS SIGNS OF ILLNESS

Infections, infestations, and allergies

CATS IN THE WILD were generally solitary animals and, as a result, infectious viral diseases did not spread very rapidly. The domestication of the cat has changed all this, however, and a variety of infectious diseases are now rife among the cat population. Skin and internal parasites are common companions of the cat, but can be kept under control with a little human help. Like human beings, cats can suffer from allergies, which may cause breathing difficulties.

Abscesses

An abscess is a pus-filled cavity in the skin that contains bacteria, as well as white blood cells and various other bodily fluids. Often the result of a scratch or bite, if left untreated, an abscess can spread toxic infection throughout the cat's body, sometimes resulting in fever, profound illness, amputation, or even death.

Cats allowed outdoors often develop abscesses as a result of being bitten by another cat. The affected area will most likely be swollen and warm to the touch, often with a small puncture wound at its center. It might be oozing pus-like fluids or even blood.

■ **Fights over territory** *are common among cats allowed outdoors. An untreated bite can become infected within a few days and an abscess may form.*

Treating an abscess

Your veterinarian can open up the abscess with a scalpel, drain, clean, and flush it, then either stitch it closed or put in a temporary drain so the cavity can continue to be flushed out with an antibiotic fluid. Your cat may also need to take antibiotics for a week or two to prevent the spread of infection.

You can prevent abscesses by neutering your cat (which reduces the urge to roam and fight) and by keeping it indoors.

Feline infectious anemia

Caused by a microorganism that destroys a cat's red blood cells, this infectious condition creates an anemia that weakens the cat and reduces its appetite. Though usually not fatal, most afflicted cats become carriers.

Spread from cat to cat during contact (usually during a fight), it can also be passed from mother to kitten during gestation. Antibiotics can help minimize the condition, but at the moment there is no cure. Only keeping your cat indoors can prevent this debilitating disease.

Feline immunodeficiency virus (FIV), feline infectious peritonitis (FIP), feline leukemia virus (FeLV), feline panleukopenia (FPV), and feline respiratory disease complex (FDRC) are all discussed in Chapter 11, in the "Vaccinations" section.

■ **A reluctance to eat** *may be a symptom of feline infectious anemia. Check it out with your vet.*

Fleas

No one likes fleas, and for good reason. These external parasites cause our pets (and sometimes ourselves) great discomfort and bad health due to their obnoxious habit of biting and sucking blood from their victims. Fleas can cause skin and coat damage, allergic dermatitis, and anemia, and can also pass tapeworm and serious viral or bacterial infections from host to host. Truly, they are not nice characters.

The facts of flea life

The female flea lays eggs on her feline host, as well as in carpeting, furniture, and other warm, protected areas of your home. A typical flea can live well over 6 months and will lay hundreds of eggs during that time. Most active when temperatures are above 62° F (17° C), fleas also prefer high humidity.

After hatching, the larvae feed on flea feces and become adults in about 3–5 weeks. The adults are wingless but can jump incredible distances and have very durable bodies that can endure tremendous pressures without being destroyed.

The domestic cat can be infested by two species of flea: Ctenocephalus felis, and Ctenocephalus canis.

Treating your cat

Fleas can be very hard to get rid of, primarily because owners usually focus their attention and effort upon the cat, not the home. Also, owners often do not follow up the initial treatment with repeat treatments; in neglecting to do so, they miss fleas that have escaped the initial barrage.

The first step in ridding your cat and home of fleas is to treat your pet. This is done by bathing and rebathing it in a veterinarian-approved flea shampoo. All of the cat's coat,

THE LATEST, GREATEST FLEA KILLERS

I don't like using topical flea killers on cats, because they are very small and are liable to have undesirable reactions to the products. Also, due to the cat's penchant for self-cleaning, the chances of it ingesting toxins is pretty high. Flea shampoo is usually as far as I go, because it gets thoroughly rinsed out. Fortunately, there many new nontoxic products on the market.

Spot-on products made from fipronil and imidacloprid (the brand names are Hartz Control OneSpot, Frontline, and Advantage) kill adult fleas but do not enter into the cat's bloodstream. They are easy to apply; you simply part the cat's hair in an area between its shoulder blades, then drip the liquid onto that spot. Fleas that jump on the animal are killed within a few hours.

Lufenuron (Program is the brand name) is an insect growth regulator (IGR); it prevents flea eggs from developing into blood-sucking adults. This usually comes in pill form, and is harmless to all mammals. It's generally safe to use an adult killer and an IGR together, but do check with your veterinarian first.

Some natural flea products contain citrus extracts (such as limonene) that have an insecticidal effect. Natural products are less powerful than chemical ones, though, so you must attack fleas on several fronts if you don't want to use chemicals. Vacuum daily, and wash your cat's bedding in hot water. Flea combs can also help immensely. Use daily, for best results.

When it comes to very young cats, I recommend using a flea comb to remove live fleas by hand. You should avoid putting any insecticides on your kitten until it is older than 12 weeks.

including atop its head, must be saturated with the lather in order to get all the fleas. The lather should stay on the cat's hair for a few minutes before being rinsed off to make sure the active ingredients can do their work effectively. After a second lathering, rinse your cat thoroughly, then towel dry. Be sure to get all the lather out, because your cat will probably begin to lick its coat afterward; you certainly don't want it to ingest any flea-killing substances. This type of bathing requires a very cooperative cat. If yours tends not to be, consider letting a professional groomer to do it. He or she has the technique and experience to do a good job.

By letting the groomer give the bath, you won't become your cat's enemy for the next week!

The box opposite explains some new, safe products you can also use to keep fleas away from your cat. Talk to your vet about any flea-control strategy. Read product labels carefully, and be sure to choose a product that is formulated specifically for cats.

Never use any flea-control product intended for dogs on your cat. You could poison your poor kitty!

Although flea collars can effectively kill fleas for an extended period of time, they often don't last as long as manufacturers claim and will become ineffective when wet. Some cats can develop contact dermatitis on their necks in response to the flea-killing chemicals contained in the collar. Also consider that your cat is wearing a collar containing toxic chemicals around its neck all the time. If you insist on a flea collar, I recommend breakaway flea collars, which give some measure of safety should the collar become caught on an object. Take the collar off immediately if you notice any signs of itchiness or redness around the cat's neck.

Treating your home

The next step is to treat your home. This can be difficult as a home has many creviced areas for fleas to hide in. When treating your home, keep your cat away to prevent further infestation or poisoning. Make sure your house is flea-free before bringing the cat home.

■ **Flea collars** *are fairly effective but can cause contact dermatitis in some cats. Make sure you buy the type of collar that will break if snagged.*

The products you can use to rid your home of fleas include:

1. **Commercial flea foggers** These products send flea-killing chemicals into every nook and cranny of your home in an attempt to get all of the blood-sucking devils. They can be effective, but foggers have their disadvantages, too. First, the aerated chemicals are flammable and can be ignited by the pilot lights in gas appliances such as stoves, dryers, hot water heaters, or furnaces, so you must remember to shut all these off beforehand. Second, they are inconvenient to use because you and your pets must evacuate the home for 6 to 8 hours while the fogger works. You must also pack away all dishes, utensils, clothing, bedding, or anything else that might be used by humans or pets. Plus, much of the dispersed chemicals end up settling high up in the treated rooms, on walls, ceilings, cabinets, and wall hangings – places where few fleas live. Only a small percentage of the active ingredient ever settles into the carpets and furniture, where most fleas are.

2. **Topical flea sprays** These kill fleas and their eggs on contact and pose less of a fire hazard than do commercial foggers. Unfortunately, they do not kill all the fleas – only the ones in the area you've sprayed.

3. **Flea powders** These powdery flea killers are sprinkled onto affected surfaces, then worked in with a broom. They tend to work well and contain fewer toxic flea-killing chemicals than other products. Powders are not wasted on unaffected areas, either, the way foggers are. Numerous flea-killing companies use this method to rid your home of fleas and often offer a guarantee that requires them to come back and treat your home for free if the initial treatment was not successful.

If you do not feel capable of ridding your home of fleas, call a professional. They're listed in the local Yellow Pages. They will get the job done and usually offer a money-back guarantee.

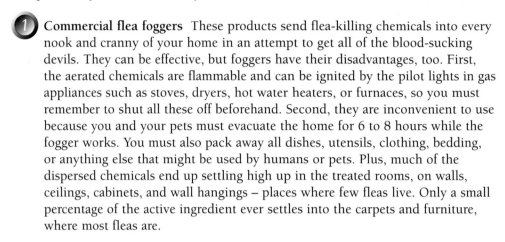

Treating your property

Once your home is flea-free, you will need to deal with the rest of your property if your cat is allowed outdoors.

The problem is that your property might be too large to treat effectively. Plus, your property borders other yards where you cannot legally spray flea-killing chemicals. If those yards aren't treated, though, your cat will simply go outside and become reinfested. What can you do?

You guessed it. Keep the cat indoors! You can rid your house and your cat of fleas, then keep them away by keeping kitty inside and by not allowing other outdoor cats (or dogs) access to your home. It's also a good idea to vacuum your home regularly, including all the upholstery, to catch stray fleas or eggs before they can infest your cat. Then throw the vacuum bag away to be safe.

Instead of throwing the bag away each time you use the vacuum cleaner (an expensive procedure), try cutting up two flea collars and inserting them into the bag. This will help kill any straggler vampire bugs before they can do more harm.

Lice

Although relatively rare on a cat, lice are not unknown in the feline world. Small, pear-shaped parasites, these tan-colored pests feed on dead skin and hair and stay on their host as long as possible.

A cat infested with lice will become itchy and may suffer from raw, red patches on its skin, mainly from persistent scratching. An affected cat may become irritable and could lose its appetite from the stress.

Treating lice

To rid your cat of lice, simply use a veterinarian-approved flea-and-tick shampoo. If the lice persist, see your veterinarian. To prevent infestation, keep your cat indoors and away from cats that are allowed access to the outdoors because they could be infested with lice (or any number of other parasites).

■ **A medicated bath** *will rid your cat of troublesome parasites – though your pet may not appreciate your efforts at the time!*

Mites

Mites are small parasites that burrow into a cat's skin, where they lay eggs and feed. They cause the affected animal to itch and scratch, often until the skin is raw and bloody. The three most common types of mites known to infest cats are mange mites (demodex and sarcoptes), ear mites, and Cheyletiella mites.

Because some mites burrow below the surface of the skin, they are not always visible to the naked eye and can be misdiagnosed as allergic dermatitis.

Mange mites

Of the mange mites, the sarcoptic mite is the more serious and usually requires close veterinary attention. The demodex variety is actually almost always present on the skin anyway and rarely causes skin problems unless the host's immune system becomes suppressed in some way, either due to a disease, old age, or stress. When that happens, the demodectic mite can begin to irritate the skin, causing itching, scratching, and even red, raw sores.

Both of these mites are contagious from animal to animal; the only way to prevent infestation is to keep your cat from coming into contact with another infected cat. Although sarcoptic mites are often contracted from other cats that spend time outdoors, demodectic mites are usually passed to kittens from their mothers.

Sarcoptic mites are usually dealt with by a veterinarian, who will use a medication called Ivermectin, either given orally or injected. Demodectic mites are usually best dealt with by improving the infested cat's overall health, thereby enabling the cat's immune system to deal with these parasites on its own.

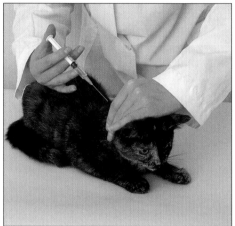

■ **If your cat** *becomes infected with sarcoptic mites, your veterinarian can get rid of them with an injection or oral medication.*

Ear mites

Ear mites are the most common infection of the cat's outer ear. Passed through direct contact with an infested cat, these mites live off of dead skin and blood and leave behind a thick black discharge that can block the ear canal and make your cat's ears smell terrible. They are painful and irritating for the cat and must be treated. Your veterinarian must treat an infestation of ear mites, and you may have to continue administering the mite-killing treatment for another 2 weeks at home. After that, the cat's ears will need to be cleaned regularly with a cotton swab dipped in baby oil or in whatever medication your veterinarian prescribes.

Cheyletiella mites

Cheyletiella mites, also known as "walking dandruff," look like small flecks of dandruff on a cat's skin and throughout its coat. Cheyletiella mites do not burrow, but live in the top layer of the skin. They move about rapidly but sometimes attach to the skin and suck fluids from it.

In contrast to dogs, cats seem to have a much milder reaction to this mite. The cat's fastidious cleaning habits probably do a great job of removing most of these mites. However, cats can still develop some scaling and slightly oily coats and what appears to be dandruff (actually the mites).

If you see what appears to be dandruff on your cat, see the veterinarian, who will be able to tell if it is an infestation of cheyletiella mites. Topical prescription medications will rid your cat of the problem.

All the mites I've mentioned are contagious to humans, so beware! To minimize the chances of mite infestations, keep your cat indoors.

Ticks

Sooner or later, any cat venturing outside will pick up a tick or two. A relative of the spider, these blood-sucking, round-bodied parasites vary in size according to their gender and how long they've been on your cat. Female ticks are generally much larger than the males, as are ticks that have been feeding for a while.

Nasty creatures

At home in grassy areas and around trees and shrubs, ticks wait for an unsuspecting creature to come by, then drop down onto it and latch on. Once a tick's jaws attach, it begins feeding on the host's blood, staying attached sometimes for days or until it is swollen with its meal. Then it usually drops off.

Ticks can carry many types of bacterial and viral infections, including Rocky Mountain spotted fever and Lyme disease – two very dangerous conditions that humans can also get. Ticks can also cause dermatitis, itching, rashes, and open sores, and a heavy infestation can cause anemia, especially in a kitten. Clearly, ticks are not very helpful little creatures.

■ **A cat wandering** *around in long grass will almost certainly pick up ticks. If your cat goes outside, try to keep the grass around your home short.*

Removing a tick

Luckily, ticks are easy to spot and can be easily removed with the right equipment and technique. Here's how to do it:

1 First, locate the tick on your cat's body. Next, drip a few drops of flea-and-tick shampoo directly onto the parasite, allowing it to soak in for a minute before continuing.

2 Now, using a pair of tweezers dipped in rubbing alcohol, grasp the tick as close to your cat's skin as possible, then pull straight toward you until the tick releases.

3 After removing the tick, swab the site with rubbing alcohol. If you use the flea-and-tick shampoo beforehand, the entire tick – head and all – should come out. If the tick's head remains in your cat's skin, don't worry; it will normally dry up and fall out on its own in a day or two. Simply swab it with an antibiotic ointment and keep an eye on it. If the head doesn't come out, or if the site appears to be red or inflamed, a trip to the veterinarian is your next step.

4 Kill the tick by dropping it into a small jar of rubbing alcohol or flea-and-tick shampoo. Screw the lid on tightly, and throw the whole thing away. Do not flush a tick down the toilet because it will survive the trip. Also, do not squash it between your fingers because you will be exposing yourself to any infection it carries.

Never use a match or cigarette to remove a tick! It doesn't usually work, and you could burn your cat badly.

The best way to keep ticks off of your cat is to keep it inside. Otherwise, keep grass height down to a minimum, and clear excess brush from your property to reduce the tick's hiding places. And examine your cat thoroughly every day for ticks so they can be removed promptly.

Internal parasites

Any organism that must inhabit and feed off another organism in order to live is a parasite. Some parasites, such as fleas, live on your cat's skin and hair, while others live inside its body, in its blood, or in various internal organs.

Some creatures living inside your cat cause it no harm. For example, certain bacteria found in your cat's digestive tract can actually aid feline digestion. However, most do cause adverse reactions, ranging from itchy skin to a damaged heart. The following parasites can invade your cat's body and wreak havoc with its health. Keep in mind that most of them can also invade your body, so it's doubly important to keep your cat parasite-free.

Roundworms and tapeworms

Tapeworms are long and flat, while roundworms are shorter and have a round body. The eggs of both are released in the feces of infected cats. Segments of tapeworms can also sometimes be seen on the hair around the anus of the cat or in the feces and resemble mobile grains of rice. Roundworms are passed to a cat if it comes into contact with the feces of another animal or by consuming prey (such as a mouse) infected with the worm. Tapeworms can enter a cat's body when it is bitten by a contaminated flea or louse or by eating contaminated meat.

■ **Cats often host** *parasitic tapeworms. These can cause diarrhea, weight loss, and abdominal discomfort and should be treated promptly.*

Most cats show no obvious signs of having either of these worms. However, heavy infections, particularly in kittens, can cause weight loss, vomiting, and even death.

If you suspect that your cat is infested with tapeworms or roundworms, see your veterinarian immediately. He or she will give your pet worming medication to kill the parasites.

Do not use over-the-counter worming medications for your cat. They don't work as well as what the vet will give you and sometimes are not specific for the parasite your cat may have.

To prevent your cat from becoming infested, keep it indoors and clean its litter box often.

Hookworms

These small worms attach to the lining of your cat's intestines, where they feed off nutrient-rich blood. Cats can be infected by ingesting larvae in contaminated soil or water, by eating an infected transport host (such as a rodent) when larvae penetrate their skin, or by a mother cat passing larvae to her kittens in the uterus of through her mammary glands.

Hookworms can cause severe diarrhea in some cats and stunted growth in kittens. An infected cat might also have a dry coat and be underweight. If you suspect your cat has hookworms, see your veterinarian, who will identify the parasite through fecal examination and administer the proper medication.

INTERNET

www.peteducation.com

Here is a great site for informative articles on cat care, veterinary articles, and pet news.

Whipworms

A parasite found in the cat's large intestine, the whipworm is less common in cats than in dogs. These small worms are blood-suckers and can cause diarrhea as well as anemia. Kittens especially can be seriously affected by these parasites.

Cats contract whipworms by ingesting the larvae. Luckily, your veterinarian can get rid of them fairly easily with the right worming medication. As with roundworms and tapeworms, keeping your cat indoors and maintaining a clean litter box are two great ways to prevent your cat from getting these nasty culprits.

■ **Give your cat worming** *medication to kill off any whipworms. Prevent infestation by keeping your cat indoors and making sure its litter box is clean.*

Giardia

These protozoans inhabit the digestive tract. Giardia are usually acquired by drinking contaminated water, and the typical sign of infestation is diarrhea. Your veterinarian can rid your cat of the infestation using the proper drugs. Prevent infestation by keeping your cat away from untested water supplies, especially ponds, lakes, and streams.

Toxoplasmosis

Toxoplasma can cause more serious damage to your cat. Also a protozoan, toxoplasma infects the cat's intestines and is acquired through exposure to affected feces.

Toxoplasma protozoans can cause birth defects in humans, so pregnant women should not clean their cat's litter box unless they are wearing rubber gloves. The risk is also much less if the cat does not go outdoors.

The primary sign of a cat with toxoplasmosis is diarrhea, which can be mild to severe, depending on the level of infection. Blood and mucus may be present in the stool. Affected pets might also vomit, lose their appetite, or become dehydrated. Young kittens can die from a severe infestation.

Diagnosed through examination of a fecal sample, your veterinarian can rid your cat of the infestation using several medications. To prevent your cat from becoming infested, keep it indoors and clean that litter box. Contact with other cats, as well as with prey animals, can infect your pet, so close the door!

Threadworms

These small, thread-like parasites can penetrate your cat's skin and infest the lungs or intestines. Too small to be seen in your cat's feces, they cause scratching, diarrhea, respiratory problems, lethargy, and loss of appetite. Only microscopic examination of the feces can diagnose this problem. A combination of medications can rid your cat of these pests.

Allergies

Initiated by exposure to chemicals, pollen, certain foods, parasites, or even dust, allergies can often cause a cat to suffer respiratory problems, skin disorders, diarrhea, and even vomiting. Just as with allergic humans, allergic cats each have their own profile of substances that they are allergic to.

Trivia...

Threadworms exist in two forms: the parasitic and the free-living – a form of the pest that can live outside of a host. Curiously, among the parasitic form of the threadworm, all worms are females. The eggs these creatures lay need not be fertilized by a free-living male worm.

What is an allergy?

Caused by a distorted response of the cat's immune system, the cat's body mistakenly identifies substances such as a harmless food product or a certain type of pollen as a dangerous invader. When the immune system goes to battle these harmless "invaders," various chemicals are released into the bloodstream. These chemicals are responsible for the symptoms of the allergy.

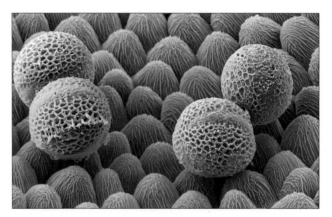

■ **Exposure to pollen grains** (*seen here magnified many hundreds of times*) *can cause allergies in some cats.*

Histamines are chemicals found in almost all body tissue, especially the skin, lungs, and bowels, which increase blood flow. In some cats, the release of histamines as a result of an allergic response can cause unpleasant reactions such as swelling, itchy skin, labored breathing, or cold-like symptoms whenever they come into contact with an allergic substance.

Cats are often allergic to fleas and can also show allergic reactions to certain types of food, shampoos, pollen, or almost anything else, depending on the cat. Even an overly stressful environment can bring on an allergic reaction.

Treating allergies

Treatment for an allergy involves first discovering what the *allergen* is and then keeping the cat away from it if at all possible. Your vet can help you discover just what your cat is allergic to and can also give the poor sufferer antihistamines, which can help relieve the symptoms, among them itchiness and congestion.

Skin and coat disorders

NON-PARASITIC SKIN and coat disorders that can affect the feline include dermatitis and ulcers. The main symptoms of these common complaints are irritation, inflammation, and hair loss. The cat may make the condition worse by constantly scratching and biting at its sores.

Dermatitis

When your cat's skin becomes red or inflamed, chances are your pet is suffering from a form of dermatitis. Cats with this problem often feel itchy and may also have dandruff, rashes, open sores, or loss of hair.

Types of dermatitis

Three types of dermatitis trouble cats: allergic, contact, and parasitic. All three can bring on the same symptoms, and all are highly irritating to the cat.

Allergic dermatitis is caused by an allergic reaction to some substance, such as a food or a new brand of kitty litter. Contact dermatitis occurs when the cat's skin comes in contact with an irritating substance such as paint thinner or flea shampoo. The symptoms for both allergic and contact dermatitis are very similar; which type it is must be determined by your veterinarian.

■ **Persistent scratching** *and raw patches of skin may indicate that your feline is suffering from dermatitis.*

The third type, parasitic dermatitis, is (you guessed it) caused by unwelcome little freeloaders such as fleas, ticks, and mites. They make the poor animal scratch incessantly, causing the skin to become raw. Fleas, in addition to being annoying and itchy, can also set off an allergic reaction in many cats, making the cat's life even more miserable.

Treating dermatitis

Curing dermatitis depends on which type your cat has. If it's allergic dermatitis, the allergen must first be discovered – a process that can take a while, even with the help of your veterinarian. Once the offending substance is found, it must be removed from the cat's environment.

If your cat has contact dermatitis, you simply need to discover what irritant is causing the problem, then remove it. This can take some thought but usually isn't as hard to discover as an allergen.

With parasitic dermatitis, at least one medicated flea bath will be required. Your vet may want to take care of this if your cat's skin is severely irritated. Then you must rid your home of the pests – always a difficult task.

Several flea-busting businesses exist that guarantee their work; in my experience they work well.

You can try using commercially available flea-killing sprays and bombs, but they tend to spread toxic chemicals into every nook and cranny of your home. Instead of spraying, the flea-busting companies use much less toxic powders that they work into your carpets.

Skin ulcers

Although an ulcer is usually thought of as a disorder of the stomach, an ulcer is actually defined as any open sore on an animal's skin or on a mucous membrane.

What causes skin ulcers?

Open sores on a cat's skin can result from parasitic infection or from some form of dermatitis. The cat scratches incessantly until it opens up a sore on its skin, which will not heal as long as the cat continues to scratch.

Treating skin ulcers

Treatment of this type of ulcer involves diagnosis and elimination of the offending parasite or the discovery and removal of the allergic substance.

Digestive disorders

THE MOST COMMON *problems affecting the feline digestive system are diarrhea and vomiting. These require immediate attention since they may lead to severe dehydration in a very short time. Other complaints include liver disease and stomach ulcers. Overfeeding your cat may precipitate more problems.*

Diarrhea

Any disorder of the digestive tract can result in diarrhea, a condition causing uncontrolled elimination, often to the point of dehydration. Kittens and young cats are often the most susceptible and can become easily dehydrated – a potentially life-threatening problem. Older cats can also be at serious risk if the diarrhea continues for too long a period, because they are also less hardy.

■ **Dairy products** *may cause diarrhea in your kitten or cat. If symptoms persist, take your pet to the veterinarian; dehydration is serious, particularly in the young kitten.*

What causes diarrhea?

Often a sudden change in diet can provoke an attack of diarrhea. Eating milk products or other human foods can also bring it on. Allergies, bacterial or viral infections, stress, or spoiled food can all cause this disorder. Serious diseases such as cancer, diabetes, or panleukopenia can have diarrhea as a symptom, in which case the problem becomes secondary to the more pressing health issue.

Always take diarrhea seriously since it may indicate a potentially life-threatening disorder.

Treating diarrhea

If diarrhea lasts for more than a day, it should always be treated by your veterinarian, who may hydrate the cat with intravenous fluids in addition to discovering and treating the cause. He or she may need to take blood, fecal, and urine samples to properly diagnose the cause.

In most cases, you should withhold food from a cat with diarrhea, usually for at least a day, to avoid further irritating the digestive tract. Be sure to provide plenty of water, though, to encourage hydration.

Always avoid a sudden change in diet, if possible, since this can often bring on diarrhea. When switching foods, do so gradually over a 2-week period. Keep your cat's food and water dishes as clean as possible, and avoid sudden changes in its environment, which could create stress – often the cause of temporary diarrhea.

Vomiting

Not always a sign of illness, vomiting can be a normal, painless activity for your cat. Many cats will actually consume plant material in order to induce vomiting.

The causes of vomiting

Sometimes vomiting can be a sign of illness, though. Conditions that can cause vomiting in your cat include:

- Worm infestation
- Poisoning
- Hairballs
- Diseases of the digestive tract
- Cancer or ulcers
- Heat exhaustion
- Viral or bacterial infection

If your cat vomits only once after eating grass or a small meal, it's probably nothing to worry about.

■ **Eating plant material** *can cause vomiting or more serious reactions in cats. So try to limit your feline's access to greenery.*

If the cat vomits repeatedly, however, especially right after meals, take it to your veterinarian for a checkup. He or she might catch a serious problem in its early stages and be able to treat it effectively.

Prevention

To prevent vomiting:

- Groom your cat regularly to reduce the chance of hairballs
- Feed smaller portions
- Limit your cat's access to plants
- Keep fresh water available, particularly during hot summer months
- Limit your cat's exposure to outdoor cats to prevent infection

Hairballs

Hair swallowed during the grooming process collects in the stomach, sometimes forming a large, matted mass called a hairball. Hairballs are a common problem in cats (especially the longhaired varieties). They can move into the intestines, where they are often passed out of the body when the cat eliminates. Sometimes these masses are vomited up by the cat, though, and sometimes they get stuck, causing a blockage.

■ **As a cat grooms,** *it swallows hair. Sometimes hairballs form in the stomach – these may be vomited up or eliminated in fecal matter.*

Prevention first

To prevent this problem, be sure to groom your cat regularly to remove as much loose hair as possible. Also, keep your cat clean to minimize its need to groom away dirt and grime. Keeping the cat indoors will help.

If your cat tends to get hairballs, you can try dabbing a tiny amount of petroleum jelly on its nose; this will be licked off and swallowed, helping to loosen up the problem. There are also commercial products that are basically flavored petroleum jelly, made in yummy cat flavors. Some common brand names are Laxatone, Petromalt, and Katalax. If your cat has a serious blockage, your veterinarian will prescribe a feline laxative, which should take care of the problem.

Liver disease

The liver is the largest gland in the cat's body and is responsible for filtering toxins, regulating chemicals, and controlling overall metabolism. The liver manufactures essential substances such as proteins, bile, and blood-clotting factors. It also plays a role in processing fats, carbohydrates, and proteins, and removes many waste substances and potentially damaging drugs or chemicals from the bloodstream. Liver failure is a life-threatening condition.

Symptoms of an unhealthy liver include:

- Lack of appetite
- Weight loss
- Lethargy
- Jaundice (yellowing of the skin)
- Distended abdomen
- Increased thirst
- Dark-colored urine
- Diarrhea or vomiting

What causes liver disease?

Liver disease can have many causes. The most common are dietary deficiencies, viral or bacterial infection, ingesting toxic substances (such as antifreeze or alcohol), and hereditary abnormalities. Tumors can also affect the cat's liver, although this is rare.

Age and the liver

The chance of your cat developing liver disease increases with age. Therefore, your veterinarian may recommend an annual blood test that monitors liver function as your pet nears its seventh or eighth year.

Treating liver disease

Fortunately, an ailing liver is often able to regenerate itself when proper supportive therapy is provided. Most times, when liver disease is caught early there is a good chance for recovery. Dietary changes are usually the most important therapy and can have the most effect on improving liver function. Pets with liver disease are often put on a low-protein diet that is high in carbohydrates and fats. Foods high in protein should be avoided by animals with liver disease, since they force the liver to work harder.

You can help avoid liver disease in your cat by:

- Limiting viral and bacterial contamination by keeping your cat indoors, away from infectious cats
- Eliminating all toxic chemicals and plants from your cat's environment
- Feeding your cat a nutritious, veterinarian-approved diet

Remember, a healthy liver is necessary to any cat's health. See your veterinarian immediately if your pet experiences any symptoms of liver disease.

HEPATIC LIPIDOSIS

Cats that do not eat for several days can develop a life-threatening condition called hepatic lipidosis, or fatty liver syndrome, in which fats build up in the liver until it is no longer able to function. Unique to cats, hepatic lipidosis is one of the most common liver diseases seen in the feline population.

Typically, a cat with hepatic lipidosis has recently gone without eating for several days. Because of the lack of nutrients, fat in the cat's tissues is broken down to supply fuel for the starving cat's body. This fat gets deposited too rapidly into the liver for it to properly process. The fat is, therefore, stored in and around the liver cells, eventually resulting in liver failure. The cat often becomes jaundiced, as evidenced by yellowed eyes or skin. If not treated, hepatic lipidosis will result in death.

Diagnosis is made from blood tests for liver function and from a liver biopsy, in which a small number of cells are removed from the liver through a needle, then examined under the microscope. Generally, other tests are then performed to determine why the cat stopped eating in the first place. If the cause for this is treatable, the prognosis for recovery is usually good.

Treatment of hepatic lipidosis requires the cat to receive a consistently high-quality diet to allow the liver to resume functioning and so remove the fat. Recovery can take 6 or 7 weeks or more.

Obesity

An all too common problem facing domestic cats today, feline obesity is a more serious condition than most owners realize. An overweight cat has greater stress put on all of its bodily systems and on its entire skeletal system, particularly the hips, shoulders, and knees. A chronically fat cat, in addition to not being able to groom properly, is much more susceptible to diabetes, as well as heart and liver disease.

OVERWEIGHT CAT

It's usually your fault

Feline obesity, except in rare cases involving problems with the thyroid gland, is an owner-induced disorder. The cat is simply fed too much and exercised too little. When calories taken in exceed calories burned, you get a chubby kitty.

Most cats should weigh about 8–12 pounds, with some breeds falling below or above those figures a little bit. If your shelter tabby is weighing in at 17 pounds, then someone is not feeding the brute correctly. It's as simple as that.

Time to cut back

If you cannot feel your cat's ribs easily, or if its belly is scraping the ground, your cat is overweight. The first thing to do is go back and reread Chapter 9. Then, stop feeding your cat treats and stop leaving food down all of the time. Instead, feed your cat two measured meals each day, making sure that you follow the calorie guidelines found in Chapter 9. Most adult cats shouldn't need more than 300 to 400 calories per day to maintain their weight.

Next, start exercising your cat (see Chapter 10). Get it moving up and down the stairs or playing with some toys. Anything to increase its metabolism will help. You will have to experiment with food and exercise amounts until you begin to see a drop in your cat's weight. Be sure to weigh your cat at least once a week and take it in to see the veterinarian, whose advice on diet and exercise will help you enormously.

■ **If your cat is obese,** *weigh it every week. Your vet can advise you on a weight-reducing regime for your fat cat.*

Stomach ulcers

A stomach ulcer is a break in the protective lining of the stomach.

What causes stomach ulcers

Ulcers in the digestive tract are often caused by viral or parasitic infection, ingestion of toxic substances, or, in some cases, a disorder of the cat's immune system.

Though occasionally they require surgery to correct, most often a combination of drugs and diet will suffice to heal the ulcer.

Avoiding stomach ulcers

Stomach ulcers in your cat can be minimized by:

- Feeding a quality diet
- Keeping toxic substances away from the cat
- Minimizing stress
- Regular exercise

Heart disease

THE MOST VITAL MUSCLE *in the body, the heart is responsible for pumping blood throughout the cat's body. If it fails, the cat will die. Heart attacks are extremely rare among cats. But cats can suffer more long-term or chronic cardiac ailments.*

Congenital defects

Malformed valves, heart chambers, veins, or arteries can all impede the action of the heart, causing the affected cat to be short of breath, move slowly, and often small in stature. Fortunately, congenital heart defects are not very common in the feline world.

■ **Your vet can detect** *a heart ailment through a stethoscope. Fortunately, heart disease is comparatively rare in the feline world.*

Feline cardiomyopathy

Most common in Persian cats, this condition is evidenced by a structural or functional abnormality of the muscle of the heart, weakening the heart muscle so that the heart cannot pump blood efficiently. Often an hereditary condition, cardiomyopathy can also be caused by toxins in the diet or by dietary deficiencies.

Infections

Numerous bacterial or viral infections can damage a cat's heart. Valvular endocarditis, for example, can cause a deformity of the heart valves.

Other infections, such as myocarditis, can damage the heart muscle itself, impeding blood flow through the cat's body. Treatment normally involves drug therapies.

■ **Persian cats** *are more likely to contract feline cardiomyopathy, or weakening of the heart muscle.*

Tumors

Though rare, tumors and other malignant growths can attack the feline heart. If small and benign, often these growths will not have dire consequences to the cat's health. If large and malignant, though, they can kill.

Treatment for cardiac tumors includes drug therapy, diet changes, and rest. If possible, a skilled surgeon will remove a tumor from the heart's surface, but tumors cannot be removed from the heart's interior.

Arrhythmia

Defined as an irregular heartbeat, cats can suffer from this serious (but not often fatal) condition. It can sometimes be a symptom of a more serious heart problem, though, and must be investigated by a veterinarian.

A heart murmur, caused by an abnormal turbulence of blood in one of the chambers, is evidenced by a sudden skip in the heartbeat. Though rarely fatal, this, too, should be dealt with carefully by your veterinarian.

HEARTWORM IN CATS

Though much more prevalent in dogs than cats, veterinarians are discovering cases of heartworm in cats as well, particularly in warmer, more humid climates. Heartworms live in the right side of the pet's heart and in adjoining blood vessels of infected cats. The female worm is 6–14 inches (15–35 cm) long and an eighth of an inch (5 mm) wide; the male is about half the size of the female. Adult heartworms live in the heart and pulmonary arteries of infected cats. They have been found in other areas of the body, but this is unusual. They survive up to 5 years.

Heartworm in cats can be even more serious than it is in dogs because cats are generally more sensitive to the damage caused by the worm. The disease is also harder to detect and cure in cats. The best way to protect your cat from heartworm is to prevent it.

Heartworm can only be transmitted through the bite of a mosquito. The life cycle of the parasite begins when a mosquito bites a pet infected with heartworm. The mosquito picks up the immature forms of the worm, called microfilaria, that circulate in the bloodstream. A mosquito with the infective form of heartworm then feeds upon an uninfected cat, transmitting the larvae to that cat. These larvae travel in the bloodstream to the heart, where they mature into adults. Though they do not produce more microfilaria (as they do in dogs), the adult worms can severely damage the cat's heart. The most common signs of a heartworm infection in a pet are a loss of energy and coughing.

Heartworm medication for cats has only recently been approved. The drugs kill the immature form of the heartworm before it reaches the heart. They are given monthly or daily, depending on the type prescribed, throughout the mosquito season. Before you give any preventive medication to your pet, your vet should perform a simple blood test to determine whether your pet is already infected.

If the cat is found to have heartworms, treatment to eliminate the adult form is available, but it is very difficult and can be quite harsh on the pet. As with most diseases, heartworm is much easier to prevent than to treat. Your veterinarian will know whether heartworm is a risk in your area, and whether preventive medication is appropriate for your cat.

Respiratory disorders

MOST RESPIRATORY DISORDERS *in the cat, as in humans, are caused by viral or bacterial infection, and generally affect the upper respiratory tract. Breathing problems can also be caused by an allergy. Symptoms include difficulty in breathing and discharge from the nose. Respiratory complaints must be treated by a veterinarian to prevent the condition from becoming life-threatening.*

Bronchitis

Bronchitis can be caused by an allergic reaction or an infection caused by a virus or bacteria. An infection caught from another cat can also bring it on – this is more common with unvaccinated cats that are allowed to go outdoors. Bronchitis is also more common in older cats.

The kitty with bronchitis develops inflamed bronchial tubes (the airways that lead to the lungs). It may cough, sneeze, or gasp for air. It may develop a fever and can have mucous discharge from the nose. In serious cases, bronchitis can close off the airways, threatening the pet's life.

Treating bronchitis

If you suspect your cat has bronchitis, see your vet, who will be able to prescribe antibiotics and an expectorant to help relieve the symptoms of bronchitis. Keep the cat warm and quiet, at least for a few days, as well.

If the bronchitis was brought on by an identified allergen, keep that nasty substance away from your cat to help prevent further attacks. Keep all vaccinations current, and consider humidifying the air in your home if you live in an arid climate.

■ **Your veterinarian will check** *your cat's breathing for symptoms of bronchitis. He or she will prescribe antibiotics, if necessary.*

Pneumonia

When a cat's lungs become inflamed, pneumonia can often result. Usually prompted by some type of infection, this serious disorder can cause pronounced difficulty in breathing, coughing, and lung congestion, often causing the cat to bring up sputum. More common in older cats and kittens, if left untreated pneumonia can be fatal. Examination of the sputum, as well as an X ray of the lungs, are both normally used to diagnose the condition.

Treating pneumonia

Treatment usually involves discovering what bacteria or virus caused the original infection, then treating it with the proper medication. In addition, all strenuous activity must be stopped for several weeks to allow the cat's lungs to heal properly. Indoor cats suffer much less from pneumonia than do outdoor cats because the cause is usually a contagion picked up from another cat.

Musculoskeletal disorders

NATURALLY AGILE, *the cat relies on a finely tuned musculoskeletal system for movement. Most disorders of the bones and muscles are degenerative, that is to say, age related, though some, such as hip dysplasia, are genetic.*

Arthritis

A debilitating disorder of the joints, arthritis can cause pain, swelling, and inflammation. Arthritis often occurs in older cats, particularly those who have spent a great amount of time outdoors or those who have suffered some type of trauma to one or more joints at some time in their lives.

Cats can suffer from two types of arthritis: **osteoarthritis** and **rheumatoid arthritis**. Whatever the cause, both are painful and will slow your cat down markedly.

A cat suffering from arthritis will no longer want to jump or leap very far due to the pain. The cat may also become more irritable and will most likely meow more than it used to.

> **DEFINITION**
>
> **Osteoarthritis** *is a degenerative condition that causes cartilage at the end of joints to wear away, causing pain, swelling, and sometimes unwanted bone growth.*
> **Rheumatoid arthritis,** *rare in cats, is a disorder of the immune system that attacks healthy joints and tissues, resulting in pain, swelling, and deformity.*

Treating arthritis

If you suspect your cat may be suffering from some form of arthritis, see your veterinarian immediately. There are medications that can make the pain more bearable. In the meantime, an arthritic cat will suffer less if it is kept moderately active and slim and trim. You can reduce the chance of your cat developing arthritis by keeping it indoors, feeding it a nutritious diet, and exercising it regularly.

Never give a cat aspirin, ibuprofen, or acetaminophen painkillers. All are highly toxic to cats.

Hip dysplasia

The hip is a ball-and-socket joint. Hip dysplasia is a deformity of the hip joint in which parts of the joint are abnormally shaped so that the ball does not fit properly into the socket. This allows the head of the femur to move easily out of the joint. Over time, degenerative joint disease can result.

INTERNET

users.netropolis.net/
kazikat/FelineHD1.htm

The Feline Hip Dysplasia Awareness web site is the best place to go to learn more about this disorder. The site offers up-to-date information and positive support.

Signs of dysplasia

Due to their small size and the fact that cats are not exercised as much as dogs, along with their natural agility, they may have hip dysplasia and still function normally. But some cats with hip dysplasia may appear to be stiff when they walk and be hesitant to jump or climb. Cats with symptoms of hip dysplasia can have the diagnosis confirmed with X rays of the hips.

Treating hip dysplasia

Many cats with hip dysplasia will show no signs of discomfort at all. An overweight cat, however, might feel pain due to the added stress on its malformed hip joints. Therefore, any cat with this problem should be kept at a reasonable weight. If your cat is obese, consult your veterinarian for the proper way to reduce the cat's weight, and so relieve the pain.

Your veterinarian can prescribe anti-inflammatory drugs if your cat is suffering from this condition. It's also probably a good

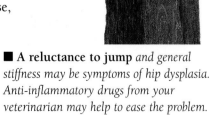

■ **A reluctance to jump** *and general stiffness may be symptoms of hip dysplasia. Anti-inflammatory drugs from your veterinarian may help to ease the problem.*

idea to limit exercise, especially activities involving leaping or climbing. In rare cases, surgery can help reconstruct the dysplastic hip, relieving the pain.

Luxating patella

The patella, or kneecap, is located in the center of your cat's knee joint. The term "luxating" means dislocated, so a luxating patella is a kneecap that has moved out of its normal location. Although relatively rare in cats, this problem seems to occur more often in Abyssinian and Devon Rex cats.

The anatomy of luxating patella

The muscles of your cat's thigh attach to the top of the kneecap. The patellar ligament runs from the bottom of the kneecap and attaches to the cat's shin bone, or tibia. When the cat's thigh muscles contract, the force is transmitted through the patella and patellar ligament, causing the leg to straighten. Ideally, the patella stays in the center of the leg during this process, because the patella slides in a groove on the lower end of the femur, or thigh bone.

■ **The Abyssinian** *cat is more likely to suffer from a luxating patella than most other breeds.*

When the patella luxates, or dislocates, it's because the point of attachment of the patellar ligament is not on the midline of the tibia, or shin. Instead, it is usually too far toward the middle of the body, causing an off-center pulling pressure on the patella.

After months or years of this, the inner side of the groove wears down, causing the patella to move haphazardly. At that point the cat begins to have trouble putting weight on the joint.

Treating luxating patella

Although some cats can live with a luxating patella, others need help from the veterinarian, usually in the form of corrective surgery. Surgery should be performed if your cat has a persistent lameness and cannot walk on the affected leg.

Nervous disorders

NERVOUS PROBLEMS are rare in cats, but when they do occur they tend to be serious. Convulsions can occur and may be due to a number of causes including tumors, poisoning, or an inherited condition.

Epilepsy

Characterized by spasms and convulsions, a loss of bladder and bowel control, and excess salivation, epilepsy also causes profound behavioral changes, often evidenced by aggression and chaotic behavior. Caused by random, aberrant electrical activity in the cat's brain, the poor feline's nervous system is short-circuited, resulting in total temporary loss of control.

A cat undergoing an epileptic seizure can often be a very dangerous animal to be around.

It can show profound aggression, often resulting in serious biting. Although your first instinct will be to help your pet, be aware that it will not recognize you during a seizure. If you cannot easily restrain an epileptic cat, consider leaving it be until the event has passed. Then, see your veterinarian as soon as possible.

■ **A cat having a seizure** *may become extremely aggressive. Leave it alone until the fit has passed, then take it to your veterinarian.*

Treating epilepsy

Often difficult to diagnose properly, your veterinarian will need to perform a series of neurological tests before confirming that your cat has epilepsy.

Anticonvulsant medications, diet changes, and even surgery are all treatments used to deal with this most unfortunate disorder.

If your cat is epileptic, be sure to keep it indoors to prevent any chance of injury. Do not put a collar on an epileptic cat because it could catch on something during a seizure. Also, be sure to discuss with your vet any dietary or environmental changes that might help minimize the attacks.

Hormonal and metabolic disorders

HORMONES ARE CHEMICAL messengers responsible for controlling many body processes. If hormone production becomes imbalanced or does not work properly, a number of life-threatening medical conditions may develop.

Diabetes

When the pancreas fails to manufacture *insulin*, diabetes is the result. Most common among older or overweight cats, the sudden increase of glucose in the cat's blood can lead to:

- Weight loss
- Diarrhea
- Blindness
- Dehydration
- Kidney damage
- Fatigue or coma
- Death

DEFINITION

Insulin, *a hormone normally produced within the pancreas, is necessary for the metabolism of glucose, the body's fuel.*

A urine sample taken by your vet will confirm the diagnosis. From that point on, your cat will need regular injections of insulin to live. Its diet must also be adjusted to regulate blood sugar levels.

Taurine deficiency

Vital to a cat's metabolism, taurine is an amino acid that is used to form proteins in the feline body. The cat's body does not manufacture taurine, so it is essential for you to supply taurine in your pet's diet. A taurine deficiency can lead to breakdowns in many of the cat's systems, including the nervous system and the cardiopulmonary system. Blindness can also result from a taurine deficiency.

A cat is not a dog

One common cause of a taurine deficiency in cats is feeding dog food to a cat. All quality cat foods have added taurine to keep your cat healthy. But dogs do not have the same need for taurine in their diets, so dog foods do not have the added taurine that cat foods do.

Feeding dog food to a cat will always result in a taurine deficiency. Do not feed dog food to your cat!

Thyroid disorders

The thyroid gland controls the cat's overall metabolism. The two disorders that can affect the thyroid are hyperthyroidism, in which the cat's thyroid gland produces too much thyroid hormones, and hypothyroidism, in which too few hormones are produced. While thyroid disorders are not as common in cats as they are in dogs, they do occur.

Hyperthyroidism

With too much thyroid hormone, the cat will lose weight, become hyperactive, and develop a greater appetite. It will also urinate more and become more thirsty. Diarrhea can result, as can heart arrhythmia and eventually, heart disease. If not treated, hyperthyroidism can also result in death.

■ **An unusual thirst** *may be an indication of hyperthyroidism. Take your cat to the vet if you suspect a thyroid problem.*

Diagnosed through a blood test, an overactive thyroid can be treated with surgical removal (followed by hormone replacement therapy), or with radioactive iodine (also requiring hormone replacement therapy afterward).

Additionally, some new drugs are now being used that seem to help reduce the output of an overactive thyroid gland. Which treatment your cat receives will depend on your veterinarian's assessment, as well as your cat's age and level of health.

Hypothyroidism

An underactive thyroid gland results in a reduced metabolic rate, causing weight gain, coat loss, and lethargy.

Treatment for hypothyroidism is simpler than for hyperthyroidism; the cat is simply given replacement hormones. Most cats affected with this problem will need to take the replacement hormones for the rest of their lives.

Urinary disorders

PROBLEMS AFFECTING *a cat's urinary system need to be investigated urgently. Difficulty in passing urine or frequent urination may be indication of a bladder infection or, more seriously, kidney disease. To help prevent urinary problems, make sure that fresh, clean water is always available.*

Kidney disease

The kidneys filter your cat's blood and regulate water in its body and produce urine as a waste product. Without proper kidney function, toxic buildup in a cat's body will quickly kill it.

The kidneys have four basic functions:

- Filtering waste products from the body
- Regulating electrolyte (potassium, calcium, phosphorus, and sodium) levels in the body
- Chemically stimulating the bone marrow to help initiate red blood cell production
- Producing renin, an enzyme that controls blood pressure

Chronic renal failure

Chronic renal failure (CRF), an always-fatal kidney disease, is a major killer of domestic cats today. It occurs when tiny holes in the kidneys called nephrons, designed to eliminate waste products and regulate electrolytes in the body, begin to die off. When this happens, waste products and electrolytes can no longer be processed effectively. A cat in CRF is poisoned by the waste that the kidneys are unable to filter. Electrolyte imbalances, anemia, and blood pressure problems may also occur as the kidneys deteriorate.

CRF may have several causes, the most common being age, heredity, environment, and disease. Some breeds, including the Abyssinian, Burmese, Maine Coon, Siamese, Russian Blue, and Balinese, appear to be more likely to develop CRF.

Although CRF can occur at any age, it is usually a disease of older cats. If your cat is 7 or older, it's a good idea to have it checked for CRF during each annual exam. With early detection, proper diet, and hydration, cats may remain happy and active for quite some time before the inevitable decline.

Trivia...

Kidney transplants are now possible for cats. Though not a total cure, a transplant can save a cat's life. The transplant donors are usually cats from shelters, who give one kidney, and the owners of the transplant recipient must adopt the donor cat.

Signs and symptoms

Although CRF can only be diagnosed through urine and blood tests, some symptoms and behaviors can point to its presence. These include:

- Increased thirst
- Excessive urination
- Loss of appetite
- Nausea and vomiting
- Weight loss
- Poor coat

DEFINITION

Dialysis *is the process of removing waste materials from the blood by means of some filtering technique or mechanism.*

Treating CRF

Unfortunately, there is no cure for CRF, although the condition can be managed for a time. The key is to reduce the amount of waste in the cat's bloodstream to a level that the kidneys' remaining healthy nephrons can accommodate. This is done through a combination of diet and medication, plus a form of blood filtering called *dialysis*.

In cats, the technique usually involves using the cat's own peritoneum (the thin lining of the abdominal cavity) as the filter for separating out waste products. A veterinarian first fills the cat's abdominal cavity with dialysis fluid. Waste products in the body gradually pass into the fluid. The doctor then removes the now-contaminated fluid from the abdominal cavity and repeats the procedure until the level of waste products is minimized.

This type of dialysis is easy to perform in cats – unlike the kind done to humans, which involves being attached to a dialysis machine for an extended period of time. Cats cannot endure this procedure, making peritoneal dialysis necessary. CRF is a terminal disease. With proper treatment, however, a cat may have from several months to a few years of relatively high-quality life left, depending on its overall health.

POLYCYSTIC KIDNEY DISEASE

Polycystic kidney disease (PKD), an inherited disorder, almost always affects Persian cats. Cats with the disease will have many cysts within the kidney. This enlarges the organ, reducing its ability to function properly. Eventually, the condition results in total kidney failure.

This disease causes lethargy, reduced appetite, weight loss, and excessive thirst and urination. Diagnosed by means of ultrasound, PKD has no effective treatment, but can be slowed through changes in the diet. Kidney transplants are also possible. Breeders of Persian cats are working hard to eliminate this fatal disease from their breeding stock.

Other kinds of kidney problems

In addition to CRF, other conditions can cause kidney failure. These include:

- Stones
- Diabetes
- Infection
- Poisoning
- Tumorous growths

Each of these conditions can be fatal, but the good news is that all are treatable if they are caught early. This is yet another excellent reason to pay attention to your cat's overall health and to see the veterinarian at least once each year, or when any unusual symptoms occur.

Incontinence

Incontinence, the inability to control urination, often affects older cats because the urethral sphincter loses its muscle tone. In some cases, younger cats can also experience incontinence, due either to stress or to injury. Stones, infections, tumors, diabetes, or kidney or bladder disease can also cause this problem, as can cystitis, a disorder of the bladder. An incontinent cat needs to see a veterinarian.

Incontinence should not be confused with marking or spraying behavior, common among unneutered male cats trying to mark their territory and express dominance over other cats. The incontinent cat will urinate at random times and in any place, while the marking or spraying cat will select an exact time and place to urinate in order to make his claim on the territory.

Feline urologic syndrome (FUS)

Feline urologic syndrome, or FUS, is a general term describing a group of lower urinary tract disorders, including kidney and bladder *stones*, urinary blockage, and cystitis (infection or inflammation of the bladder).

FUS will affect about 25 percent of all cats at some point in their lives. The pain associated with it can cause extreme anxiety and grief.

Symptoms include poor urinary flow despite repeated visits to the litter box, a bladder that feels hard to the touch, constant licking of the genital areas, or even blood in the urine. An affected cat might also meow incessantly.

DEFINITION

*A **stone** is a hard, small object that can form in the cat's bladder, urethra, or kidney. Consisting of minerals such as calcium or magnesium plus mucus, these stones can vary in size from the microscopic to the size of a dime, or even larger.*

What causes FUS?

FUS has several causes, including stress, abnormal urinary pH, or improper water, ash, magnesium, or fiber intake in the animal's diet. A combination of two or more of these can also be factors.

Cystitis, one of the causes of FUS, is a condition that irritates and inflames the inner wall of the bladder. Cystitis can be caused by retaining urine for an extended amount of time, stones or crystals rubbing against the bladder wall, or infectious organisms inside the bladder. If you notice your kitty trying to urinate frequently to no avail, it could be suffering from cystitis. You should take it to the veterinarian.

If left untreated, FUS can completely block the flow of urine, which is still being produced by the kidneys. This leads to uremic poisoning, an accumulation of poisonous wastes in the blood stream. Permanent damage to the bladder and kidneys, as well as eventual death, can follow without treatment.

Preventing FUS

To prevent FUS, first be sure to provide plenty of fresh water for your cat or kitten. Next, look very carefully at the foods you are feeding your cat; some cat food manufacturers have supplemented their dry and canned food with pH-controlling acidifiers to help to keep the cat's urine pH in the normal range of between 6 and 6.5. If you're in doubt about the best food for your cat, consult your veterinarian.

Dry foods generally contain more fiber than canned and semi-moist foods, and fiber draws water as it travels through the bowel, creating more concentrated urine, especially if the cat doesn't drink enough water. Dry foods generally also have more ash per gram than moist foods. But moist foods alone cannot prevent FUS.

■ **Canned food,** *which contains more water and fat than dried food, should be given to a cat with FUS.*

Keeping stress levels down to a minimum for your cat may also help prevent FUS, since a stressed cat might tend to avoid both the litter box and the water bowl for extended periods.

If you are feeding a dry food, supplement it with canned to increase the food's water and fat content – two ingredients known to help minimize FUS. Finally, be sure to exercise your cat to stimulate its overall health and help prevent infections from gaining a foothold. Remember to take your feline in to the vet as soon as you see any of the symptoms, as an acute blockage can cause death within 48 hours.

Eye and ear disorders

THE CAT HAS INCREDIBLE sense organs, designed for its life as a predator. Eye and ear disorders may result from genetic or congenital defects, trauma, or infection. However, most commonly they are a result of old age.

Cataracts

As your cat gets older, it eyes may become clouded. The cloudiness is caused by the buildup of proteins within the cat's lenses. This occurs very slowly and is part of the aging process. If one of your cat's lenses clouds up over a short period of time, however, the resulting cataract could seriously impair its vision. Often caused by trauma to the eye, cataracts can also be caused by diabetes or as a result of ingesting certain toxic chemicals, including many household solvents. Although they are relatively painless, a cataract renders the affected eye almost completely useless.

Treating cataracts

Treatment for a cataract almost always involves removing the affected lens and inserting a plastic lens in its place. Some owners choose not to have the surgery performed on their cats, however, especially if the pet is over 8 years old, because the trauma of anesthesia and surgery can be more dangerous than the cataract. Cats with cataracts do surprisingly well, relying on their senses of smell and hearing to get around.

Although they are hard to predict or prevent, you can minimize the chances of your cat developing a cataract by keeping it indoors. This will lessen the chance of another cat scratching your cat's eye during a fight – an injury that can cause cataracts. Keeping dangerous solvents away from your cat will also help, as will feeding a nutritious diet.

Poorly fed cats can develop diabetes or become obese – two of the disorders that may contribute to cataract growth in the feline.

■ **A veterinarian can inspect** *your cat's eyes for cataracts with an ophthalmoscope. Surgery may be carried out on young, fit cats to restore vision.*

Deafness

Cats can develop a partial or total loss of hearing in one or both ears. A deaf cat, though otherwise healthy, will still suffer from the loss of a key sense – one that a cat relies on to escape injury or death.

Deafness results from a break in the acoustic nerves leading into the brain or by faulty operation of the mechanisms of the outer ear, including the ear drum and the three tiny bones responsible for transmitting sound to the inner ear.

What causes deafness?

A cat's deafness can be caused by either genetic or congenital defects, by some types of trauma, or by a severe ear infection. Diminished hearing can occur due to ear-wax buildup, congestion in the middle ear, or from being constantly subjected to loud noises. Though still capable of hearing, these cats may have trouble hearing the approach of a car or a barking, territorial dog.

Mammals with white coats, including cats, have an abnormally high incidence of hereditary deafness. The gene for the white color also seems to harbor the defective gene that causes deafness. Its prevalence among domestic pets is a result of breeding programs that encourage the color. In my opinion, this is an example of form taking precedence over function.

Dealing with deafness

Apart from carefully selecting your cat in the first place, there isn't much you can do to prevent hereditary or congenital deafness. Any breeder who discovers the trait in one of his or her animals should have the common sense to neuter it, to prevent those defective genes from entering the feline gene pool.

You can minimize deafness caused by injury or illness by keeping your cat indoors in a safe environment, free from infectious agents. Be sure to vaccinate and keep all unvaccinated cats away from your pet. Regularly examine your cat's ears to make sure they are clean, and see your veterinarian at least once a year to catch a potentially dangerous ear infection in its early stages, before it can cause actual tissue damage.

Trivia...

When the vestibular apparatus in the cat's inner ears is damaged, the cat's righting reflex, or the ability to always land on its feet, becomes compromised. The vestibular apparatus consists of three semicircular, liquid-filled canals and two other liquid-filled compartments. Filled with microscopic hairs, any change in the cat's physical orientation is detected by these structures, which instantly signal the cat's brain of the change. The three semicircular canals are situated at right angles to one another, enabling the cat's brain to precisely calculate changes in direction and speed.

Dental problems

A cat's teeth are vital to its health, because without them the cat can't eat properly. In the wild, they also help a cat catch and hold prey, as well as defend itself from other animals. Adult cats have 30 teeth; it is in your cat's best interest for it to keep them all.

Cats, like humans, can develop problems with their teeth, including:

- Cavities
- Loose, broken, or missing teeth
- Gum disease
- Tartar and plaque buildup

It's important to minimize the formation of plaque on the cat's teeth (see Chapter 8), to prevent problems down the line. Your veterinarian can clean your cat's teeth for you once a year to keep those pearly whites looking good. Not having your cat's teeth cleaned once a year might raise the risk of serious dental problems down the road. Lost teeth can lead to loss of appetite, which can affect the cat's overall health. Oral infections can also spread to other parts of the body and become extremely serious.

Be sure to inspect your cat's teeth at least once each week, and see the vet if anything unusual appears.

Cancer

PERHAPS THE MOST FEARED *word in the English language, cancer can be loosely defined as any uncontrolled growth of cells in the cat's body. Cancer can occur in any part of the body, including the blood and the skin.*

Different kinds of growths

A true cancerous growth is malignant – it grows uncontrollably. Other unwanted growths, such as cysts or warts, stop growing at some point and are benign. A malignant, cancerous growth can metastasize, sending cancer cells off to other areas of the body through the circulatory or lymph systems, where they can take root and cause more uncontrolled growths.

What to look for

Common in cats of all ages, cancerous growths can go undetected for long periods of time until they become large enough to be seen or felt by an owner. This is especially true with cancer that forms inside the chest or in the digestive tract. If left untreated, cancer is almost always fatal.

Apart from actually seeing or feeling a growth on the cat's body, detecting cancer can be difficult. Some symptoms to watch for include:

- Increased irritability
- Increased vocalization
- Obvious pain
- Loss of weight
- Loss of appetite
- Difficulties breathing, moving, or eliminating
- Coughing
- Bloody stools or urine
- Diarrhea

Treating cancer

If you notice any of these symptoms, or anything else out of the ordinary, see your vet. Luckily, many forms of feline cancer are treatable, either with surgery, drugs, radiation, chemotherapy, or a combination of several of these. A change in diet and/or lifestyle might also be suggested. Prevention is hard, as many cancers seem to have a genetic predisposition but a healthy diet can help reduce the risk.

The earlier a cancer is detected, the better a cat's chance for survival. Regularly monitoring your cat's body for any lumps or growths is a good way to ensure early detection.

A simple summary

✔ A good number of maladies can affect your cat. Fortunately, there is almost always an effective treatment available to bring it back to good health.

✔ You are your cat's best defense against illness. If you notice your cat behaving differently, a trip to the vet is a good idea. A checkup can find a health problem before it gets serious.

✔ Keeping your cat indoors will greatly minimize its chances of contracting many diseases.

✔ A simple regimen of good diet and plenty of exercise will stave off a great many maladies.

Chapter 13

The Older Cat

THERE'S NO GETTING AROUND IT: All of us, including our cats, age. Although it may be impossible to halt the aging process, we can still slow it down a bit, for both ourselves and our cats, by living well, eating a nutritious diet, and avoiding situations and substances that tend to accelerate the aging process. We can also learn how to compensate for the lost abilities and prepare ourselves for the inevitable. In this chapter, I will discuss how aging affects the domestic cat and how you can learn to make the process as painless as possible, for both your cat and yourself.

In this chapter...
✓ What changes to look for
✓ Dietary considerations
✓ Grooming the older cat
✓ Make it simple to get around
✓ Trips to the veterinarian

What changes to look for

AGING IS A PROCESS THAT *slows the body's regenerative powers and reduces the efficiency of every biological system. It seems as if both cats and humans are pre-programmed to slowly wind down like old clocks, until we ultimately run out of time. As your cat ages, it will inevitably experience many changes in the functions of its body. Its internal organs begin to function less effectively. It becomes more vulnerable to disease and injury and takes longer to recover from illness. Mental processes also slow, and weight can increase, due mainly to a slowing metabolism.*

■ **Though old age will eventually catch up** *with your cat, regular checkups by your veterinarian and gentle, loving care by you will considerably improve your elderly pet's quality of life.*

Some cats may have more pronounced changes than others, and in some cats the changes may start to occur at a younger age. Knowing what changes to expect can help you and your cat adjust to them when and if they do come.

Your aging cat

As it enters its seventh or eighth year of life, begin to monitor your **older cat** more closely.

Do not chalk up every little problem to old age, though, because many changes can also be signs of a serious disease that has nothing to do with age. If you are in doubt, consult your veterinarian and be sure to discuss any concerns you have about your older cat during its regular physical exam.

> ### DEFINITION
>
> *How old is an **older cat**? The Academy of Feline Medicine recommends beginning a senior preventive health care program by 7 to 11 years of age. At 12, almost all cats start experiencing the effects of aging.*

The immune system

As a cat ages, its immune system will not work as well as it once did, making it more prone to infectious diseases. This reduces the older cat's ability to fight off illness. Because of this, it becomes increasingly important to keep your older cat up to date on its vaccinations.

Heart and lungs

As a cat's heart ages, it loses some efficiency and cannot pump as much blood in a given amount of time. The feline heart tends to become slightly heavier with age, with the major arteries becoming thicker and less flexible. Arrhythmia, or an unsteady heartbeat, can develop, making activity more difficult. Because circulation decreases, the older cat begins to have a harder time keeping warm.

The older cat's respiratory system begins to lose some efficiency in its job of supplying the body with oxygen and removing carbon dioxide. The lungs lose their elasticity, and the bronchial passages become constricted. Overall, the older cat may be more prone to respiratory infections.

■ **Respiratory diseases** *are more common in the older cat. Oxygen supply may become depleted as the lungs lose efficiency.*

Kidneys and liver

With age also comes an increased risk of kidney disease. This may be due to changes in the kidney itself or result from the dysfunction of other organs such as the heart, which, if it's not functioning properly, will decrease blood flow to the kidneys. The most frequent early sign of kidney disease is an increase in water consumption and urination, but this generally does not occur until much of the kidney function is lost. Over time, the kidneys begin to lose their ability to filter the blood, resulting in an increasing level of toxic materials in the cat's body.

Liver function also declines with age. The liver's ability to detoxify the blood and produce the necessary chemicals and proteins gradually decreases, hampering the cat's overall metabolism.

Without its liver operating at peak efficiency, the aging cat's body won't be able to detoxify itself in the proper manner. This accelerates the aging process.

The glands

Some glands tend to produce fewer hormones as they age, while other glands may produce more. Hormonal problems, especially hyperthyroidism, are common disorders in many older cats (see Chapter 12). Some older cats also develop diabetes as a result of the pancreas not secreting enough insulin.

Movement

Reduced mobility and the onset of arthritis can occur in older cats, especially those that injured their limbs or joints earlier in life. As in people, arthritis in cats may only cause a slight stiffness, or it can become debilitating. Physical tasks that once were easy, such as jumping up to the arm of a sofa, may become increasingly difficult as time goes by. Cats may have difficulty jumping onto favorite perches or going up and down stairs. Bones become more porous and brittle, increasing the chance of a break or fracture.

The aging cat will tend to lose muscle mass and tone, making athletic maneuvers more difficult. Because moving about becomes harder, the older cat will choose to become more sedentary; this further atrophies the muscles.

■ **An arthritic cat** *will find it increasingly difficult to jump up onto a favorite sleeping place. To help your ailing cat, make sure that you provide it with a comfortable place to sleep that is easy to reach.*

Coat and nails

Some aging cats, especially black cats, may develop gray hair. The coat may also become thinner and duller. The skin of the older cat may become less elastic and subject to injury. Dry skin and coat can also become a problem for older cats, because the aging cat's sebaceous glands secrete less oil onto the skin and through the coat.

You may also see changes in the nails. They tend to become more brittle, just as they do in humans. The nails of an older cat may need to be clipped more often because it may not use scratching posts as often as a younger cat.

Trivia...
The oldest cat on record lived in Austin, Texas. He recently died at the age of 34.

Teeth and gums

Dental problems are also common in older cats. Most older felines suffer from varying levels of gum disease and can lose teeth because of it. A gradual buildup of plaque on the cat's teeth causes receding or bleeding gums and can lead to the loss of bone that surrounds and anchors the teeth into the jaw. Older cats can also suffer from broken teeth and from bad breath. All these dental problems can affect a cat's appetite.

Hearing and vision

Some cats will lose some hearing as they age, due in part to the thickening of the ear drums. Often the hearing loss must become pronounced before you are aware of the problem. The first sign of this problem can appear as unprovoked aggression. The deaf or hard-of-hearing cat is

■ **Your elderly cat's teeth** *must be checked regularly by your veterinarian. Decaying teeth can cause loss of appetite, leading to rapid weight loss in the older cat.*

startled when you approach or pet it, because it didn't hear you coming, and it reacts defensively. The cat simply acts instinctively to what it perceives as a threat.

Although hearing loss generally cannot be reversed, changes in how you interact with the cat can minimize the problem. Cats with hearing loss can still sense vibration, so clapping your hands or stamping on the floor may alert the cat to your presence.

Cats may also lose some vision as they age. Cataracts (see Chapter 12) can develop, causing the cat to seemingly ignore objects that are in plain sight. It might even have difficulty finding its food dish or may bump into furniture that has been moved recently.

Behavior changes

As cats age, they have a decreased ability to cope with stress. This often results in behavioral changes. Aggression, inappropriate elimination, and increased vocalization can develop, as can increased irritability and fear.

Dietary considerations

DIET PLAYS A BIG ROLE *in keeping your older cat healthy. As cats age, the movement of food through their digestive tracts slows, as does the cat's metabolism. Additionally, the cat's stomach and intestines do not do as good a job of digestion and absorption as they once did; this can lead to malnutrition. Your cat's sense of taste may also diminish over time, perhaps causing it to lose interest in its regular food. Some older cats will actually eat more, however, in an attempt to feel satisfied. Decreased saliva output can also contribute to the aging cat's dissatisfaction with meal time.*

Too thin

With an aging, thin cat that has lost interest in eating, you may need to add taste enhancers to its food to compensate for the pet's failing taste buds. If you usually feed a dry cat food, try adding a tablespoon of canned food to the bowl. With some cats, you may need to switch over completely from a dry food to a canned food, because canned cat food has much more taste and smell than dry food. The stronger scent will help activate the cat's appetite. Canned food will also provide the older cat with more water – an essential part of its diet that often gets ignored by the aging animal.

■ **Tempt an aging, thin** *cat with a soft tasty treat. The older cat may find it difficult to eat hard food.*

Older cats who are missing teeth or suffering from dental disease might also appreciate soft food to eat rather than hard dry food. To remedy this, either switch to canned, or soak the cat's dry food in warm water or chicken broth for 10 minutes before serving.

Too fat

Because the cat's metabolism is slowing down, you may need to cut back on the total calories fed to avoid obesity. The best way to do this is to gradually switch your plump 8- or 9-year-old cat over to a lower-calorie senior food, which will provide a nutritious diet with about 10 to 20 percent fewer calories.

Older cats that do not drink enough water may have a tendency to develop constipation as well. Constipation can also be a sign of other serious disease conditions; a cat suffering from this problem should therefore be taken to your veterinarian for evaluation. To fight constipation, consider adding a quarter teaspoon of olive oil or flax seed oil to its food each day; this should help keep things moving right along!

Consider serving smaller, more frequent meals once the pet has reached its eighth or ninth birthday. This will stress the digestive system less than would feeding one or two large meals.

FIGHT FREE RADICALS!

The chance of your cat developing tumors increases with age. Although the reason for this is not completely understood, it might be caused by the increasing number of free radicals – extremely active, unstable charged atoms and molecules that attempt to bond with other atoms and molecules in the cat's body.

A process called oxidation occurs in your cat's body as the result of the formation and presence of free radicals. These free radicals damage cell DNA, causing all manner of health problems.

In a healthy cat, these free radicals are neutralized by the body's antioxidant defense system, consisting of vitamins, enzymes, and amino acids that combine with the free radicals to make them harmless. The older cat's antioxidant defense system is weaker, however, and cannot neutralize the free radicals as effectively.

You should strongly consider adding a vitamin-mineral supplement to your aging cat's diet each day. This supplement will help support the pet's immune and antioxidant systems, which usually begin to function less effectively by the cat's eight or ninth year. Available at quality pet supply stores and veterinary clinics, a good vitamin-mineral supplement will help ensure proper digestion and absorption of food and also support the pet's flagging metabolic functions. These supplements can be given as pills or can be sprinkled onto the cat's food. For the best advice on which supplements to use, consult your trusty veterinarian.

INTERNET

www.peteducation.com/
drugs_supplements.htm

Click here to learn about drugs and supplements for older cats.

Grooming the older cat

WHEN A CAT *reaches 8 or 9 years of age, it may begin to have some trouble grooming due to achy, stiff joints and reduced flexibility. Dirt, bacteria, dead skin cells, hair, and airborne pollutants will collect on the cat, creating an unfriendly environment for your older feline's skin. The result of this can be a dirty, matted coat, or even a parasitic infection.*

When a cat's coat becomes matted and filthy, it can easily become irritable and withdrawn. After all, cats are, by nature, fastidiously spotless in their grooming habits. An instinctively clean animal forced to live in filth would feel like Felix Unger going without a shower for a week. Yuck!

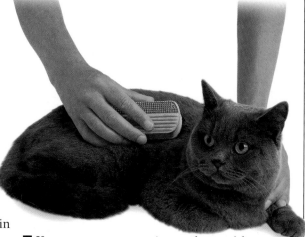

■ **Keep your mature cat's** *coat clean and free of disease with regular grooming sessions.*

Get out the brush

You may need to help the aging cat with its grooming chores regularly. Keep a close eye on your older cat's coat, especially if it's a longhaired variety. Chances are the area between its shoulder blades and its anal area will get dirty the quickest, as these spots can be hard for the aging cat to reach. Brush and comb the cat out at least twice a week and consider giving it a bath once a month, or as soon as it needs one.

When brushing and combing the aged cat, be as gentle as possible because it will have a lot less tolerance for any discomfort.

Clean and inspect

Be sure to continue to clip your older cat's nails often. They tend to dry and split with age, and keeping them trimmed will help minimize this. Inspect and clean its ears, too, because an aging cat can develop wax buildup. Ear mites can also appear in the older cat's ears, due in part to its less-thorough grooming habits.

Try to inspect and clean your older cat's teeth at least once a week, especially if it has gum disease. Doing so will help extend the life of the teeth, which will enable the cat to continue eating a nutritious diet without pain. If the teeth are too dirty for you to clean, have your veterinarian take a look. He or she should be able to clean them with little trouble.

Don't fight with your older cat over grooming issues.

If it puts up a fight every time, throw in the towel and take the cat to a professional groomer. Let him or her do the dirty work. Your cat will be clean, and you won't become the villain.

Make it simple to get around

ONCE YOUR CAT BEGINS TO SLOW *down physically, it may not be able to get around the house as easily as it once did. Jumping up to its favorite perch might become difficult or impossible. Reaching its food dish, placed atop a counter or the clothes dryer (to prevent the family dog from getting to it) may now be a daunting task. Even climbing into a litter box with a high edge could prove hard for a cat with arthritis. Clearly, changes to its living space are in order.*

A place to rest and eat

First, if the pet cannot reach its favorite resting spot, try to create a comfortable spot that it can reach. If you have a kitty condo with a 6-foot-high perch, cut it down to 2 or 3 feet. If it can't jump up to get its dinner, relocate the dish to an area it can get to. To continue to keep the dog away, consider putting the cat's dish on the floor in a small room, with the door propped open about three inches. The cat will be able to get in, while only the dog's nosy nose will be able to poke through. Be sure not to put the food or water dishes upstairs or downstairs, though, because climbing steps may be painful for your older pet.

■ **Locate your elderly cat's food dishes** *in an easily accessible spot. Older cats won't be as agile as a youngster and will be reluctant to jump up onto high surfaces. Make sure that other pets are still kept away though.*

A place to eliminate

If your aging cat has arthritis, consider cutting down its litter box or getting a new one so that the edge is only 2 inches high, instead of the more customary 4 inches. This will allow easier access. In doing so, however, you will need to use less litter, which means you'll have to change the litter more often.

A place to be safe

Finally, keep your aged cat at home to protect it from disease and infection, which older cats are more vulnerable to.

Cold or hot weather outside can also take its toll on the old cat, whose slowing metabolism won't be up to dealing with temperature extremes. The older cat won't be able to move as fast as it once did, either, making car dodging or cat fighting nearly impossible.

PET KITTENS?

Often the owners of elderly cats bring a new kitten into the home, thinking the company might perk the old codger up. They also reason that the new cat will be able to model its behavior on the older resident cat, making the first few months of kittenhood easier to deal with.

My advice to you is this: Don't do it! A new, perky, rambunctious kitten will only annoy and stress the older cat – the last thing you want for a senior citizen. The stress of having to compete for territory after so many years of total control is something your old cat does not deserve to go through. Take my advice and let the old cat live out the rest of its life in peace.

■ **A bold and inquisitive kitten** *will cause stress to the elderly cat. Is it really fair to make your aging cat put up with a boisterous rival in its old age?*

Trips to the veterinarian

AS YOUR CAT GETS ON IN YEARS, it will become essential for you to take it in to see the veterinarian more frequently. I recommend a checkup twice a year for an older cat.

Your veterinarian will know what age-related disorders to look for and will be able to catch a potentially serious problem before it has a chance to become life-threatening. He or she will be able to clean the cat's teeth, give it the proper booster vaccinations, and examine it from head to tail in an effort to catch problems before they get out of hand. When taking your aging cat in for its biannual physical exam, request that the cat's stool, urine, and blood be analyzed, because these tests will most often catch a serious illness. Be sure to have the veterinarian discuss the test results with you, so you can get a clear picture of the state of your cat's health.

A simple summary

✔ As your cat ages, it will experience several physical and behavioral changes that you need to make provisions for.

✔ The aging cat will need you to re-evaluate its dietary needs in order to keep it healthy and fit. Lower-calorie foods, flavor enhancers, and nutritional supplements may all be needed to ensure that your older cat stays in the best shape possible.

✔ As a cat ages, it may be less able to groom itself, and you may have to brush, comb, bathe, and trim it more than you might have when the cat was younger.

✔ When a cat ages, its decreased mobility may require you to alter its environment to enable it to continue to enjoy its life. I recommend locating all essentials on one floor of the house, as well as keeping the more disease-prone, aged pet inside the home.

✔ Seeing the veterinarian twice a year for a thorough examination will help prevent a minor condition from developing into a serious one.

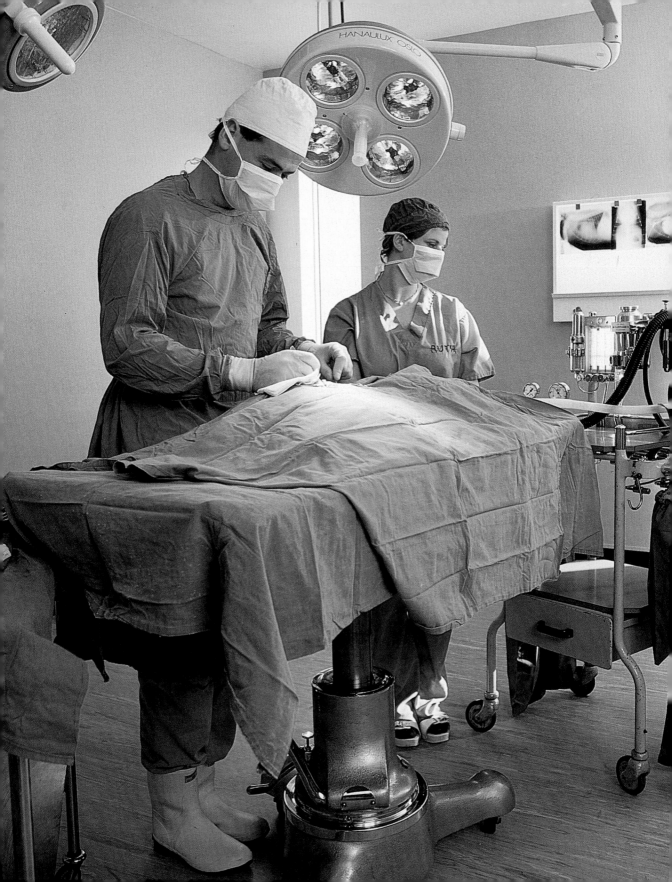

Chapter 14

Feline Emergencies

SOMETIMES EMERGENCIES occur that require a cat owner to think and act quickly to save the cat's life. Car accidents, poisonings, dog attacks, or acute illnesses can all threaten the life of your cat and call for prompt action. Luckily, with the right training and preparation, you can be ready for nearly any situation that comes along. If you stay focused and calm, you will be able to perform first aid on your cat, perhaps saving its life.

In this chapter...
- ✔ Your cat's vital signs
- ✔ Dealing with minor injuries
- ✔ Dealing with more serious injuries
- ✔ Taking your cat to the vet
- ✔ Giving your cat medication

SERIOUS INJURIES OR ILLNESSES MAY REQUIRE AN OPERATION

Your cat's vital signs

IF YOU SUSPECT SOMETHING *is wrong with your cat, you will need to take its* pulse, *check its breathing, and measure its body temperature. Knowing these things will help you quickly decide if your cat is in distress. Let's take them one at a time.*

Pulse

A cat's normal resting pulse should be about 120 beats per minute. Ten or 20 beats more or less is probably still normal, because cats have individual differences and because the cat's activity level just prior to taking the measurement affects the heart rate. If it is substantially higher or lower, it could indicate illness.

To take a cat's pulse, place your fingers on the inner surface of a rear leg, right where it joins the body. A large femoral artery comes close to the surface here; placing two or three fingers at this juncture should give you a strong pulse.

■ **The cat's pulse**
can best be felt high up on the hind leg. An abnormally high or low pulse may be an indication of illness.

Try it right now. Find your cat and hunt around for the spot until you can feel a pulse. It will take some practice at first, both for you and the cat. All you need to do is count how many pulses you feel in 15 seconds. Take that number, multiply by 4, and you have it! If you're calling the veterinarian, you will be able to report this statistic to him or her, perhaps helping in an initial diagnosis.

Taking the cat's temperature

Another great diagnostic tool, a high or low temperature could point to an infection or some other problem. Knowing your cat's temperature can help you discover if something unsavory is going on inside its little body. A normal temperature for your cat should be between 100.5° and 102.5° F (38° and 39° C).

Taking a cat's temperature isn't as easy as taking its pulse, however, particularly if the cat isn't very fond of being handled. Of course, you have been handling, grooming, and examining your cat's body from kittenhood on, though, in which case you shouldn't have much of a problem. Still, if your cat vehemently resists having its temperature taken, don't force the issue. You could get badly scratched or bitten. Instead, let the veterinarian do it when you bring the cat in.

First go into your cat first aid kit (described in Chapter 5) and get your trusty rectal thermometer. Clean it with soap and water, then lubricate it with petroleum jelly. Make sure you have shaken it down to below 98° F (37° C) first, of course.

Next, place your cat on a table top, preferably in a standing position. At this stage, you might want to have a friend gently hold the cat under the tummy so it remains standing. Lift its tail gently and place a small amount of petroleum jelly onto the cat's anus. Then slip about an inch of the thermometer into its anus. Be careful not to push the thermometer in at a sideways angle because this can hurt the cat or break the thermometer. Leave it in for about a minute, then pull it out and read it. If the cat's temperature falls outside of the normal range, give your veterinarian a call.

I have found the new plastic digital thermometers easier and safer to use than the old-fashioned glass models. They tend to be sturdier, give better readings, and do not pose a danger to the cat if they break.

Respiration rate

A resting cat's rate of **respiration** should be about 20 to 30 breaths per minute. If it has been active or frightened, expect it to be a little higher. If it's substantially lower, get the cat to a veterinarian because it might be suffering from shock or some form of respiratory failure.

Dealing with minor injuries

CATS ARE USUALLY QUITE CAREFUL *not to injure themselves, but there may be a time when your cat gets a minor cut, abrasion, or burn. This kind of injury is certainly not life-threatening, but it will need treatment to prevent infection from setting in and turning a little cut into a serious problem. You can treat many minor feline mishaps at home. If you have a good first-aid kit put together (see Chapter 5), you should be able to deal with these minor injuries.*

■ **A cat with minor injuries,** *such as a surface wound, can be safely nursed at home. Make sure that you have an up-to-date first aid kit that includes such essentials as gauze.*

When to see the veterinarian

A puncture wound, a cut that continues to bleed despite your attentions, or a serious burn covering an area larger than a pencil eraser should be seen by your veterinarian, though, to be on the safe side.

Scrapes and abrasions

Try to keep the cat as calm as possible while you examine its injury. For a minor abrasion (often found on the cat's foot pads or nose), first clean the area with a suitable antibiotic cleaning solution such as Betadine, making sure to get any blood, dirt, or other debris out of the damaged area. Then apply a thin coat of antibiotic ointment to the affected area.

A bandage is often not necessary, and it's usually hard to convince a cat to wear one, but be sure to clean the abrasion two or three times a day for a few days, or until it appears to be healing well with no swelling or inflammation. Don't worry about your cat licking at it; the ointment isn't toxic, and the licking might actually help to keep the cut clean.

If the abrasion does not begin healing well after 3 days, make sure that you see your veterinarian.

Cuts

If your cat has a minor cut on its skin, you should be able to effectively treat it at home. A minor cut is one that stops bleeding on its own after a few minutes; if it doesn't, your cat will need to see the veterinarian.

Treating a minor cut

To treat a minor cut, follow these simple steps:

1. Press down on the cut with a clean gauze pad for a minute or two, or until the bleeding stops.

2. Remove the gauze and clean the cut with an antibiotic cleaning solution. The cut may start to bleed again, and if it does, apply another gauze pad and press down lightly until the bleeding stops again.

3. Apply a small amount of antibiotic ointment, then wrap the area with a roll of gauze. If the affected area is on a limb or tail, this should be a straightforward task. If it's on the body, you may be able to wrap the gauze around the cat's torso. If not, don't worry; you can just apply a generous amount of antibiotic ointment, which will act as a coagulant.

4. After wrapping and securing the gauze with adhesive tape (no tape on the cat's fur, please!), be sure to place the cat in a restricted area where you can observe it. It will probably try to remove the bandage by chewing it off; try to discourage this if you can. If you can't, applying a good coat of ointment to the cut should be sufficient.

Minor burns

A burn affecting more than a very small area (about the size of a pencil eraser) should be seen by your veterinarian immediately.

You can deal with a small, minor burn. First, soothe a scald or burn with a cloth dipped in cool water, then apply an ice pack wrapped in a damp cloth. Apply the ice pack for a few minutes, then remove it for a few minutes. Keep alternating in this manner for about an hour.

A minor burn should then be cleaned with an antibiotic cleaning solution, then covered with an antibiotic ointment. Finally, cover the burn with a light gauze pad or bandage. Try to keep it on the cat for the remainder of the day. Also, consider putting a call in to your veterinarian to get his or her professional input.

Insect stings

For most cats, insect stings are little more than a minor irritant. But for a pet who has an allergic reaction, a sting can be serious – even life-threatening. Unfortunately, there is no way to know if your cat is allergic to insect stings until it has been stung.

Cats most often get stung in areas that have little hair protection – often the face, feet, or inside of the mouth (insects can make interesting prey). If you have seen bees, wasps, or hornets flying around, then find your cat acting hurt or scared, it may have been stung. Look for any red, swollen area with a bump in the middle. If your cat is allergic to the *venom*, serious swelling will develop quickly. The cat's throat may also swell, causing great difficulty in breathing. If this happens, get the pet to the vet as soon as possible.

If your pet is not having an allergic reaction, check the area for any stinger that may have been left behind. Stingers are very small and difficult to see; they usually look like tiny black splinters. You should try to remove the stinger because it may still contain venom.

Remove it by quickly scraping across the area with a flat object (like a credit card). Do not use tweezers, as this might actually cause more venom to be pumped into the affected site. Then wash the area with mild soap and water and apply a cold pack.

You can keep your cat away from any stinging insects by not allowing it outdoors. Also try to remove any insect nests you find in the vicinity of your house.

If your cat has a history of allergic reactions, speak to your vet about having the correct dose of antihistamines on hand, as these can save a cat's life. Keep the medication in a first-aid kit close at hand, especially during the warmer months.

Trivia...

Burns of the skin are rated according to their severity. A first-degree burn is a superficial burning of the skin, akin to a sunburn. A second-degree burn is more severe, with blistering of the skin and more pain. A third-degree burn results in permanent skin death, with great pain and a high danger of infection since the skin's primary job is to seal the inside of the body off from germs.

DEFINITION

Venom, *a poisonous, liquid substance often secreted by snakes, scorpions, bees, and spiders, is injected into a prey animal or enemy, chiefly by biting or stinging.*

Dealing with more serious injuries

WITH A MORE SERIOUS INJURY, *any treatment you offer will be to simply stabilize the cat so you can bring it to the veterinarian. You cannot deal with breaks, serious cuts, poisoning (which I discussed in Chapter 5), animal attacks, or motor vehicle accidents. Your cat must see a veterinarian. Know your regular veterinarian's policy about after-hours or emergency care. If it's after office hours for your vet, take your cat to the nearest emergency veterinary clinic.*

In most cases, the answering machine at your vet's office will give you the phone number of the nearest emergency facility. Better yet, find out before there's an emergency, and write the number down in your feline first-aid kit.

Car accidents

Every cat owner's nightmare, a cat never fares well when struck by a motor vehicle. Only a problem for cats allowed outdoors (or for cats that have escaped), few cats survive a collision with a moving vehicle. Only some cats who receive glancing blows live to tell the tale.

Any animal in pain has the potential to bite and should be handled very carefully.

Take the time to place a soft muzzle, such as a tube sock or a man's tie, around the injured cat's muzzle. This will prevent it from biting anyone who handles it.

If your cat has been struck by a motor vehicle, the first thing not to do is lose your cool. Instead, take stock of the situation and answer these questions:

- Does the cat appear to be mortally wounded or just badly shaken?
- Is the cat conscious?
- Is the cat losing blood?
- Is there evidence of broken limbs?

The answers to these questions will determine what actions you take first. The following sections describe what emergency action to take.

If your cat has been hit by a car, take it to the veterinarian even if it appears to be fine. Cats are very good at hiding their discomfort, and your cat could be seriously injured, yet show no signs.

For cats with no discernible injuries other than shock, carefully move a blanket or towel underneath the cat. Then, with the help of a friend or bystander, gently place the cat into your car and get it to the veterinarian. If possible, have someone ride with you to prevent the cat from moving around. Be sure to keep the cat warm by placing a blanket or coat atop it.

Do not call 911. This service is already inundated with human emergencies and will not help you with your cat.

Instead, have a bystander or the driver of the vehicle contact your veterinarian or local veterinary emergency hospital. The staff can guide you about how to proceed and will be prepared for your arrival if necessary.

Bleeding

Severe bleeding must be stopped; if not, a drop in blood pressure could send the cat into shock, killing it. To stop severe bleeding, apply firm and steady pressure to the area using a clean cloth or gauze pad. Hold it for 4 or 5 minutes before slowly releasing the pressure.

If the bleeding continues, try compression and bandaging. Hold another clean pad over the wound, and after 4 or 5 minutes bandage the compress and wrap and tape it firmly. Make sure you don't put the bandage on so tight that it cuts off all circulation, then get your cat to the vet.

Avoid using a tourniquet because most of the time they do more harm than good. A tourniquet should only be used as a last resort.

The only time to use a tourniquet is when a major artery has been severed or when a venomous snake has bitten your cat.

To make a tourniquet, use either surgical tubing, a clean strip of cloth, or even a shoelace. Tie the tourniquet around a limb between the wound and the heart. Insert a stick or a pen or pencil under the tie, then twist it to tighten the tourniquet and control the bleeding.

Every 10 minutes loosen the tourniquet briefly. Do this while you are on your way to the veterinarian.

Broken bones

Prevent a cat with a suspected break or fracture from moving about on its own by wrapping a small towel around the limb and securing it with tape. Then, very gently, carry your cat to your car for the trip to the veterinarian.

If your cat is limping even slightly after an accident, suspect a break and get the cat to the vet for an X ray.

Shock

Shock, a phenomenon that occurs whenever an animal's body and brain are not being adequately supplied with oxygen, can be fatal. A cat in shock will:

- Have pale gums
- Be disoriented and nonresponsive
- Have a low body temperature
- Have a fast, weak pulse that can become nearly impossible to measure

If you suspect that your cat has shock, keep it warm and get it into an emergency clinic as soon as possible.

Back injury

If you suspect any damage to the cat's back or spinal cord, the safest thing to do is keep it still while you place a call to an emergency clinic. Place a jacket or blanket over the cat to prevent it from moving. Do not let it get up and move on its own, as any movement could paralyze or even kill the cat. Then grab someone's cell phone and call the veterinarian. Someone there will be able to tell you what to do next.

> ### Trivia...
> *Cats are much less apt to break a bone in a fall than are other animals. Amazingly, the elasticity of cats' bones is only one-tenth less than that of rubber! If a cat falls 10 stories, it has a 90 percent chance of survival. If a dog or human falls the same distance, they have less than a 10 percent chance of survival.*

■ **Restrict movement** *if you suspect your cat has a back or spinal cord injury. To do this, place a towel or something similar over the injured animal to prevent it from struggling.*

CARDIOPULMONARY RESUSCITATION (CPR) FOR CATS

If your cat is not breathing, you can give it mouth-to-mouth resuscitation. If its heart has also stopped, you can attempt to perform cardiopulmonary resuscitation (CPR). Keep in mind that even when CPR is performed in an animal hospital by trained professionals, the results are often unsuccessful. However, you can at least try to resuscitate your pet so that you feel that you have done all that is possible. And sometimes it does save an animal's life.

1. Lay the cat on its side and check its mouth for any obstructing object and remove it if you can. Check for breathing by watching the chest rise and fall and feeling the nose for the movement of air. If you do not detect breathing, hold the mouth shut, cover the cat's nose with your mouth, and administer two short breaths. Remember, a cat's lungs are much smaller than yours, so don't breathe too hard! If the cat does not start breathing on its own, continue with short breaths at the rate of 12 to 15 per minute

2. Check for a heartbeat by feeling across both sides of the chest at the level where the elbows normally rest. If there is no heartbeat, begin chest compressions. With the cat on its side, place your thumb on the sternum (breastbone) and your index and middle fingers onto the back of the cat. If you cannot reach, brace the back of the cat with one hand, and apply compressions with the thumb of the other. Apply compressions at a rate of 100 to 150 per minute. After every ten heart compressions, give a breath of mouth-to-mouth resuscitation (this is a lot easier if two people are performing the CPR).

3. Keep trying for at least 5 minutes. But if you have administered CPR for 5 minutes with no response, it is highly unlikely that you will be successful in reviving your cat.

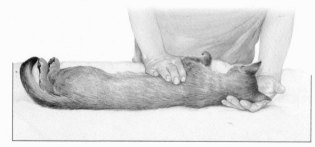

PERFORMING HEART
COMPRESSIONS

Animal attacks

If your cat is attacked and seriously hurt by another animal, you will need to act quickly. Dogs are usually the guilty parties, but other cats and even wild animals such as a coyote or raccoon could be the attacker. In addition to a serious bodily injury, your cat could contract rabies or some other infectious disease from an attack – another reason to make sure all its vaccinations are up-to-date.

The most common types of injuries from an animal attack are puncture wounds from the attacker's canine teeth (what we might call the fangs). These

■ **Dog attacks** *on cats are quite common and can inflict nasty puncture wounds. For this reason, make sure you keep your cat's vaccinations up-to-date to prevent infection.*

should be cleaned out as best you can with an antibiotic cleaning solution, dressed, then seen by your veterinarian as quickly as possible. If the punctures are bleeding heavily, pressure must be applied for 4 to 5 minutes at a time with a short respite in between. In this case, a helper will be needed to drive you to the emergency clinic so you can keep pressure on the wounds.

Scratches, tears, or gaping wounds should all be treated as discussed previously in this chapter. In all cases, be sure to clean the wounds and control the bleeding. Throughout the treatment, be aware that the cat is quite likely to bite you if it has not been muzzled.

The most effective way to prevent attacks on your cat is to keep it indoors. Barring that, be sure to have a talk with any neighbors who insist on allowing their pets (especially aggressive dogs) to wander the neighborhood. If they're being uncooperative, call animal control.

INTERNET

www.learnfree-pets.com/pet-rescue/

This is a great site to learn more about feline first aid.

Snake bites

Usually much more serious than an insect sting, a bite from a poisonous snake can kill your cat if it is not treated quickly by a veterinarian. Rattlesnakes, water moccasins, copperheads, coral snakes, and Gila monsters (a lizard, not a snake) can all kill your cat with a single bite. If you live in an area with venomous snakes around, do not let your cat outside!

If your cat does get bitten, you will need to act quickly. This is one of the few times when a tourniquet should be used (follow the directions on page 244). If you have a snake-bite kit with suction cups, those should be applied to the bite areas as well, although they may not stick to the cat's hair.

By using a thick coat of petroleum jelly, however (or by shaving the bitten area with an electric razor), you might get the cups to stay in place. These will help keep the venom close to the wound, instead of circulating through the cat's body. Before using the cups, be sure to irrigate the punctures with antibiotic cleaning solution, if available. If not, use soap and water or, at the very least, a wet cloth. Then get to the veterinarian, pronto!

Heat stroke

Any cat suffering from heat stroke needs to be cooled down quickly. Signs of heat stroke include rapid breathing and a high pulse rate. To treat it, run cool (not cold!) water over the cat's back and underbelly, using the sprayer in your sink or bathtub or a garden hose. Reevaluate the animal's condition every 5 minutes until the breathing pattern returns to normal. The animal should be seen by your veterinarian immediately after this treatment because numerous serious complications can occur as a result of heat stroke.

The most common cause of heat stroke in animals is being shut inside a car. The temperature inside a closed car can be more than 20° F (11° C) higher than it is outside the car – even if you leave the window open a crack.

Never shut any pet inside a car, not even for a few minutes.

Seizures

A seizuring cat must be prevented from injuring itself. Place blankets around it and move it away from stairs or other hazardous places in the house. Speak calmly to the pet because your soothing tones may help bring the animal out of the seizure more quickly. Do not attempt to place your hands in the animal's mouth; cats rarely bite their tongues during a seizure.

Call your veterinarian to alert him or her to the problem and get ready to transport the cat as soon as the seizure ends.

Choking

Although it's rare in cats, a large piece of food or part of a toy can obstruct the airway, choking the cat. The first thing to do is see if you can grasp the foreign object with your fingers or a pair of tweezers. If you can't, you will have to perform the Heimlich maneuver. Here's how to do it:

With the cat lying on its side, place the heel of your hand just below the last rib, on top of the diaphragm. Then give two or three inward pushes. If this does not dislodge the object, try again using more force.

While performing the Heimlich maneuver, make every effort to get the cat to an emergency clinic. You can perform the Heimlich maneuver in the back seat of a car while another person drives you to the clinic. If the cat has no pulse, you will need to perform CPR (see the box on page 246).

Taking your cat to the vet

AFTER YOU HAVE STABILIZED your cat's injury, you must get your cat to an emergency clinic as quickly as possible. This isn't always an easy thing to do, though, because many of the things you need to stabilize the injury (such as applying compression to a bleeding wound) will exclude you from driving. Also, there aren't any pet ambulance services (yet). What can you do?

Call on a friend

It pays to have friends, I always say. Always try to have someone, either a friend or family member, who can come over quickly and drive you to the clinic. Even a neighbor who you might not be too friendly with will often be happy to help in a time of crisis. The trick is to have someone in mind to fall back on, just in case.

Have the address and telephone number of your veterinarian's office, and an after-hours emergency clinic, clearly posted somewhere in your home; the refrigerator door is a good place.

That way you won't need to frantically rush around looking while your cat suffers. Also, have a clear idea of how to get to both places, so you can direct the friend or family member without any problem.

Giving your cat medication

ONCE YOU HAVE GOTTEN YOUR *injured cat back home, you will probably need to give it some kind of medicine each day to aid in healing and fight infection. The problem is, many cats hate taking pills.*

Don't worry! First, many medications can be given in powder form, sprinkled right onto the cat's food. Others in capsule form can be opened up and sprinkled on the food as well. For a solid pill, though, see below.

Giving a cat a pill

Getting your cat to take a pill needs a gentle but firm approach. Place the cat on a raised surface, and follow the steps outlined here:

1 Hold the pill between the thumb and index finger of one hand, while you place your other hand atop the cat's head.

2 Work the thumb and index finger of the hand that's atop the head into the corners of your cat's mouth, hooking them into the mouth until they are nearly touching the cat's molars.

3 Tilt the cat's head straight back until its nose is sticking up into the air. At this point, if the cat hasn't bitten you, its mouth should be wide open.

■ **To give your cat a tablet,** *simply hold the cat firmly and put the tablet on the back of the cat's tongue. Then close the mouth and massage its throat.*

4. Drop the pill as far back as you can into the cat's mouth, then close the mouth and massage the cat's throat for a few seconds. You can also blow a quick breath into its nose. Both these actions make a cat swallow reflexively.

With practice you should be able to do this quickly, before the cat knows what hit it.

If your cat tends to be a biter, do not try this; you could be seriously hurt.

Instead, have your veterinarian give you a medication that can be sprinkled onto the cat's food. A solid pill can even be crushed and sprinkled, if necessary. Or "pill guns" can be purchased at pet supply stores; these shoot the pill far back into the cat's throat so you don't have to use your hand to lever its mouth open wide.

A simple summary

✔ One of the first steps in diagnosing the condition of a sick or injured cat is to measure its vital statistics. These include the cat's pulse, temperature, and rate of respiration.

✔ You can deal with most minor injuries to your cat at home. If you have any doubts, however, call the veterinary clinic for professional advice.

✔ Serious injuries to your cat need professional care as soon as possible. Stabilizing the injured cat before transporting it is essential in order to maintain the life of the cat.

✔ Be sure to have a friend or family member that you can rely on to drive you and your cat to the emergency clinic if necessary. Have the address, telephone number, and directions to the emergency veterinary clinic on hand to ensure there are no unnecessary delays.

✔ Administering medications to your cat doesn't have to be an impossible task if you use the correct technique.

Chapter 15

Cats Behaving Badly

WHEN WE BRING AN ANIMAL into our home, it's inevitable that there will be some disagreements about what is acceptable behavior. Fortunately, most objectionable cat behaviors can be corrected.

In this chapter...

- ✓ What is a behavior problem?
- ✓ Simple strategies
- ✓ Feline aggression
- ✓ Biting and scratching
- ✓ Begging
- ✓ House-soiling
- ✓ Finicky eating
- ✓ Jumping up

- ✓ Eating plants
- ✓ Scratching furniture
- ✓ Too much meowing
- ✓ Separation anxiety

KEEP TEMPTATION OUT OF YOUR CAT'S WAY!

What is a behavior problem?

BEFORE I CAN HELP YOU change the behavior of your felonious feline, I would like to spend a few moments discussing just exactly what a behavior problem really is. After all, what you find distasteful behavior might be cute to another cat owner. I personally do not care to have my cats meowing noisily all day and all night, but I know quite a few Siamese owners who just love to hear their cats chattering away. To each his own.

■ **Incessant meowing** *may annoy and disturb some cat owners, but it can't really be classified as bad behavior on the part of the cat.*

What's normal to the cat

Anything a cat does is a normal behavior as far as the cat is concerned. It is choosing to behave in this way for a reason and is not thinking at all about whether or not the behavior is going to be offensive to you.

Cats never act out of revenge or spite. Those are human emotions, not feline ones.

So you thinking a behavior is inappropriate doesn't mean a whole lot to the cat. For instance, scratching up the trunk of a tree is a normal marking behavior for a leopard in the wild. Scratching up the arm of your leather sofa is a normal marking behavior for a domestic cat.

So what is inappropriate behavior?

In my opinion, improper feline behavior occurs whenever something that your cat does clashes with what your expectations are. You do not expect or desire your cat to urinate on your bed or scratch up your couch. Therefore, those behaviors are undesirable – to you. The cat might not initially see anything wrong with it at all. A cat who chases a pet gerbil all around the house isn't doing anything unusual. Nevertheless, it has to learn otherwise in order to get along with everyone in the family.

Simple strategies

WHEN YOU ASK YOUR CAT *not to perform certain instinctive behaviors,*
you are going up against millions of years of evolution. You can't just tell your
cat, "Stop being a cat."

You must find a way for the cat to express its natural instincts in
an acceptable manner.

Acceptable alternatives

Redirecting the cat's natural instincts is a
much more effective solution to the problem
than any overt punishment ever could be.
The cat continues the behavior, only in a fashion more
acceptable to you. You have given it an acceptable
alternative. For example, if your cat is scratching the
couch, place a scratching post near the couch, so the cat
can mark that particular territory in an acceptable manner.

Instead of letting your cat decide what is going to
amuse it, give the cat interesting environmental
distractions that will keep it amused and away from
the things you want left alone. Again,
you are providing it with acceptable
alternatives. A cardboard box filled
with newspaper, a feather toy, a wind-
up mouse, or whatever your cat likes
will take its mind off of those less
interesting things you want left alone.

■ **Provide a scratching post** *for your cat as an*
alternative marking territory.

Eliminating the causes

Cats don't have a lot of self-control, and sometimes things are just too tempting for them.
You can help them out by removing as much temptation as possible. Don't want your cat
unrolling the toilet paper? Then keep the bathroom door closed. No eating off the kitchen
counters? Don't leave food out.

Try to think like a cat. Wouldn't you find a caged canary a delicious temptation? Isn't that
dirty litter box much less appealing than the rich potting soil around the plant in the living
room? If you're a cat, you bet! Avoid these disasters waiting to happen by putting the canary
in a cat-proof, off-limits area and scooping and cleaning the litter box regularly.

Modifying the environment

Sometimes you can make an area less attractive to a cat with a few simple modifications. For example, cats don't like to walk on tin foil or on pebbly surfaces. So leaving a piece of foil or a plastic doormat turned spiky-side-up on top of the stereo will keep kitty from sleeping up there. Double-sided tape is also a super feline foe. Try it on the arm of your couch and see how fast kitty learns to prefer the scratching post.

INTERNET

www.lovethatcat.com

At this site, you can find books and videos on dealing with undesirable cat behaviors, as well as lots of other useful cat products, including toys, beds, and even kitty mobiles.

Relieving boredom

Again, think like a cat; do you want absolutely nothing to do all day? If you do not supply your cat with interesting things to do and see, it will find ways to entertain itself that might drive you bonkers. A bored cat will get into cupboards and closets, simply out of curiosity. By providing the cat with activities and an interesting, stimulating environment, you will help minimize problem behaviors stemming from an idle feline mind. Make sure your cat has a perch with a good view out the window. To spice up the view, try adding a bird feeder just outside. Or, simply leaving the television on for enriching visuals and sounds. By creating an interesting atmosphere, you can often head off problem behaviors before they start.

Discouraging a behavior

When passive, nonconfrontational methods fail, gentle forms of discouragement may be needed to stop an undesirable behavior. For instance, if your cat continues to jump up on the kitchen table when you're eating, a timely squirt of water from a spray bottle or water pistol can help stop the behavior.

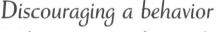

When spraying water at your cat to discourage a behavior, aim for the cat's rump, not the face!

The beauty of the spray bottle or water pistol is that the unpleasant consequence (the stream of water) does not erode the trust the cat has in you. That's because the water, though shocking, is detached from you and does not seem to come from you. Even combining it with a firm "No!" command won't cause the cat to fear your presence or touch. The pet will only become conditioned to the word itself, quickly realizing that "No!" means "I am doing something wrong and should stop it now."

Never physically abuse your cat! It is less than a tenth of your size and can be seriously injured from being struck in any way.

Feline aggression

CATS ARE PREDATORS, *and predatory behavior comes naturally to them. However, when that behavior is directed at you in a way that makes you feel threatened, it's a problem. Aggression has different solutions, depending on what caused it in the first place. Let's look at each type.*

Dominance or territorial aggression

This is when a cat feels that its status or territory is being usurped by another animal, often a fellow cat. The offending cat uses force or intimidation to control others and to possess whatever it desires. The aggressive cat will hiss at, chase, or physically attack the intruder.

Cats are, at best, tolerant of others attempting to share their domain. You are perhaps the only exception to that, because most cats see their owners as big, hairless cat parents. Remember that your cat has the same territorial instincts as any wild feline. Your home is its territory, and any time another creature comes around, it will initially be seen by your cat as an intruder. Some level of aggression, at least in the beginning, should be expected if you bring a new pet into the house. Though it may not escalate past hissing and swatting, it could, and you need to be prepared for that.

Apart from territorial concerns, your cat may want to express its dominance over the intruding animal (or person). Whenever two or more adult cats get together, for instance, they will immediately begin working out who is the more dominant of the two. Kittens are better at tolerating others of their

■ **A cat will display aggression** *toward any animal that threatens its territorial rights. The affronted animal will hiss, spit, and even attack its perceived rival.*

own kind because they still have fond memories of being part of a litter. Once they are 4 to 5 months old, though, the more solitary mindset of an adult cat kicks in, making dominance contests with other cats more likely.

Rarely will a cat be overtly territorial or dominant over a human. When it does happen, it's a sign of an extremely pushy cat.

FIGHTING LIKE CATS AND DOGS

Cat-to-cat aggression is often limited to some posturing, hissing, and perhaps a few well-timed swats from the more dominant animal. Cat-to-dog aggression can be more serious, for obvious reasons; most dogs are larger than most cats and may respond to a cat's dominance or territorial aggression by turning on their prey or by invoking their own territorial, dominant inclinations. If either of these happen, it could be curtains for the cat. If the dog in question is a friendly one, it may trustingly get too close to a wary cat and get scratched. Though this usually doesn't have dire consequences, the dog's eyes can be seriously hurt.

Dealing with dominance or territorial aggression

Try the following if you have a dominant or territorial kitty:

- Have your cat neutered before 6 months of age. Whether your pet is a male or female, leaving it unneutered will only encourage territorial and dominance disputes, as well as create tension between you and the pet over issues of marking, scratching, and roaming.
- Keep your cat indoors as much as possible. Allowing it access to the outdoors will ensure that it will eventually get into fights with other cats, causing your cat to view any other cats as dangerous and threatening. Once that happens, you may never be able to successfully socialize it with another animal.
- Keep your cat's home environment as calm and predictable as possible, avoiding traumatic episodes such as a group of small children suddenly chasing it or the neighbor's Labrador retriever rushing in to say hi.
- Socialize your cat as early on as possible. Allow it to be around different adults and responsible children right from the beginning, as well as any other pets you may have in the home (provided they are not aggressive). If you want your cat to get along well with another cat, or a dog, consider raising them together. Two kittens, raised in the same home from the time they are 8 to 10 weeks old will get along far

better than an established adult and a new kitten or adult cat. Likewise for a dog–cat combo; raise the puppy and kitten together and odds are they will be the best of friends.

● Choose a kitten that seems to interact with its littermates in a reasonable way. Avoid overly dominant, pushy kittens that seem to bully the others, as well as the kittens who shrink away from any contact. Pick one that shows curiosity, yet knows when to back off. Also, make sure not to take a kitten that was separated from its mother and littermates before the eighth week, so you can be sure it got the proper maternal care as well as the right amount of early socialization with its siblings.

● If you're adopting an adult cat, be sure to observe its behavior closely before you make your decision. Is it in with other cats or by itself? Does it have any fresh (or old) scars on its body? Offer the cat a toy or treat, then take it away and watch the reaction. If the cat shows any possessiveness, move on to a different cat.

Fear aggression

Fear aggression occurs when a cat decides that something is threatening and unavoidable and attacks. A cat displaying fear aggression will show clear body language cues, including:

● Ears flat against the head
● Hair standing on end
● Pupils dilated
● Tail thrashing back and forth
● Hissing
● Arched back
● Slow retreating movement, often followed by a quick attack

A fear-aggressive cat will strike out at anyone or anything coming inside of what it decides is its safe space. It's what the cat decides is dangerous, and not the intentions of the approacher, that count here. Some fearful cats, when left no other recourse, will lie on their side and brandish all four paws up into the air, claws ready to slash away at the attacker. Often, children and dogs will mistake this posture as an invitation to play, only to find out otherwise.

■ **Signs of fear aggression** *in the cat include flattened ears, arched back, hissing, bristling fur, and wide-open pupils.*

The level of socialization a kitten receives while still in the litter plays a big role in determining whether or not it will exhibit fear aggression later in life. Kittens separated from their litters before the eighth week, for instance, often become antisocial, fearful, and timid adults. Bad experiences can also trigger fear aggression in a cat. If a young child accidentally trips over a 4-month-old kitten, the cat will remember the experience for a long time and probably always be somewhat nervous around children. Likewise, a cat attacked by a dog will certainly show fear and possibly aggression as well around dogs for the rest of its days.

Dealing with fear aggression

- Discourage friends from handling your fearful cat. Instead, let visitors toss a few treats down on the floor. By doing this regularly, you may be able to ease the cat's fears enough for it to eventually investigate visitors and perhaps allow a pat on the head. At no time, however, should a visitor try to initiate the contact.
- Place a fearful cat's litter box and food and water dishes in low-traffic areas. Do not place the litter box in a guest bathroom, where the cat stands a chance of being trapped inside with a stranger.
- Tell children and adults never to chase the cat or surprise it in any way.
- Choose a kitten carefully. Never buy a pet from a pet store or "backyard breeder," as these venues rarely produce high-quality, well-socialized cats. Also, do not take a kitten from any breeder who is willing to let it go before its eighth week of life. The kitten needs to stay with its mother and siblings at least that long to learn the proper socialization skills. Look for a breeder who allows his or her kittens to socialize regularly with humans from 2 weeks of age and on, or a shelter that regularly socializes its kittens. Choose a kitten that appears confident, friendly, and curious. If it shows any timidity or fear, pass on it.
- Do not bring a kitten or cat into a home filled with lots of unpredictable goings on. Try to set up a quiet, predictable environment for the new cat so that it can acclimate to its new surroundings with as little worry as possible.
- Socialize a new kitten as much as possible. The more socialization the kitten gets, the less likely it will be to show any signs of fear aggression later on.

■ **A kitten should stay** *with its mother and siblings until it is at least 8 weeks. The young cat needs this time to learn socialization skills.*

Food aggression

Food aggression, in which the cat attacks to protect its food or to steal the food from another animal, is much less common in cats than it is in dogs.

A cat will show food aggression, however, under several circumstances. If the cat has spent part of his life as a stray, odds are it had to fight for some meals. Bring a stray cat into your home, then, and you might find that it beats up your other cat at dinner time. Shelter cats may very well have the same mindset; many of them came from the streets, where food was scarce.

Food aggression can also accompany dominance issues. The problem comes when you have two cats that have not yet been able to resolve the dominance issue. Food becomes a great bone of contention between them. Often it can escalate to a full-out battle, with possible injury to both cats.

Sometimes a real bully of a cat might exert its dominance over a less domineering cat at dinner time and not know when to stop the intimidation. The attacked cat becomes frightened and goes into fear-aggression mode. One cat fights due to an inflated sense of importance, while the other fights from fear.

Dealing with food aggression

- Feed your cats on opposite sides of the kitchen during feeding. Buy extra food and water dishes, and set each cat up in his own corner. This solution will work with cats who simply do not feel comfortable having another cat so close by during feeding time.
- Feed each cat in a separate room if the aggression is severe. By doing so, you will relieve the stress that the attacked cat has been experiencing, letting it eat in peace. You will also be halting the aggressive behavior of the dominant animal; allowing the behavior to continue only serves to reinforce it.
- If the aggression is between a cat and a dog, feed the cat where the dog can't get at its food. Your cat can easily able to jump up to a counter several feet above the floor, so consider simply feeding it atop a kitchen counter while the dog eats undisturbed below.

Hereditary aggression

Hereditary aggression is caused by poor breeding. If your cat has exhibited unpredictable aggressive tendencies right from the start, it might simply be genetically predisposed to do so.

A stranger walking too close, a child innocently trying to pet it, or even a sudden loud noise can set off a cat with this problem. Unfortunately, the cause of hereditary aggression is biological, not environmental, making solutions few and far between.

Dealing with hereditary aggression

- See your veterinarian, who will help determine if the cat really does have a genetic predisposition for aggression. Sometimes hereditary aggression can be mistaken for fear aggression; your veterinarian will help you make that determination.
- Ask your veterinarian about the use of tranquilizers and mood-altering drugs to minimize the dangerous behavior. Just as Lithium, Prozac, Xanex, and Valium are used to modulate human behaviors, similar medications can be used on cats. There are also several natural remedies that can help a cat behave more calmly.
- Avoid getting a cat from an amateur or disreputable breeder. Never buy a kitten from a "backyard breeder" or a pet shop, as they are almost all driven by profit and have little or no concern for the genetic stability of the cats they sell. Instead, go to a reputable shelter, a professional breeder, or a private party who you know is not in the business of selling cats. Good shelters will be able to screen out genetically aggressive cats before they are ever seen by the public; odds are any kitten or cat you see there will be mentally sound.

Maternal aggression

Maternal aggression can occur whenever someone or something comes too close to a mother cat's litter, particularly when the kittens are newborns. The aggression might even be directed at you, the owner, if the cat feels you are taking too many liberties with her kittens.

Maternal aggression in domestic cats is unpredictable. Some feline mothers will become aggressive upon your approach, while others don't seem to care at all. Most feline mothers have a good sense of who is and who isn't a threat to their kittens, though.

■ **The mother cat** *may be very protective toward her kittens and become aggressive if any person or animal ventures too near to her family.*

Dealing with maternal aggression

- Provide the mom cat with a quiet, warm, secure nesting area if she is about to give birth, then simply allow her to be a mother to her babies.
- Respect the mother's wishes and wait a few weeks. Luckily, maternal aggression tends to subside on its own as the kittens become less vulnerable.
- Keep your cat indoors, away from roaming tomcats, who can smell a female in heat a mile away.
- Spay her; it's the best way to avoid maternal aggression in your cat.

Paternal aggression

This extreme behavior occurs among wild and domestic cats. Males sometimes kill the kittens of a nesting female who has mated with one of his competitors. Male cats exhibit paternal aggression for a simple reason: By killing a competitor's kittens, the male cat prevents that competitor's genes from being passed on. After the kittens are dead, the female will rapidly come back into heat, opening up the opportunity for the murderous male to mate with her and spread his genes.

Dealing with paternal aggression

- Have your male neutered before he becomes sexually mature (usually by 6 months of age). By removing hormonal factors from the picture, you will effectively prevent your male cat from ever participating in this horrible form of aggression.
- Keep him indoors and away from any nesting females to prevent him from getting at any kittens. If you know of any nursing females in the area, make sure the owner ensures the safety of the kittens by making sure the nest is indoors and protected.

Prey aggression

Prey aggression, as evidenced by a cat stalking and/or killing another animal, occurs most often with cats allowed outdoors. Cats are born predators, and you cannot change that very basic part of their nature. All you can do is minimize the danger to the prey.

Dealing with prey aggression

- Have your cat neutered. Doing so will reduce its level of prey drive somewhat and help keep its mind off predatory urges.
- Keep your cat indoors. Cats that regularly hunt and kill animals quickly learn how much fun it is.
- Avoid having pets that might be considered delectable to your cat. Rodents, birds, rabbits, ferrets, small reptiles, and fish are all prime candidates.
- Place all small pets you insist on having in the most inaccessible areas of the home. Place a secure lid on all fish tanks, and apply several strips of doubled-sided transparent tape around the perimeter of all small pet containers.

Putting a bell on the collar of an outdoor cat will not protect the birds in your neighborhood.

Cats are born for stealth and will very quickly learn how to walk and even pounce without making the bell ring. Meanwhile, when the bell does ring, it will drive your cat crazy because felines are very sensitive to high-pitched sounds.

Sexual aggression

Sexual aggression, which takes place between a female and a male during courtship, can be a hard one for owners to tolerate. During mating, the female usually rejects the male's sexual approaches at first, then eventually allows the male to grasp her by the nape of the neck and mount her. It is toward the end of this process that the real conflict can occur. The male's penis has barbs on it that help stimulate ovulation in the female. When the penis is removed, these spines can hurt the female. She will scream, then slash out at the male.

Rather than be horrified at this aggression, what you should be asking yourself is this: Why am I allowing my cat to breed? If you are not an experienced cat breeder, you shouldn't be letting your pet breed at all.

■ **During mating,** *the female may display aggression toward her partner. She will reject his first advances, lashing out at him with her claws.*

Play aggression

Play aggression is seen mostly in kittens and adolescent cats. During the first few months of life, kittens learn to stalk and attack primarily through playing with their littermates. They will take turns sneaking up on one another from all angles, pouncing on an unsuspecting brother or sister. If your cat has maintained a juvenile, kittenish mindset into adulthood, it may still be exhibiting this playful stalking and pouncing behavior, directed either toward other pets in the home, a visitor, or even you.

Dealing with play aggression

- Allow two cats playing roughly to work it out between themselves without your intervention, unless it gets too aggressive.
- If you or another person are the target, clap your hands together briskly and say "No!" in a fairly stern tone if the cat play-attacks roughly.
- Sit quietly in a chair in your living room with a water pistol or plant sprayer bottle filled with water by your side. If your cat begins to stalk you or another person or pet in the home, spray it with the pistol or sprayer bottle (which should be set to emit a solid stream of water).
- Don't encourage biting games by using your hands to play with your cat. Play with toys that are acceptable targets of your cat's aggression.
- Watch your cat's body language, and accept its message when you have gone too far or when the cat prefers to stop playing. Pushing the cat beyond this point will only encourage aggressive behavior.

Redirected aggression

With redirected aggression, a stressed cat lashes out at an innocent person or animal. Have you ever tried to mediate an argument between two friends, only to have them both attack you? This is an example of redirected aggression.

Cats are very capable of this type of aggression. For instance, have you ever tried to break up a cat fight? If so, you may have had one or both of the cats attack you instead of each other. That's redirected aggression.

Another example is when a cat, after being injured, scratches or bites its owner, who might simply be trying to examine the cat or take him to the veterinarian. The animal is scared and in pain; to release the stress, it attacks you.

Dealing with redirected aggression

- Minimize the number of cats you have in the home, and don't crowd them.
- Don't try to break up a cat fight. You may get scratched badly. Throw a glass of cold water onto two fighting cats.
- Avoiding picking up your cat if it has just undergone a traumatic experience and is still scared. Instead, let it come to you, or give it a few minutes to calm down before trying to comfort it.
- Make sure your cat's environment is safe and secure to prevent stress and injury.
- Keep hold of your own temper. Remember that your cat's redirected aggression is a nonthinking, instinctive reaction to pain or fear and is not a calculated plan to hurt someone.

Biting and scratching

NOT TO BE CONFUSED WITH *outright aggressive behavior,
unpredictable biting or scratching by a seemingly well-adjusted cat can be
upsetting and even scary. Without warning, a seemingly happy cat will bite or
scratch you not necessarily hard enough to break the skin, but enough to hurt.*

I'm not talking about unprovoked, serious biting. I'm talking about biting in
response to a stimulus that the cat finds threatening or annoying.

*No owner should have to deal with a cat who shows serious, unprovoked
aggression toward the human members of your family.*

A cat bite is one of the most infectious wounds a person can suffer. Even a scratch
from an angry cat can send you to the doctor. If your cat is acting in this manner, see
your veterinarian, who may be able to diagnose what the cat's true problem is.

Why cats bite

A number of reasons can explain this behavior. Some cats will
simply reach a saturation point for handling or petting; a quick
bite or swat is used to say "enough." This type of behavior is
common among unneutered cats, as well as those who
have spent a great deal of time outdoors, because
both have had to deal with the
physical attentions of other cats.

Sensitive spots

Some cats will bite or
swat at you upon being
petted simply because
they are extra sensitive in the
areas in which they are being
touched. The neck and the
rump of the cat are two extremely
sensitive areas; most cats will
tolerate being handled in these areas
for a short time only. Linger too long
(especially at the rump), and the cat
may warn you to quit with a small
bite or a swat.

■ **A cat may bite and scratch** *its owner during
play if touched in a particularly sensitive area.
Most cats dislike having their stomach touched.*

Unneutered females may not enjoy too much petting and handling about the neck because during mating the male grabs the female roughly by the nape of the neck.

A cat you play roughly with is more likely to bite or scratch, thinking that the behavior is simply part of the playing process. Kittens, used to playing rough with their littermates, will often bite their owners, thinking it a part of the socializing process. They need to be taught that this is not acceptable behavior. An insecure cat may also bite or scratch without warning. Finally, a biting cat may be injured or have a disease that causes it pain. If your normally sweet cat suddenly becomes a biter, a trip to the vet is in order.

Preventing biting and scratching

- Get your cat neutered before it reaches sexual maturity.
- Keep your cat indoors to prevent fights with other cats. Many house cats learn to play rough and bite from these interactions.
- Socialize, handle, and groom your cat as early on as possible to desensitize it to touch.
- Allow your cat time to itself.
- Let your cat initiate your petting sessions.
- End petting sessions while the cat is still enjoying itself.
- Take your cat's warning body language and sounds seriously, and respect its wishes about physical contact.
- Make sure your cat has no hidden injuries by taking it to the veterinarian regularly.

■ **Petting sessions** *should be an enjoyable experience for both cat and owner alike. End these sessions before your cat gets bored and respect its need for time to itself.*

Dealing with biting and scratching

- Limit petting and grooming sessions to under a minute, and stop any type of physical contact before the cat reaches its saturation point. Keep the cat wanting more attention, and avoid letting it decide when to stop.
- Pay attention to your cat's body language while petting it. If you see its tail begin to thrash back and forth or feel its body tense up, end the touching session.
- Consider giving your cat a small tasty treat after each short handling session. This will stop it from worrying and redirect its attentions and thoughts to the reward to come.

Begging

WHEN YOUR CAT MAKES *a pest out of itself every time you are preparing food or eating, it is begging for a free handout. There could be several reasons your cat does this.*

Why cats beg

First, you might actually be underfeeding it. An underfed cat will try to find more to eat and may resort to begging. Most owners feed their cats enough, though, and can tell if their pets are underweight simply by looking and feeling. If you are in doubt, consult your veterinarian, who will tell you the ideal weight for your cat.

A former stray or shelter cat probably had to struggle for food. If this is the case, it might retain a very high food drive for much of its life, which could precipitate the begging behavior.

It's your fault!

The most common cause of begging behavior in a cat, though, is you. If you give your cat a little something whenever it begs, you're teaching your cat that begging brings rewards. This encourages the cat to keep begging.

Dealing with begging

- First, make sure your cat is at a good weight, to ensure it is getting enough food.
- Feed it on a regular schedule, at precise times, instead of free-feeding all day.
- Give your little beggar treats only when you are trying to encourage or teach a particular behavior, such as "Come" or "Sit." If you feed it random treats throughout the day, you will condition the cat to beg for more.
- Never feed your cat from the dinner table or from your plate, and do not feed it food intended for human consumption.
- Never give your cat food while you are preparing a meal at the kitchen counter. If you do choose to give it something, place the treat in the cat's food dish instead. That way it will look for food only in its dish and not at your table.

If your cat continues to jump up onto the table or the kitchen counter looking for food, simply keep a spray bottle filled with water handy. When the silly feline jumps up, give it a spritz while saying "No!" It will quickly get the idea.

House-soiling

THIS IS THE NUMBER-ONE REASON *cats are turned in to shelters. Certainly any feline that fails to use the litter box makes life miserable for everyone. But it's important to remember that the cat has a reason. When you figure out what the reason is, you will be more than half way to a solution.*

Illness

This is the first possibility to eliminate, and you can do this by taking your cat to the veterinarian. A kidney, bladder, stomach, or intestinal problem could cause your cat to lose control, as could an allergic reaction, change of food, or even poisoning.

■ **Soiling indoors** *may be caused by a urinary problem. Do not scold your cat – take it to the vet to see if it requires medical treatment.*

Accidental defecation usually involves diarrhea, a clear sign of illness. Medical problems may also cause painful urination or defecation, and the cat will then avoid the litter box because it thinks something in the box has caused the pain. A medical cause is more likely in cats that seem to have accidents in different locations each time or in those that are older than eight or nine years, but it is always a possibility with any cat.

The litter box isn't just right

Your cat's litter box is important to it. Proper disposal of feces and urine is an ancient feline drive motivated by the cat's need to hide its identity and location from predators. In your home, your cat's preferred spot to eliminate is its litter box, where it will carefully bury all waste materials. Trouble occurs when the condition or location of the box changes. The cat may seek out a new place to eliminate. Even changing brands of cat litter can upset a cat and cause it to abandon the litter box.

Obtaining a second cat and failing to buy a second litter box can often prompt the less dominant animal to search out a more secure spot to eliminate, which might end up being the floor of your closet.

269

Stress and change

As I've already mentioned, cats love a stable, predictable environment. Changing things can provoke some cats to temporarily ignore the litter box. Moving to a new home, acquiring a new pet, going on a vacation, or even buying new furniture can do it, as can the loss or addition of a family member.

Abuse, conflict, illness, injury, or a change in environment can cause stress for your cat, also resulting in accidents. Even a stray cat wandering around outside your home can upset your cat enough to cause an accident. An unwanted bath or grooming session, a dramatic weather change, or even a change in feeding time can trigger improper elimination habits.

Marking behavior

Cats are very territorial. In the wild, they mark the boundaries of their territories by urinating, defecating, scratching, and depositing scent from numerous glands on their bodies. Any other cat that approaches these marked-out boundaries gets the message that it is on another cat's turf. By respecting one another's territory, they avoid fighting and make sure there will be enough prey to go around.

Cats do not normally mark inside their own territories, unless they perceive a threat to their status. A very dominant cat will certainly do so, particularly if a new pet or person suddenly appears in the home. Unneutered cats, particularly males, are more likely to spray or defecate in the home as a way of marking territory or objecting to the presence of a competitor. Furniture, beds, and doorways are likely spots for the unfortunate action. Strays and shelter cats are also known to spray in their home because they have gotten used to doing so while living outdoors.

■ **Cats mark their territory** *by scratching or urinating. Marking sends out a message to any other felines in the area that the marked-out territory is strictly out of bounds.*

Often even neutering these kind of cats won't have an immediate effect on the behavior because it has become such an engrained habit.

Any cat that chooses to leave its feces unburied is clearly displaying dominance. Fecal marking is more rare than spraying, but it does occur, especially among extremely dominant cats forced to live with a new pet or pets. Indoor–outdoor cats living in a neighborhood with a high density of outdoor felines may mark with feces as well. The small territories each cat has often require them to take these drastic measures to mark out a tiny yet valued domain.

Playing litter box detective

The first step in trying to solve a feline house-soiling problem is to take the cat to the veterinarian for a full examination to rule out any chance of illness.

If you suspect the litter box is the cause of the house-soiling, switch to a good clumping litter, then make sure to scoop it out at least two times a day and change the litter completely at least twice a month. Place the box in a quiet area that's easy for the cat to get to. If you are a multiple cat home, add a second litter box, preferably in a different area. This will ensure that a less dominant cat won't get spooked by the presence of the more dominant feline in or near the only litter box in the house.

If you suspect a change in litter has caused the problem, go back to the old brand. This could end the problem immediately. Stay with the same brand of litter once you find one the cat likes. Keep the same box, if possible. Cats get attached to the look and scent of the old one and might object to a newer design.

If you must get a new litter box, leave the old one down for a while, and place the new one next to it, filled with litter. This will allow the cat to remain comfortable, while still having the chance to explore the new box.

Less change and stress

Try to avoid major change in the cat's life. Changing the look of your home alters your cat's territory, which could disturb your cat. If you must change things, do it slowly. Try to minimize stress in your home. Don't let kids chase the cat, and don't introduce other pets into the home unless necessary. Keeping your cat relaxed will help prevent many forms of behavior problems, including house-soiling.

If you must move house, first clean any carpets in the new place with a good odor-neutralizing product, available at all good pet supply stores.

This will eliminate the odor of any pets that lived there previously, minimizing the chance that your cat will spray in order to claim territory. Also, don't buy used furniture, since it may have the scent of other animals on it. When you do move, confine your cat to one room of the new place for a few days until you are sure it is not having any accidents. Then allow it access to the rest of the home, being careful to observe the cat closely for a few days.

No marking!

The best way to prevent marking is to have your cat neutered. An unneutered cat will absolutely spray in the home. I guarantee it. Males and females can both be guilty of the behavior, so don't think getting a female will save you. If you eliminate the mating drive, you will reduce the need to mark.

If your cat has sprayed or defecated in the home, immediately clean the area thoroughly to prevent a repeat performance in the same spot. Use an odor-neutralizing product such as Nature's Miracle (available in all pet supply stores). This type of product removes the cat's scent from the area, while plain soap and water will not. If the cat can smell its old mark, it will mark there again.

■ **An unneutered male cat** *will hold its tail upright and spray against the leg of a chair or any other piece of furniture that it wishes to mark.*

The water spray

If you see your cat getting ready to mark, spray it with water from a plant sprayer while saying "No!" If it is targeting one area, treat the spot with an odor neutralizer, then with a commercially available cat repellent. Or try sprinkling black pepper onto the area. You can also try placing strips of double-sided tape down around the spot or even strips of aluminum foil. Shallow pans of water or crinkled sheets of newspaper can also work. If all else fails, place small dishes of food down at the spot. This usually works, because cats won't mark near food.

Solitary confinement!

If nothing works to stop the marking behavior, confine the kitty to a small room in your house for a week. Reducing its territory in this manner gives the cat little reason to mark. After about a week, slowly introduce the cat back into the rest of the home, making sure that all old marked areas have been thoroughly cleaned with an effective odor neutralizer.

Finicky eating

UNLIKE DOGS, *who seem to gobble up everything in sight, many cats are quite picky about their food. Some cats become spoiled by owners, who feed them treats throughout the day. When then presented with a dish of kitty kibble, most pampered cats will ignore it. The end result is a cat that will only eat snacks and treats, often your leftovers, or rich food with a strong scent.*

What causes finickiness?

The biggest cause of finicky eating in a cat is free-feeding. Leaving food down all day means the cat never really gets hungry so it just picks at its food from time to time – often just out of boredom.

Another cause of finicky eating could be your cat's health. If it becomes sick or injured, its appetite may fall off dramatically.

If you notice that your cat's normally good appetite has taken a nose dive, call your vet, because it may point to a health problem.

Trivia...

After cats eat, they always immediately clean themselves. This is because their instinct tells them to get the food scent off them so that predators will not smell the food and come after them.

Feeding a finicky feline

The best way to feed a finicky cat is to make food available only twice a day at fixed meal times. Put the cat's dish down and call its name, ring a bell, or blow a whistle. If the cat comes and eats, great. If not, pick the food up after 15 minutes and wait until the next meal. You may need to repeat this for a day or two, but it won't take any longer. The cat will quickly become hungry enough to figure out the schedule. Don't fret; your cat won't starve itself. Sooner or later it will learn that dinner time means "Get it while you can!"

■ **Finicky eating** *may be a sign of ill-health. However, if your cat is free-fed, it could be that the cat never gets the chance to feel really hungry.*

273

Jumping up

CATS CAN LEAP UP onto surfaces many times higher than their height. This means they can easily get up on the kitchen counter, the dinner table, your computer, the knickknack shelf, the stereo, or other places you don't want them to be. It's not so hard to teach them that there are boundaries. You just need to be consistent in how you enforce the rules.

Off the counter and table

To keep your cat off the kitchen counters and the dining room table, try the following:

1. Make sure no food items are ever left out to tempt the cat. Be sure to leave the counter tops clean and wipe up all the crumbs and greasy spots. Wiping them down with a soapy sponge after you're finished in the kitchen will further discourage your cat, because the soap will leave behind a bitter taste.

2. Never reward begging behavior. And if you plan to give your cat any human food, do so at regular mealtimes in the cat's dish. And consider scheduling the cat's meals just before yours, so kitty will be happily munching away while you are preparing dinner.

3. Keep a water-filled plant sprayer bottle next to you while you cook and eat. If your cat jumps up onto the counter or table, spray it while saying "No!" Even if no food is out on the counters or table, enforce this every time – the counters and table should always be off limits. Otherwise, you'll just confuse the cat.

4. To prevent your cat jumping up onto counters, place double-sided tape or sheets of aluminum foil on the counter tops. Cats hate to walk on these. If you do, your cat will quickly learn where it is and is not allowed to go. Keep a few spray bottles handy around the home. The moment the cat jumps up onto a forbidden item, spray it on the rump and say "No!" To stop it from going onto the forbidden furniture while you are gone, try placing a few strips of double-sided tape or a sheet of aluminum foil on the spot. They'll act as a deterrent in your absence.

Trivia...

The cat, the giraffe, and the camel are the only animals that walk by moving both left legs simultaneously, then both right legs. Other animals move the front left with the rear right, then the front right with the rear left.

You need to decide right from the start what the boundaries will be for your cat and then enforce them consistently.

Whatever behavior modification technique you use, stick with it for several months until the cat is completely out of the habit of jumping up in that spot.

Eating plants

I TALKED IN CHAPTER 5 about ridding your home of toxic plants, and I want to start by emphasizing how important this is. No matter how well you train your cat, you cannot take the chance that kitty will munch on something poisonous. So, while I am sure no remaining plants in your home are toxic, you still do not want any pretty, nontoxic, expensive plants to be destroyed.

Why cats eat plants

Although cats are carnivores, they do sometimes consume vegetable matter. In the wild, a cat eats all of its prey, including the contents of the prey's stomach. The partially digested vegetable matter may provide the cat with vitamins and minerals not necessarily found elsewhere. In a distant echo of this behavior, domestic cats seem to love chewing on plants. Young, tender plants are especially at risk. The cats may be instinctively searching for nutrients or feel a need to vomit up something disagreeable. Or they may simply like the taste.

Plant-munching is bad for your plant, though, and may also be bad for your cat. You might bring home a plant that is unsafe for cats and not know it. The plant may have been sprayed with a pesticide at the nursery or the florist. You just can't tell.

■ **Cats love to chew the leaves** *of houseplants, so make sure that any plants you have are nontoxic.*

Some simple solutions

It's not difficult to remedy the cat–plant situation:

1. Get your nontoxic houseplants off the floor and the windowsills. Put them atop tall stands that a cat can't climb or hang them from mounts.

2. Cover the soil of the plant with marbles or rocks to discourage digging.

3. Wipe down the plant leaves with a dilute soap and water mixture or spray them with a dilute vinegar and water mixture; it won't hurt the plant, and it will taste terrible to the cat. You can also buy a veterinarian-approved cat repellent and spray it on the plant's leaves.

4. Place double-sided tape around the area where you keep your plants to keep the cat away from temptation.

5. If you can catch the cat in the act of chewing on a plant, spray it with water (water only!) from a plant sprayer bottle.

Make sure your cat has an interesting environment to prevent boredom — one of the main causes of improper behavior. Lots of toys and play time should keep your plants safe.

GROWING A CAT GARDEN

Because cats really do like to munch on plants, it would be nice to grow some nutritionally suitable plants that are just for the cat.

If you would like to do this, try sprouting some grass seedlings indoors in a pot so that your cat has a regular supply of fresh greenery to chew on. Grow them yourself from grass seed or buy already-sprouted grass at your local pet supply store. Place the cat garden far from your houseplants. You can't expect your cat to realize that it may chew the grass but not the begonia, when both are side by side, but it can learn that the plants in the kitchen are okay for chewing, while the plants in the living room are off limits.

When given an acceptable, tasty alternative, most cats will forget about the houseplants entirely.

Scratching furniture

SCRATCHING IS A NORMAL, *necessary behavior that enables your cat to shed the outer layers of its claws. It is also a way for cats to stretch out their muscles, much in the way that we stretch our arms when we wake up in the morning. Scratching is also a marking behavior to demarcate the boundaries of a cat's territory. Unneutered cats, both male and female, tend to scratch more because territory is more of an issue for them, and males tend to scratch more than females because they have larger territories and guard them more zealously.*

Scratching solutions

The best way to deal with this problem is to redirect it to an area where scratching is acceptable.

Buy several quality scratching posts that are at least 3 feet tall and at least 8 to 10 inches wide. Choose scratching posts covered with a rough surface, such as hemp rope or thick carpet. A kitty condo or cat tree will provide additional scratching surfaces. Cover the spot your cat likes to scratch, such as the sofa arm, with strips of double-sided tape or something that has a nontextured feel to it, such as a plastic tarp. Place the new scratching post right in front of that spot. Try to arrange things so your cat can't even reach the forbidden spot. Show the cat the new scratching posts, and scratch at them yourself so it can model the behavior.

■ **Scratching furnishings** *is not acceptable, but you must provide your cat with an alternative place to scratch.*

Once your cat is using the scratching posts instead of furniture, you can move them to places that are more convenient for you. But you still can't hide them away in the basement because scratching marks territory, and who wants territory in the basement? Not your cat! Placing the posts near favorite catnap spots can work well because cats like to stretch right after they wake up.

Caught in the act

If you do catch your cat scratching at the furniture after you've provided it with a scratching post, give it a squirt of water from a plant sprayer bottle while saying "No!" in a firm voice. When the cat uses the scratching posts, though, don't forget to praise it!

277

Too much meowing

SOME CATS HAVE BIG MOUTHS. *Whether it's a meow, squeak, chirp, scream, or howl, all cats are capable of a variety of vocalizations and need to make a little noise now and then. But cats that vocalize all the time can drive their owners crazy.*

What's there to say?

A frequent cause of excess vocalization in a cat is the desire to mate. Females in heat will howl nonstop to locate or attract a male. If your female cat is not neutered, expect her to wail whenever her heat comes (which, unlike dogs, can be all year long). The actual act of mating will cause your female to howl and scream in pain. An unforgettably haunting sound, the female's cries during coitus can sober even the most stoic of owners. I hope you're getting the idea here that spaying a female will definitely cut down on the caterwauling.

Excess vocalization in an otherwise quiet cat could be a sign that it is ill or in pain. Although most cats tend to internalize their discomfort, some will express it through constant meowing or howling, often combined with pacing. If your cat shows these signs, take it to the veterinarian for a checkup.

Some cats vocalize when they're stressed. Cats become attached to places, companions, and offspring. If any of these are taken away, the cat may meow or wail in lament.

> ### Trivia...
> *Some cat breeds are more vocal than others. Siamese, Burmese, and Tonkinese are all quite talkative (especially the Siamese), meowing and caterwauling often to get attention or to just comment on life in general. Abyssinians can also be quite vocal. This is normal behavior for these breeds. If you don't want a talkative cat, don't go near these four breeds.*

Some simple solutions

Here are some ideas you can try to cut down on excessive meowing:

1. See the veterinarian. He or she will check the pet for illness or injury so you can eliminate them as a cause.

2. Have your female cat neutered. You'll love the quiet!

3. If your cat is calling out because it has lost a loved one, try to distract it with play, toys, and treats. Introduce new distractions, such as a cardboard box stuffed with newspaper or a kitty condo. Do not rush out to get a new kitten, as this could increase the stress. Instead, simply be there for the cat.

Separation anxiety

THERE ARE SEVERAL REASONS WHY a cat might suffer from **separation anxiety**. A cat acquired before its eighth week has not received enough socialization and interaction with its mother and littermates to feel really comfortable on its own. When a 5- or 6-week-old kitten goes home with a new owner, it bonds closely to that person – so close, in fact, that the absence of that owner can create a lot of stress. Bottle-fed orphans are particularly susceptible to the problem because the owner becomes the surrogate mother.

> **DEFINITION**
>
> A cat with **separation anxiety** shows increased fearfulness and stress when its owners leave the home.

■ **A bottle-fed kitten** *will come to regard its owner as a surrogate mother and may become distressed when separated from its human mom.*

Dealing with separation anxiety

Once a cat has shown profound separation anxiety, it is hard to modify the behavior. Techniques worth trying include:

1. Have a friend or neighbor stop by once a day while you are gone to interact with the cat for at least a few minutes. Or pay a professional pet sitter to do this for you. This can help relieve much of the stress your cat feels.

2. Make your cat's environment as exciting as possible by leaving out numerous cat toys, putting a newspaper-filled cardboard box down on the floor (perhaps with some catnip under the shredded newspaper), hiding treats around the home, and leaving a radio or television on while you are gone.

3. Buy a pet videotape and play it for the cat while you are away. These videos, available at many pet supply stores, show cats, dogs, and other animals on the screen in a size that appears lifelike to your cat.

Avoid the problem

The best way to deal with feline separation anxiety is to avoid it from the beginning. First, if you know you are going to be gone 12 to 14 hours each day, be sure to avoid getting the breeds mentioned in the box below, particularly the Siamese. These cats insist on having regular companionship and are nearly dog-like in nature.

Another way to minimize the problem is to get two kittens instead of one right from the start. Regardless of the breed, the two littermates will amuse themselves all day and won't worry about you and your whereabouts. Just be sure not to take them home until they are at least 8 weeks old.

■ **The Siamese** *craves human company and will not tolerate being ignored. Avoid this breed if you are out of the house for long periods.*

SOMETIMES IT'S THE BREED

Certain cat breeds are more prone to separation anxiety. They include:

- Abyssinian
- Balinese
- Burmese
- Cornish Rex
- Devon Rex
- Havana Brown
- Siamese
- Sphynx
- Tonkinese

All these breeds are very sociable and don't do well left alone all day.

BROWN-AND-WHITE SPHYNX

Choose your cat wisely. Always pick the kitten who seems curious and confident yet not overbearing. Never choose the shrinking violet in the corner just because you feel sorry for it.

A simple summary

✔ Defining exactly what a feline behavior problem is depends on what your expectations of the cat and the relationship are. Therefore, "improper behavior" on the part of a cat will vary from owner to owner.

✔ Accept your cat's basic feline nature, and resolve to work with it rather than against it. Cats can't change the fact that they must scratch, require a clean litter box, and need something to keep them amused during the day. When you understand what your cat really needs, it will go a long way toward helping you cope with behavior problems.

✔ Successfully dealing with your cat's inappropriate behavior depends on you choosing the proper strategy. Effective strategies include providing alternatives, elimination of the cause, relieving boredom, desensitization, and negative reinforcement.

✔ If you understand why your cat is misbehaving, you should almost always be able to eliminate the problem, including the most common ones.

✔ Dealing with behavior issues requires patience, understanding, and creativity.

✔ A sudden change in behavior can signal a serious illness. If your good cat suddenly starts behaving badly, take it to the veterinarian right away.

Chapter 16

Saying Farewell

DESPITE THE BEST OF CARE, inevitably the time will come when your cat will no longer be able to live a comfortable, worthwhile life. In this chapter I'll deal with the heartbreak of having to say goodbye to your dear feline friend. Hopefully, I can give you the knowledge and the courage to make the best decision for your cat, when that time finally comes.

In this chapter...
- ✓ Tough decisions
- ✓ Euthanasia
- ✓ Burial options
- ✓ Your own grief
- ✓ Helping children deal with the loss
- ✓ Pets also grieve
- ✓ The right time for a new friend

SAYING GOODBYE TO A LOVED PET IS NEVER EASY

Tough decisions

PART OF THE RESPONSIBILITY

of owning a pet is that we must take responsibility for the quality of life of our furry friends. Sometimes a cat passes away peacefully in the night. More often than not, however, the end of a cat's suffering must come as a result of its owner's decision to have the pet put to sleep by a caring, competent veterinarian. Making the decision to end a terminally ill cat's pain and misery will probably be one of the hardest things you will ever have to do.

■ **Your vet** *can put your cat to sleep painlessly once its quality of life is poor.*

How will you know?

How can you possibly make such a decision? What can you base it on? First, you have to assess objectively the cat's state of health and its level of comfort. If it's a young cat suffering from a serious but curable illness, most owners would choose to do anything possible to save the animal. If that same illness struck a 15-year-old cat, though, the decision might be different.

If a cat is in terrible pain and has little chance of recovering, most owners would make the decision to have the cat put to sleep, whatever the pet's age. Likewise, if an elderly cat could no longer walk and had no control of its elimination habits, most owners would likewise decide to have the cat put to sleep.

I think the key factor in making the decision is in attempting to prevent needless suffering while still maintaining a sense of dignity for the cat. If the pain my pet is enduring cannot be ended or minimized, and if the indignity of suffering becomes all too apparent, I can, with regret, come to terms with the reality of the situation and make the decision to put an end to the pet's physical and emotional suffering.

It's still not easy

I don't write these words lightly. I have gone through this several times and can tell you it is not easy. People without pets sometimes make light of the grief and suffering pet owners face toward the end of a companion's life. The truth is that a pet is a part of the family and is loved and cherished. Losing a family member is grievous; having to make the choice to put one to sleep is doubly so.

I can't pretend to tell you exactly how to go about making the decision to put your cat's suffering to an end. All I can say is that it is a decision for you and you alone to make. By all means talk it over with your veterinarian so that you understand exactly what the medical options are. But don't let someone else convince you to do something your instincts tell you isn't right. If you don't make the choice, you won't be able to live with yourself for a very long time. You owe it to your cat to decide when the time is right on your own.

The only advice I can give you is this: Don't put off the inevitable just because you can't cope with the thought of it. That is, in my opinion, a selfish act. Try to think only of the cat's well-being and not your own. Your feline buddy gave you many years of love and companionship; respect this by making a selfless decision at the right time.

Euthanasia

IF AND WHEN YOU MAKE the decision to have your cat put to sleep, call your veterinarian and make an appointment. He or she will assess the situation and give you competent, candid advice. If you and the veterinarian are in agreement, the procedure can be scheduled. Called euthanasia, the veterinarian uses a combination of intravenously administered drugs to quietly and painlessly end the life of the suffering feline.

> **DEFINITION**
>
> **Euthanasia** *is the voluntary termination of a life. In the case of a cat, the animal is administered an overdose of an anesthetic to bring on a painless death.*

Prepare yourself

You can decide to have your cat euthanized during that visit or schedule it in a few days, if you feel you need some time to prepare. Consider waiting, just so you don't feel pressured to make a decision. Try to schedule a time when the veterinarian isn't going to be too busy or rushed, perhaps at the end of the day. Also, paying for the procedure in advance will prevent you from having to go through those tedious tasks on the actual day.

Some veterinarians will come to your home to perform the procedure. Local laws may not allow this, however; be sure to check with your veterinarian to make sure.

Perhaps the best advice I can give you regarding the actual procedure is to take someone with you. Afterward, you will be in no condition to drive or even cope with the situation. A trusted friend will be able to take care of the details, allow you to grieve, and give you a shoulder to cry on.

■ **Don't be alone** *when the time comes to have your pet put down.*

You can decide not to be present during the procedure if you think it would be too painful to endure. Many pet owners do just this. Others wouldn't let an army interfere with them being right there, and their beloved pet slips away in their arms. That decision is up to you.

What happens?

To euthanize your cat, the veterinarian must first gain access to a vein in the cat's leg. As this is not always easy with a cat, he or she will most likely sedate the cat first, injecting a mild sedative that will make the cat relaxed and sleepy.

When the veterinarian is ready, he or she will shave a small area of your cat's leg, then find a vein in which to insert the needle. Once done, an overdose of anesthetic is delivered into the vein. The drugs used act to relax muscles and stop nerve transmissions. This puts the cat into a deep sleep, after which its heartbeat and breathing cease.

Within moments, the pet's life is painlessly and peacefully ended. Although some cats will take a few additional breaths or perhaps shudder involuntarily, most often they quietly slip away.

Most veterinarians will allow you to spend some time alone with your cat at this point. After this, he or she will ask you what you want to do with the body.

I strongly advise against having young children present during this procedure, since it can be extremely traumatic. Also, if the vet comes to your home, be sure to remove all other pets from the home for the day. They will be acutely aware of their companion's death and could be severely stressed.

Burial options

SOME OWNERS TAKE THE CAT *home*
for a private burial, while others opt for cremation,
in which case the veterinarian makes arrangements
with a local pet crematorium to pick up the body.
Some owners have a pet mortician prepare the cat for
burial in a pet cemetery. The decision is up to you,
though local laws may have some say in what is done.

■ **You may choose** *to bury your*
cat in a pet cemetary.

You should make the decision about burial options before your cat is euthanized so you don't have to think about it on that day.

Home burial

A popular choice, interring your cat on your own property means that you can visit your pet's grave whenever you want. Local laws may prohibit this option, though. Check with your veterinarian, who should know the correct procedure. Also, this is not an option for those who rent or live in a city.

Pet cemeteries

There are many pet cemeteries across the country. You can find pet cemeteries in the Yellow Pages, through pet mortuary services, or through your veterinarian. Many owners prefer this option, as the cemetery offers a certain sense of respect and permanence. If this is your choice, be sure to investigate the cemetery beforehand, because the quality of management can vary quite a bit.

Prices vary, but expect a plot to cost at least $100, with additional regular maintenance charges. You can supply your own casket or buy one from a reputable retailer (see your local Yellow Pages). Prices can vary from $50 for a no-frills plastic shell, up to over $500 or more for a custom-made casket.

Cremation

An increasingly popular option, cremation enables you to keep your cat's ashes in an urn inside your home, bury them, or even scatter the ashes in a location that will be meaningful to you and your cat. Prices vary but should not exceed $200.

Trivia...

The pet-casket business has become a multimillion-dollar industry, with caskets for pets of many species now available, from a tiny gerbil or parakeet all the way up to a horse. Top-of-the-line pet caskets come with fully lined, color-coordinated interiors, lace trim, pillow, padded bottom, and an airtight steel shell available in many colors.

The biggest problem with cremation has been the doubt over whether or not you are truly getting your own pet's ashes.

Some cremation services have been caught doing mass cremations, then handing the ashes over to unsuspecting clients who are not aware that the ashes they hold are those of their pet, plus a dozen others. If the cremation service you contact will not allow you to be there for the start of the procedure, find one that will.

Your own grief

AS I'VE ALREADY SAID, be sure to have a close friend bring you home from the procedure and stay with you, if that is what you want. Some cat owners decide to be alone, and some really need the company. The last time I had to make that difficult decision, I chose to go away for a few days on a hiking trip, all by myself. You should do whatever helps you cope with the loss.

There is help

As the cat's owner, you bear the brunt of the grief over the death of your cat. For some, dealing with the loss can be an overwhelming ordeal filled with sadness, regret, and even guilt over not being able to do more. If you find yourself unable to come to terms with the loss, I heartily suggest talking to a grief therapist or a member of the clergy – as either will be able to help put things into context.

Speaking once or twice to a professional can often be enough to get you through the worst of it, so don't be too proud to seek help.

Time does heal

The weeks and months following the passing of your feline friend will not be easy ones. Eventually, though, after finding a place to put the sadness, you will begin to think of the happy, funny times you spent with your beloved cat. The grief will ebb, leaving only loving memories in its wake.

When a pet of mine passes, I always make a generous donation to a local animal shelter, in the hope that it might help save some lives. I make the donation in the name of my departed pet, out of respect and love.

GRIEF SUPPORT

If you feel the need to speak to someone specifically trained to help with grief over the loss of a pet, several veterinary colleges in the United States offer the telephone services of social workers. Some of the schools participating in these types of programs are:

University of California School of Veterinary Medicine:
(916) 752-7418

University of Florida College of Veterinary Medicine, Pet Loss Support Hotline:
(904) 392-4700, ext. 4080

University of Pennsylvania School of Veterinary Medicine:
(215) 898-4529

Washington State University College of Veterinary Medicine:
(509) 335-1297

INTERNET

www.iaopc.com/
petloss.htm

This page of the International Association of Pet Cemetaries' web site is dedicated to dealing with the loss of a pet.

Helping children deal with the loss

CHILDREN CAN BE HELPED *to understand that life eventually comes to an end. When the family cat dies, tell them the truth, be there for them, and acknowledge their sadness. This can actually be a good opportunity to help a child learn how to properly express his or her feelings.*

Be honest

When a pet dies, it may be more difficult for a child to deal with feelings of grief if he's not told the truth. Avoid using the term "put to sleep" when discussing euthanasia of a cat with a young child, because he could misinterpret this and develop a fear of bedtime.

Even suggesting to a child that "God has taken" the pet might create a problem, because the child might grow to resent the higher power for doing such a callous thing.

Understanding death

Children under the age of four really have no concept of what death means. A child of this age should simply be comforted and reassured that the pet's failure to return has nothing to do with the child.

Children from the age of 4 to 7 do have a rudimentary understanding of death, at least in the finality of not seeing the cat again. They are even capable of feeling some guilt for the cat's death, especially if the cat and the child didn't get along. If your child feels in any way responsible, reassure him or her that the cat's death had nothing to do with anyone in the family; that the cat had simply lived a good, long life and was ready to die.

Some children in this age group can also interpret death as an illness that can be caught, like a cold. If this happens, they could begin to fear that they might die soon. These children should be comforted and reassured that this is impossible. Short talks with children this age can help relieve them of their fears and allow them to release any emotions that might be bubbling just beneath the surface.

■ **Young children** *will miss their pet, but won't really understand what death truly means. They simply need comfort and reassurance.*

INTERNET

www.pet-net.net/
bookstore.htm

Log onto this site for a great list of books about pets. There are some specifically targeted at helping grieving pet owners and their children come to terms with their loss.

Seven- to 10-year-old children understand the finality of death. Some children in this age group, rather than fearing for their own mortality, begin to worry about the health and safety of their parents, siblings, or friends. After all, if the beloved family cat can die, why not a family member or some other beloved person? If these types of fears go unresolved, further problems can result, including antisocial behavior or problems at school. These children must be talked to and comforted, just as you would with younger children. If necessary, the parent of a grieving child of this age can attend one or more grief and loss seminars with the child. When the time comes to choose a new cat, be sure to involve the child in the process, as it will help empower him or her and give a sense of new hope.

Children over 10 years of age usually show the same reactions to a pet's death that adults do. They are more likely to mask their real feelings, however, in order to avoid the powerful emotions at play. If they're not allowed to express their grief, these children can suffer tremendously. Talk to these children, and, if necessary, read a book about pet loss together with them. As with the younger kids, involve these children in the process of choosing a new pet when the time comes and all are ready for the new commitment.

If your child becomes increasingly sullen and withdrawn after the death of the family cat, be sure to speak to your family pediatrician, who can put you in touch with a pediatric grief counselor.

Pets also grieve

WHEN THE FAMILY *structure is disrupted by the death of a cat, life changes for the surviving pets. In some cases, animals react much as humans do. They might cry, lose their appetite, oversleep, or become withdrawn and sullen. More than ever, these depressed pets need you to help them through this period of loss.*

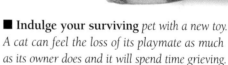

■ **Indulge your surviving** *pet with a new toy. A cat can feel the loss of its playmate as much as its owner does and it will spend time grieving.*

Behavior changes

Look for changes in the surviving pet's behavior right after the death of your cat. Loss of appetite, housetraining mistakes, disobedience, and even running away are all possible. Plus, the sudden change in the pet hierarchy can add to the pet's confusion.

If your surviving pet seems to be grieving, chances are that this behavior will lessen with time – the great healer. Try to help this process along by offering the cat extra attention, new toys, or even a nice treat once or twice a day.

Do not go right out and get a new cat, since it would be a stranger and a territorial invader in the surviving pet's eyes. Instead, renew your relationship with this pet, and let time take care of the rest.

The right time for a new friend

AS YOU BEGIN TO come to terms with the loss of your dear feline friend, you are probably thinking you don't ever want to go through those feelings again. I don't blame you; I've been there. How could another cat ever duplicate the joy and camaraderie that you shared with your departed cat?

Not a replacement

The answer is, it can't. No other cat could ever come close to replacing the deceased pet. To assume it could would be disrespectful, in my opinion. Instead, a new cat will relate to you in new, unique ways. It will have its own personality, mannerisms, and habits. In time, it will find profoundly different ways to endear itself to you.

■ **Your new cat** *should not be treated as a replacement for your departed feline; it will have its own personality.*

Wait a bit

My advice is to wait a while, to allow the grieving process to take its course among all family members. If you don't wait, you may take home a cat on impulse and end up with the wrong pet for you. You might be looking for a carbon copy of your deceased cat, and that just doesn't exist. The new cat would sense your disappointment and would not be comfortable or happy.

You will know when the time is right. When it is, take your time in selecting a new friend, and be sure to involve the whole family in the decision. Then, when you get the new cat home, allow it to be its own cat. Let it develop its own personality, and, for heaven's sake, don't name it after the departed cat! You will find that, rather than being a replacement, the new cat will instead be a new book in a series: Just as entertaining, but with a different main character and plenty of new adventures to entertain and amaze you.

■ **Involve the whole family** *when the time comes to choose your new kitten. In doing this, you can be sure that the new kitten or cat will be welcomed in the household by everyone.*

A simple summary

✓ Saying farewell to your feline friend will be one of the hardest decisions you'll ever have to make. To help you at this difficult time, be sure to have the support of friends and family on hand and the help of a compassionate veterinarian.

✓ The ultimate factor in helping you make the decision whether or not to euthanize your cat should be the pet's potential to recover, its level of suffering, and the retention of its dignity.

✓ Euthanasia, a painless procedure performed by your veterinarian, will end the cat's pain and suffering in the most humane manner possible.

✓ There are numerous burial options. Choose the one that makes the most sense for you.

✓ Be sure to pay attention to the children in your family after the death of the family cat. If they are not allowed to grieve properly, they can bury unresolved feelings of loss, which might affect them for years to come. Talk about the death with them, and, if necessary, bring them to a grief counselor.

✓ Don't forget that the surviving pet or pets in your home will also go through a period of grieving. Be there for them, and try to spend some extra quality time with them.

✓ Don't immediately go out and obtain a new cat in an attempt to replace the old one. Instead, wait until the grieving process runs its course for all members of the family, including children and the surviving pets. When the time seems right, don't try to replace the departed cat; look for a pet with its own unique personality.

PART FOUR

ACCOLADES FOR THE PERFECT CAT

THE WIDER WORLD OF CATS

MOST CAT OWNERS ARE CONTENT to simply interact with their pets at home, enjoying each day as it comes. But there's a lot more you can do with your cat. Do you want to *train* your cat to perform tricks? How about *showing off* Miss Kitty at the cat show?

Perhaps you're ready to commit yourself to improving, modifying, and protecting cats through carefully planned *breeding* programs.

Let's take an in-depth look at how you can get more *involved* with cats than you ever thought possible.

Chapter 17

Hollywood Calling!

MOST PEOPLE THINK cats are incapable of performing complex behaviors on command, the way dogs do. Guess what? They're wrong! Believe it or not, your little feline critter is totally capable of learning and performing a whole repertoire of complex behaviors and tricks on command. This chapter is dedicated to showing you how smart your cat really is. By training your cat, you'll be expanding its mind and strengthening the bond between you. Plus, you'll be showing up that stuck-up circus poodle down the street!

In this chapter...

✓ Can your cat learn tricks?

✓ Why teach tricks to your cat?

✓ How to teach your cat tricks

✓ What equipment do you need?

✓ Five tricks you can teach your cat

THE WELL-TRAINED CAT WILL PERFORM ON COMMAND

Can your cat learn tricks?

DON'T DOGS LEARN TO PERFORM *tricks much faster and more easily than cats? The short answer to that is yes, they do, because they are wired to learn complicated behaviors more efficiently than cats. The reason is fairly straightforward: Dogs are more motivated to please you than cats are. A dog will learn how to sit or shake paws fairly quickly, not just for a food reward, but out of respect and devotion to its pack leader, in this case its owner or trainer.*

■ **A dog will learn** *to perform tricks much more easily and willingly than a cat. This is due to the dog's desire to please its "pack" leader.*

Leader of the pack

Once a dog identifies its leader, it will do almost anything to please and obey him or her, because that's the way dogs are designed to be. The *hierarchy* of the dog pack requires all members to obey the leader.

So when you teach your dog to sit, it will do so not only for a reward of food, but for praise and affirmation from the leader (you). This desire to please another is the key to teaching a dog to do almost anything.

Not so with a cat. Cats did not evolve as part of a hierarchy, and they are not genetically predisposed to follow the leader. Cats have different motivations than do their more accommodating canine cousins. To be honest, they have little desire to please others and will basically only do something if they perceive there to be some personal benefit to the action. In other words, they are narcissistic little rascals! There won't be any kissing up for the cat!

> **DEFINITION**
>
> A **hierarchy** *is a power structure, or pecking order. At the top is the alpha, or leader, the most powerful, successful animal (usually but not always a male). Below him in descending order are animals with less and less power and authority. At the very bottom is the animal in the group with the least power and influence.*

This more independent, self-serving attitude of the cat is one of the reasons we like them so much. Dogs are great, but sometimes their submissive neediness can be emotionally draining. We choose to keep company with cats precisely because they do not define themselves and their happiness by our love and attention. They do not live for us; they live with us.

The best bribe

So does this narcissistic attitude render cats untrainable? Not at all! It simply requires trainers to take a different approach. In the absence of pack loyalty and the desire to please, the only remaining motivation left to the cat trainer is the world's oldest: Food.

Cats have a high predatory drive. This means they also have a strong desire to eat. Think about it: If you were a cougar who hadn't made a kill in a week, wouldn't you tear into a nice, juicy antelope if given the chance? The "eat when you can get it" attitude, an ancient one for cats in the wild, makes food a highly desirable thing in their minds. You never know when you will eat next, so pounce on it when you can!

■ **The predatory instincts** *of all felines are well developed. You can use this natural drive to bribe your cat into learning tricks.*

Domestic cats have that same instinctive desire to eat. In our society, however, it has been effectively reduced by cat owners who leave food down all the time for their cats. When food is always available, the desire for it decreases. If you had pies, cakes, sandwiches, roasts, and salads covering your table all day, your appetite would eventually decrease (although your waistline would most likely expand). If you were fed once or twice each day, however, you would look forward to feeding time with great anticipation. In fact, this tends to be the way most of us eat – at regular mealtimes. We're a little hungry when we sit down to eat, and it doesn't do us a bit of harm. This same anticipation can be created in your cat by feeding it measured amounts at regular mealtimes.

Once you have established a mealtime schedule, you can use food treats to teach your cat to perform tricks. In other words, you are bribing the cat.

Why teach tricks to your cat?

THERE ARE SEVERAL REASONS *why you should teach your cat to perform a few tricks. First, training your cat is a fine way to forge a strong bond between you both. Working together on a goal will build respect and trust. Second, regular training gives the cat something to look forward to and helps relieve the boredom associated with being home all day waiting for you to come home. Neither cats nor humans deal well with prolonged boredom; it makes us both cuckoo.*

Cats learn things anyway

I know there are some readers out there who firmly believe that teaching a cat to perform tricks is just plain wrong. They feel it is an affront to the independent feline nature. My answer to them is, first, you will never, ever get a cat to do anything it does not want to do, no matter how hard you try.

■ **Strengthen your bond** *with your cat by teaching it some tricks. Your cat will look forward to your training sessions.*

Second, the plain fact is that all animals, cats included, learn to perform many new behaviors that are not necessarily instinctive but are instead unique to their normal environments. For instance, when water levels in a river go up dramatically over a 2-year period, local beavers quickly learn to build higher, stronger dams. They do this even if the river levels have never been that high before, because they have the power to adapt to their environment. Your cat is much smarter than a beaver and can easily learn new behaviors if it is in its interest to do so.

You train your cat all the time without even realizing it. Your cat learns to come to you whenever you open up the cat food, right? It also learns to avoid the neighbor's 2-year-old tail-puller very quickly, doesn't it? Both are good examples of the conditioned response. Why not add to your cat's repertoire of behaviors, to expand its intellect and relieve its boredom?

INTERNET

www.petmarket.com

Log on to this site, click on the "Cat Catalog" link, then click on "Videos." You will find a great instructional video on how to teach lots of tricks to your brainy cat.

How to teach your cat tricks

AS I'VE ALREADY MENTIONED, *cats are masters of self-interest. If performing a behavior gets them what they want, they will do it. That means your cat can easily learn how to sit on command in exchange for a yummy treat. It's all in the food and in your cat being hungry enough at the time to perform for it.*

It's not a treat if your cat doesn't love it

Besides switching your cat to a regular feeding schedule (if you haven't already done so), you will need to do a little experimenting to find out just what your feline friend likes in the way of treats. Some cats love little bits of cheese, while others prefer a dab of meat-flavored baby food on the end of a spoon. Still others will do back flips for a bit of tuna or a piece of boneless chicken. Some just want a bit of cat food. You can even buy small containers of cat treats at the pet store, although most of these do contain preservatives and other questionable ingredients. If you can, stick to healthy, do-it-yourself treats. Try a bit of this and a bit of that until you discover what works best.

■ **Tuna can be used** *in trick-training. Whenever your feline performs well, be sure to reward it with small bits of its favorite treat.*

I suggest doing this treat test when your cat is fairly hungry, say a half-hour before its regular dinner time, because this is when you will also be doing most of your trick training with your cat.

Using treats will be an essential part of teaching tricks to your cat. This means that quite a few treats will be fed to your feline friend. To make sure your cat doesn't become a portly puss, use very small treats. A bit of cheese or tuna the size of a pencil eraser is big enough!

Doing what comes naturally

You should also watch your cat's normal mannerisms and behavior patterns closely for a while to pick up on what movements and actions come naturally. For instance, some cats (such as the Siamese) are more vocal than others. If yours is, it should be relatively easy to teach the cat to speak on command because it already performs the behavior on its own. You simply need to reinforce it with treats and add a cue word, so you can elicit the behavior on command. Of course, if your cat tends to be too vocal, you won't want to encourage this!

Some cats learn better than others

Certain factors will affect how well your cat learns tricks. These include:

1 **The personality of your cat** If your feline is outgoing and confident, odds are it will learn quickly and happily. But if it tends to be on the shy, reserved side, you might have some trouble getting it to perform. Shorthaired cats tend to be a bit more active and sociable than longhaired cats; because of this they often learn faster. Also, males are slightly more outgoing and confident than females (with exceptions, of course), and therefore, learn a bit faster.

2 **The age of your cat** Generally, the younger the cat is, the more likely it will be able to learn new behaviors. An 8-month-old will be much more open to performing for a treat than an 8-year-old will. This does, of course, have limits; an 8-week-old kitten probably won't yet have the mental or physical capabilities needed to perform most tricks. Don't give up on the older cat, though. Training will just take a bit longer.

■ **The Siamese** *is an extremely vocal breed, and will learn to vocalize on command more easily than most other domestic cats.*

3 **The environment** You must teach your cat in a very quiet place, with no distractions. No other people or pets should be present. Televisions, radios, washers, dryers, and dishwashers should all be turned off. Also, choose the room in your home farthest away from street traffic. Selecting the most quiet part of the day might also help. The reason for all this is simply that cats have great senses and will become distracted by the least little thing. Even the aroma of food cooking can be enough to turn off a cat's thinking cap. Only after your cat has mastered a trick can you begin to slowly introduce some distractions.

4 **How often and how long you work with the cat** If you have training sessions regularly (say twice each day, 4 to 5 days a week), the cat will learn rapidly. If, however, you only work on teaching it tricks every now and then (say twice a week), chances are your cat won't learn much. You need to be regular and consistent because cats have a short attention spans and need to be reminded often. Also, be sure that each session lasts no more than a few minutes to prevent boredom – always the killer of any kind of learning.

Patience is a virtue

Be patient and upbeat throughout the training sessions. Realize that your cat will only participate if it is having a good time. Forcing the issue, adopting a stern attitude, or yelling at the cat will only work against you. Remember that teaching tricks to a cat is a novel activity and one that most cats are not used to. Give your kitty time to get used to the idea.

Never force your cat to do anything it doesn't want to do!

The importance of handling

Your cat must tolerate and even enjoy being handled if it is to learn tricks. During the training sessions you will be doing a lot of handling, and a cat who dislikes being handled won't be a good learner. I recommend that, from early on, you begin desensitizing your cat to your touch by grooming, massaging, and stroking it regularly. Doing so will ensure a calm, happy cat when training time comes around. Be sure to reward your cat every now and then with a small, tasty treat during these handling sessions to let it know that its patience and good behavior is appreciated.

BASIC RULES FOR TRAINING YOUR CAT

Cats do not learn as easily or readily as dogs and must be motivated and rewarded at every opportunity. Follow the simple guidelines below in your training sessions:

- Never hit your cat or get angry at it.
- Teach your cat right before feeding time, when it is hungry.
- Work on only one trick at a time, and don't move on to another trick until the previous one has been mastered.
- Always teach your cat in a quiet area.
- Always reward your cat with a treat after performing a trick properly.
- Precede each command with the cat's name.
- Never force your cat to do anything it seems hesitant or scared to do.
- Never overwork your cat. Sessions should only last a few minutes.
- Remember to use the release word "Okay!" to end a training session.

- Change the type of treats you are using often to prevent your cat from getting bored.
- The same person should teach the cat a trick. Only after the trick has been perfected should anyone else command the cat to perform it.
- Always end a session on a positive note. If your cat performs the trick well, or even makes a good attempt at it, praise, reward, and stop. Overworking a cat is an easy way to sabotage any work you have done.
- Once your cat learns a trick, begin working in different areas of the home so it associates the treat with the action rather than the location.
- Don't forget to have fun!

What equipment do you need?

TREATS ARE NOT THE ONLY THING you need to train a cat. You'll have to do a little shopping, as well.

A clicker

The clicker is a little metal or plastic sound-making device found in most novelty or toy stores. The clicker is a vital training device used by all professional animal trainers.

The "click" sound made by the clicker acts as a bridge between the desired behavior and the food reward.

Trainers working with dolphins use a whistle in the same way, blowing it at the exact moment the dolphin has correctly performed a trick. The whistle is then quickly followed with a fish. The clicker is used with cats and dogs because it is a very sharp, identifiable sound that doesn't occur naturally in the animals' lives.

INTERNET

www.annesanimal actors.com

Check out this site to learn about one of Hollywood's best-known animal trainers.

You click the clicker immediately after a behavior has been correctly performed and before the treat is given. Your cat will eventually understand that the click means "Yes, you did it! Way to go!" The sound will also heighten the cat's expectations for the treat that follows. The sound of the click eventually becomes nearly as important as the treat itself, because it creates a mood of excited expectation.

Toys

Any toys your cat really loves can be used as a motivational tool, and you'll need a toy when your teach your cat to fetch. A small, crocheted ball works well, as does a furry little mouse toy, because both can be easily grabbed in the cat's mouth. A rubber or plastic ball might not work as well because the cat won't be able to grab hold of it as easily.

Never let your cat or kitten play with a toy small enough to be swallowed! And don't use a toy with buttons that can be easily pulled off and swallowed. Your cat could choke to death on these.

A teaser toy such as a feather on the end of a string can also be useful, especially when teaching your cat to spin.

A table

You'll notice I've suggested starting many of these tricks by putting your cat on a table. Do not use the dining room table, or any other table where your cat is not normally allowed, for trick training. It's not fair to expect the cat to understand that it's not allowed on the table except during training. That distinction is just too subtle for a cat.

Use a table or desk your cat is allowed on anyway, or bring out a special training table for the occasion. Put a table cloth or towel on the table to help your cat get its footing.

■ **A small furry mouse toy** *is ideal for teaching your feline to fetch, since it can be easily grabbed in the cat's mouth.*

Treats

Almost any type of edible treat can be used to entice your cat to perform. It all depends on your pet's preferences. I have found that a dollop of meat-flavored baby food on the end of a spoon works well. The spoon can be used to manipulate the treat, luring your cat into certain positions, and is also necessary when using gooey or runny treats. Bite-sized pieces of chicken, tuna, or cheese work well, too.

Just use what your cat seems to like, and remember, it isn't a treat if your cat doesn't love it. Don't give too large a treat, because the cat might just carry it off into a corner and ignore the training session – and you. Also, avoid using your cat's regular mealtime food; it won't be special enough.

■ **Chicken pieces** *will be appreciated by most cats. Use them as rewards in training.*

Five tricks you can teach your cat

THE FOLLOWING FIVE TRICKS *can be taught to your cat or kitten without much difficulty, provided you have patience and follow the guidelines I have set out for you in the previous sections. So, without further ado, let's get this show on the road!*

Sit

The "sit" command is a building-block behavior for many other commands taught to cats in show business. When you begin teaching this trick to your cat, you will actually be teaching it how to learn. The most crucial and exciting moment will be when your feline friend sits on command for the first time.

1 First, choose a quiet location and a time when no one else is around. Make sure your cat or kitten is hungry by working on the trick a little bit before feeding time. Place your cat or kitten on a table, away from the edge, making sure the table top has decent traction (a table cloth will help). The pet should be in a standing position at the beginning; if the cat won't stand, simply stroke its rump once or twice. Most cats will instinctively raise their rumps when you do this.

2 Now, with your clicker in your left hand, hold a delicious treat about an inch or two in front of your pet's nose with your right hand. Let it get a good whiff, but don't let it eat it yet. The cat's focus should be on the treat and nothing else.

3 As soon as your cat shows a definite interest in the treat, slowly move the treat upward and slightly back, from in front of its nose to a point right between its ears. As you do this, say, "Fluffy, sit." Make sure the treat is never more than an inch or two from the cat at any time. (If it gets too far away, the cat will most likely stand up on its hind legs in an attempt to get at it.) As the cat follows the path of the treat, it will naturally sit. If the cat is hungry, you should be able to get it to sit within 5 to ten attempts. If not, stop, and try again in approximately five minutes. During this session, you will be learning the fine art of treat manipulation; how you present the treat and how you move it will have a direct effect on your cat's performance.

4 The moment your cat does sit, click your clicker once, say "Good sit," then give your cat the treat. If you choose to use a spoonful of food, let the cat have just a lick or two each time it actually sits. Once you have successfully gotten your cat to sit two or three times, end the session by saying "Okay!" This tells the pet that work time is over.

5 Give your cat lots of praise, then feed it dinner. Be sure not to work the trick again until right before another meal. You shouldn't work the trick more than twice each day.

6 As you practice this trick, raising your right hand up above the cat's head becomes the hand signal for "sit." Each trick should have a spoken command as well as a hand gesture.

■ **As soon as the cat sits,** *praise it and give it a treat. With a little patience, your cat will soon sit on command.*

Spin

This trick should be a fairly easy one for your cat to master. The behavior you are after is simple; you want your cat to spin around in a tight circle, as if it were chasing it own tail.

1 Start the trick with your cat standing in front of you on the floor. You can be on your knees or standing.

2 Let your cat see that you have a delicious treat in your right hand. Again, dinner time should be close at hand to ensure the cat is hungry. Hold the treat close to its nose, then very slowly guide the cat around in a tight circle while saying "Fluffy, spin." Be sure to keep the treat close to its nose. If your cat does follow the treat, click the clicker once and give it the food. Even if it follows slowly or only for a half turn, still click and reward to let it know it's doing the right thing.

3 Continue to work the trick for a few minutes in an attempt to get the cat to spin all the way around. If you can only get a half-turn, however, that's okay. Stop after a few minutes, then try again 5 minutes later. Eventually you will succeed.

4 Continue working this trick each day, slowly increasing the speed of the spinning and your distance from the cat. The circular hand motion you have been using to lure the cat

Trivia...

Among other tasks, cats can be taught to beg, eat with their paws, heel, jump through a hoop, play a piano, play dead, roll over, open a door, hide food in boxes, wave, and speak.

around will eventually become the hand signal for spin. As you begin to get farther away from the cat, continue to use the circular hand motion, but decrease the size of the circle you make. The ultimate goal is to get your cat to spin around without you having to lead it with the treat. You should ultimately be able to give the hand signal or verbal command from several feet away and have the cat spin in a circle. Click and treat when it does!

5 Take it slowly, and realize that the cat has to learn that making the desired response (a circle) gets it the treat. After perfecting the spin in one direction, consider teaching your cat to spin in the other direction, using your left hand to signal for that.

Down

Teaching this command will require a bit more patience on your part. I would suggest that you teach your cat the first two tricks before trying the "down." This will get your feline used to learning tricks.

From a cat's perspective, lying down in front of you is a vulnerable position to be in. You must, therefore, be absolutely sure that nothing scary or threatening will happen to it while in this position.

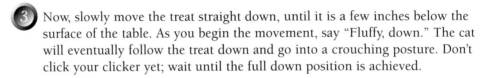

1 Place your cat in a sitting position on a table. This time, have the cat close to the edge so that when it's lying down its nose will be off the table.

2 Hold a treat an inch or two from the cat's nose. Again, make sure the cat is hungry.

3 Now, slowly move the treat straight down, until it is a few inches below the surface of the table. As you begin the movement, say "Fluffy, down." The cat will eventually follow the treat down and go into a crouching posture. Don't click your clicker yet; wait until the full down position is achieved.

4 When the cat crouching low, help it into a full down position by gently pressing down on its shoulders. As soon as the cat extends its front paws straight out, click the clicker and give the cat its reward.

5 It is very important that you do not try to force the issue here; please feel free to take a full week or even more to master this behavior. If your cat isn't too fond of being handled, you may have to settle for the crouching position instead of the full down position.

You may need to keep your hand on the cat's back at first to maintain the "down" position. Make the cat think you are petting it rather than forcing it to stay down.

 When done, always say "Okay!" This releases the cat from the session.

Shake

Though not a hard trick to teach your cat, you should know that most animals, both wild and domestic, do not normally like having their feet manipulated or held for very long. An animal's feet are its means of escape from danger, and restrained cats can get very nervous.

For this reason, when teaching the "shake" command, be sure not to overhandle your cat's feet or restrain them in any way. If the cat wants to pull away, let it. Some cats won't tolerate this trick, while others will let you handle them to your heart's content. Be sure you know your cat will tolerate having its feet touched before trying to teach it this trick.

 Start with your cat in a sitting position near the edge of a table or on the floor with you sitting in front of it.

 Ask your cat, "Fluffy, shake," while simultaneously reaching out with your right hand and gently lifting its paw. The moment you shake the paw, click your clicker once, let go of the paw, and immediately reward the cat. You can also say "Good shake" when giving the treat.

 Be positive because the cat might be confused and concerned at first. Work this stage of the trick three or four times a day for about a week before moving on. After a week of this, your cat should be understanding that when you lift its paw, this action always seems to be followed by food.

 When your cat understands the first part of the trick, reach out with your hand as if to grab the cat's paw, but this time don't actually grab it. Say "Fluffy, shake," then move your right hand up close to the cat's foot. Hopefully, your cat will anticipate what is about to happen and lift its foot all on its own. If it does, take the offered paw, click the clicker once, then reward the cat with a treat. Even if the cat moves its paw only slightly the first time, you should still click and reward. If the cat still will not offer its paw, try gently tapping on the back side of the cat's lower leg while saying "Fluffy, shake." This should help encourage the cat to lift the leg. When it does, take the offered paw, click, and reward. Reaching out your hand toward the desired paw eventually becomes the hand signal for the trick.

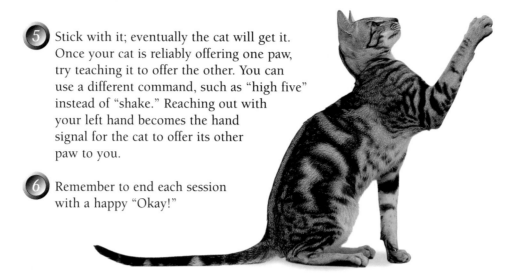

5 Stick with it; eventually the cat will get it. Once your cat is reliably offering one paw, try teaching it to offer the other. You can use a different command, such as "high five" instead of "shake." Reaching out with your left hand becomes the hand signal for the cat to offer its other paw to you.

6 Remember to end each session with a happy "Okay!"

■ **Teach your cat** *to offer a paw on command. Remember not to restrain its paw for too long though, as it will make your cat nervous, and always reward your cat with a treat when it has performed well.*

Kiss

If you shudder at the idea of having meat-flavored baby food smeared on your face, this trick might not be for you. Otherwise, it's a fun trick to teach your cat. Plus, your cat's rough tongue imparts a truly unique feeling on the skin – one that most people find fascinating.

For this trick, you will need to use a treat that has a thick consistency. A piece of tuna or cheese won't work because it won't stick to your hand or face. Meat-flavored baby food or cream cheese will work well, as will chicken spread.

> ### Trivia...
> *The cat's tongue is covered with tiny, barbed structures called papillae, which are designed to help scrape meat off of a bone and pull dead hairs out of the coat during grooming.*

1 Make sure your cat is plenty hungry before trying this trick! Place the cat on a table in a sitting position. Have a helper sit directly in front of the cat, about a foot or two away. He or she should have the gooey treat already dabbed onto his or her face or hand. You should have the clicker and an additional treat with you.

2 Allow the cat to smell and see the gooey treat on your valiant helper's face or hand. You can do this by having the helper lean forward slightly or by moving his or her hand close to the cat's nose. Then have him or her sit upright again. Many cats will have to be held back from licking your helper's face or hand at this point. If necessary, do so.

3 Now release the cat, while at the same time having your helper lean forward a bit or placing his or her hand close to the cat. Say "Fluffy, kiss." Most cats will go right over and lick the treat off of your helper. If this happens, click once and offer the cat a different type of treat, perhaps a bit of chicken or tuna. Repeat this twice a day for several days before moving on.

4 After your cat has mastered this skill, begin to decrease the amount of gooey treat smeared on your helper, while at the same time increasing the distance between them both. Eventually (after a week or so), you should be able to reduce the gooey treat to nothing and the distance to 6 feet or more. Always reward the cat after performing the trick, even when it has mastered it.

5 Begin asking the cat to kiss you. When it does, reward it. Also have friends and family members ask for a kiss, making sure they have a treat on hand. Once the cat has learned the trick well, there is no further need for the clicker, although you'll always need the treat reward.

A simple summary

✔ Cats can learn to perform a wide variety of tricks, just as dogs, but they do learn differently though.

✔ Training your cat will stave off boredom and strengthen the bond between you.

✔ Unlike dogs, cats will not perform a behavior out of loyalty or devotion. Instead, they will only learn and perform a new behavior in exchange for a bribe, almost always in the form of a tasty treat.

✔ Always train in a quiet room with no distractions.

✔ Patience and practice are the main keys to successful feline training.

✔ Never force your cat to do anything that it does not want to do.

✔ Use a clicker to help your cat associate rewards with the correct behavior.

Chapter 18

Cat Breeding: A Serious Business!

MOST OF YOU READING THIS BOOK have probably wondered what it would be like to have the experience of seeing a litter of kittens born. Seeing the miracle of birth is something one never forgets. Corny, but true. The purpose of this chapter is not only to educate you about the fine art of breeding cats, but, quite frankly, to attempt to dissuade you, if possible, from doing so. Sorry, but it's true: Whenever possible, I like to steer amateur cat aficionados away from breeding, because it's a very difficult, time-consuming, and highly responsible avocation to be involved in. Even I don't breed cats – and I write books about them!

In this chapter...

✓ A breeder's life

✓ Why you probably shouldn't breed cats

✓ It gets expensive

✓ Just one litter?

A breeder's life

WHO CAN RESIST KITTENS? Is there anything cuter or more fun to watch than a basket of the little meow machines cavorting, investigating, and vying with one another for attention? Personally, I can't think of many things more enjoyable than interacting with a litter of playful kittens, and neither can most animal lovers I know.

Making the conscious choice to breed cats, however, be they pedigreed or mixed-breed, should be a very weighty decision. Whether you intend to let your unneutered female cat have only one litter, or go full speed ahead and initiate an entire breeding program, replete with breeding stock and a state-of-the-art breeding facility, the responsibilities, expenses, and consequences you will incur will be staggering, especially if you have had little previous experience.

■ **A litter of kittens** *is undeniably delightful. However, breeding from your cat is not a decision that should be taken lightly.*

Passion, not profit

Meet a cat breeder and you will most likely find a person who is a dedicated feline fan, and, more specifically, a loyal supporter and champion of a particular cat breed. He or she will have probably been breeding and showing that breed for many years. No die-hard baseball or football fan could ever show more dedication. When it comes to that breeder's cat breed, nothing could be more intriguing, rewarding, or important.

Breeding cats properly and responsibly is not easy. In addition to having a great deal of knowledge about the science and mechanics of breeding, a breeder must have an unquenchable supply of idealism toward the craft (and it is a craft), the breed, and the species. He or she must have great foresight regarding what will be good for the breed in the long term, rather than what will best generate short-term profits. Indeed, no dedicated cat breeder ever turns much of a profit at all (more on that later).

Don't even think about breeding cats if you have no working knowledge of the basic principles of genetics, feline reproduction, or the genetic history of the breed you have chosen to become involved with.

The cats' house

Additionally, a cat breeder must surrender his or her home to the process. A cattery must be constructed, and that can cost thousands of dollars. The home itself often becomes co-opted by the cats, particularly young kittens that are learning house manners before going to their new homes. The breeder's family doesn't escape the process, either. They must be there to help out with new litters and cantankerous mated pairs or with clean-up detail. Sleep? I suppose they get some every now and then.

■ **If you intend** *to breed cats, you will need to construct a sturdy cattery suitable for the purpose. A well-designed and maintained cattery can cost thousands of dollars.*

Why on earth would anyone want to surrender their lives to a bunch of whiskered fur balls? Good question. I love to write about them, train them, and help owners with their cat-related problems, but I would never have the patience or dedication to relinquish my home and time to the art of breeding. I suppose the answer is that cat breeders are passionate about their cats and about the process. They take it seriously, because they hold the future of the breeds in their hands.

Whatever course the individual cat breeds take depends primarily on the selective-breeding programs initiated by responsible breeders.

That's big responsibility; too big for me. Too big for you? Think very carefully about it.

■ **Bundles of fun** *they may be, but kittens are very time-consuming and require a lot of patience.*

Why you probably shouldn't breed cats

I NOW WANT TO GET INTO THE sordid details of running a cat-breeding program, to give you an idea of what to expect if you ever decide to give it a go. Hopefully, I can leave you with such fear and apprehension that the idea will just leap from your head like a cat on a hot tin roof (thank you, Tennessee Williams).

All work and no play

Running a cattery isn't the glamorous job it's made out to be. First, the facility itself must be maintained. Enclosures must be cleaned and disinfected several times a day; litter must be scooped and/or replaced; floor drains cleaned of cat hair; plumbing, heating, and cooling systems maintained; and fencing and cages inspected.

Then you have to care for all those cats. Depending on the size of a breeding operation, anywhere from two or three cats up to a dozen or more might be present at any given time. These all have to be fed and watered, cleaned up after, and examined regularly for any signs of illness or injury. They also need to be groomed regularly; if the breed is of the longhaired variety, that means at least once a day for each cat. And they have to be cuddled and played with and loved – every single one of them.

Playing matchmaker

Next, you must be responsible for planning, directing, and monitoring the actual breeding procedures that take place on the premises. You might be bringing in a **tom** or **queen** from another breeder, making you responsible for that cat's safety. You must monitor the mating act itself – often a prolonged screaming, biting, and scratching match between a male and a female, with little love lost between them.

Playing midwife

Let us not forget the birthing process, which must be carefully monitored to ensure the survival of the kittens

DEFINITION

A **tom** is an unneutered male cat whose job it is to impregnate the female. A **queen** is an unneutered female whose job it is to give birth to the kittens. The centerpiece of any good breeding program, almost all breeders must own at least one worthy queen. Conversely, tom cats are often contracted out from other cat owners and brought to the cattery to service the queen.

and the health and well-being of the mother. When you are breeding cats, the health of the mother and all of the unborn kittens must become your priority and your responsibility. Sleep? Not likely, once birthing time approaches. You have to be there, no matter what the hour, to assist the mother in case anything goes wrong. At the very least, you need to talk softly to the mother during the arduous procedure, which can take many hours from the first kitten to the last.

■ **The queen** *may need assistance with kittening so you need to be on hand throughout the birthing process.*

A difficult birth may find you speeding to the emergency veterinary clinic in the middle of the night. Newborn Persian kittens have unusually broad heads, which can sometimes become lodged in the mother's birth canal. This requires the immediate assistance of a veterinarian to save the kitten and mother.

Playing mother

Then, a breeder must, of course, be responsible for the development and health of the newborn kittens.

Your veterinarian will have to check the health of all the newborn kittens and their mother – a process that will probably cost you hundreds of dollars.

If, perish the thought, the mother dies during labor, you would have to bottle-feed all of the kittens yourself. This means feeding them about every 2 hours, day and night, stimulating them to eliminate, and keeping them warm and safe.

317

If all goes well, a breeder must then find reputable, capable owners to purchase (or adopt, in the case of most mixed-breed kittens) the little ones, at about 12 weeks of age. This is not always easy; you cannot simply sell your kittens to the highest bidder. A responsible breeder cares for his or her breed and all the individual cats mightily and will insist that all prospective owners be able to properly care for the kittens in the right manner. That means having the right type of home, the proper means, a respectful attitude toward pets, and a decent amount of experience and knowledge about cats and about the breed in question. Not everyone who looks at the kittens walks out with one, even if they have the money.

Emotional stress

Plenty of emotional stress comes with being a breeder. First, some of your cats will inevitably become ill and die. And as a breeder, you'll have several cats, so this pain will be multiplied. The death of one favorite cat can be very hard for anyone; can you imagine the emotional effects of having several cats die within a span of a few years? This can happen, especially when kittens are stillborn or born with an incurable congenital disorder. Queens sometimes die giving birth; and since a queen is usually with the breeder longer than the other cats, her death can be devastating.

In addition to the emotional stress of having a cat die, there is the difficulty in letting the kittens go time after time. Breeders become very attached to their litters and don't enjoy seeing them leave, even when they're going with qualified buyers. Beginner breeders have a particularly hard time with this – letting that first healthy litter go, one at a time, can be a heartbreaking experience.

■ **When the kittens are old enough** *to leave their mother you will be faced with the heartbreak of saying good-bye to your little family. Even knowing they will have a good home doesn't help much.*

Red tape

Then there is the boring, tedious side to breeding. Lots of paperwork is involved. Pedigreed kittens must be registered with the appropriate cat registry. Contracts must be drawn up for each sale. The typical contract includes:

1. A formal bill of sale.

2. A date of birth and physical description of the kitten being sold.

3. The price.

4. The registration number of the kitten provided by the appropriate cat registry.

5. The date of purchase.

6. A health guarantee, promising the buyer that the kitten is physically sound and free from congenital defects. A veterinary certificate is included in this guarantee, stating that the kitten has been examined by a licensed veterinarian, who found it to be in perfect health.

■ **Before selling a kitten,** *you must make sure that it is in good physical health and free from any congenital defects.*

7. Registration papers, allowing the buyer to register ownership of the kitten.

8. A pedigree, or the genealogy of the kitten, showing its line of ancestors and their show titles, if any.

In the contract, most breeders specify certain conditions that the buyer must fulfill in order to keep the kitten. These can include:

- A neutering clause
- A promise not to allow the kitten to roam outdoors
- A promise not to resell the kitten
- Breeding rights or requirements, if any
- A clause forbidding declawing

In addition to all this, the breeder must supply the buyer with a record of vaccinations and worming, advice on diet and health care, and any other pertinent information about the breed.

As always, whenever contracts are involved, a lawyer must be on call to provide his or her services, if needed. This can cost the breeder a good deal, especially if any litigation arises over the sale of a kitten.

It gets expensive

HAD ENOUGH YET? Let me quickly go over what expenses you would accrue as a cat breeder. One at a time, shall we?

Acquiring breeding stock

I already touched upon this a bit earlier. To start out, you must have at least one queen. The queen is the center of the breeder's avocation; without a top-notch female representative of the breed, nothing else matters. She must be of championship stock and in perfect health. Her temperament must be as pleasant and patient as possible, with no aversion to handling. Finding a suitable queen could be a lengthy task, and one that could cost you hundreds of dollars.

If you choose to acquire a tom cat (the big, bad macho male) to breed with your queen, you won't be able to have him in your home, since an unneutered male is nearly impossible to live with. He will spray urine all over in an attempt to claim territory and attract females. He will also fight quite ferociously with any other tom he sees, especially if a female in heat is close by. Though usually not as expensive as a quality queen, a championship-caliber tom cat will cost you a pretty penny.

Facilities

A proper breeding program requires a well-constructed cattery. You just can't operate a breeding program out of a room in your home. Either a converted garage or basement or a separate building must be constructed. It must be well insulated and built so that nearly every surface can be easily cleaned and disinfected. The floors of the cattery need to be smooth and nonporous, with

■ **A well-run breeding** *establishment requires the construction of a cattery with an outdoor area. The cattery should be well insulated and easy to keep clean.*

> ## Trivia...
> *Most small catteries make do without a tom. Instead, they pay for the services of a male cat (called a stud fee) owned by another party. The tom cat visits the cattery where the queen resides and is allowed to do his thing, so to speak. Queens can also be artificially inseminated with sperm purchased from the owner of a quality tom.*

at least one built-in drain to facilitate easy cleanup. Heating and air conditioning are essential to maintain the proper temperature for the cats, which will eventually include little ones.

Within the cattery itself you will need metal cages enclosed on all sides, including the top. The number of cages will, of course, depend on the size of your operation. In addition to cages for the resident cats, at least one cage must be provided for visiting cats (such as a tom on loan).

Connected to the indoor area should be an outdoor run, for exercise, catnapping, and socializing. This, too, must be properly enclosed and constructed of materials that are easy to clean. Separate from the cat housing area should be a work area, used by the breeder to wash and groom cats and to store supplies. In total, a cattery can cost thousands to build.

Plans for a cattery must meet any state and local building code specifications that apply in your area. You will also be required to obtain a construction permit before beginning work.

Food, supplies, and utilities

A breeder with several queens, a tom, and an ever-changing number of kittens will have to feed them, groom them, and see to whatever minor health needs can be done at home. These supplies can cost a breeder hundreds per year. In addition, hundreds in heating and cooling bills will be spent to keep the cattery at a tolerable temperature.

Medical expenses

A breeder can rack up impressive veterinary bills each year, especially if problems occur with pregnancies or births. All those cats must also be properly examined and vaccinated, costing even more. Most breeders keep a local veterinarian quite busy.

Travel expenses

Most breeders also show their prize cats – a necessity for a breeder who is serious about their breed. Doing well in a cat show helps build the breeder's reputation and helps the breeder learn about what other breeders are doing. Breeders often travel to cat shows around the country. If it's too far to drive, each show costs the breeder air fare for at least one person, plus transportation charges for the cat or cats, and for all of the necessary equipment. Also, accommodation must be paid for. Though driving to a cat show costs less, it still costs a breeder a good deal in fuel, hotels, and time.

Advertising

Most breeders advertise their catteries in local and national periodicals and magazines. Pick up a copy of any cat magazine and thumb through it to see the dozens of advertisements. These can cost breeders hundreds of dollars each year.

INTERNET

www.Y2spay.org

If I still haven't convinced you not to breed your cat, may be this site will.

Employees

If a cattery is small, a breeder can make do without hiring help. But medium and large operations usually require at least one or two part-time or full-time employees to help maintain the facility. Even paying the minimum wage allowed by law, this can add up to tens of thousands each year.

What profits?

Breeding cats is an expensive calling. But, you say, that's okay; you can just breed quality kittens and sell them for high prices, recouping your financial investment. No! If you were to sit down and calculate what it costs to produce just one quality kitten, figuring in all costs, you would find that even a prized kitten from a rare breed, capable of selling for over a thousand dollars, might barely cover your costs with just a bit left over.

■ **Although top-quality** *pedigreed kittens may sell for a great deal, breeding a championship-winning litter is in itself a costly affair, with no guarantee of success. You may even find that you lose money.*

The bottom line is that cat breeding is not a very profitable venture, despite what many novices think.

The only breeders who make any money at all are the infamous "kitten mill" owners, who produce low-quality kittens in abhorrent conditions and sell the poor creatures to pet shops across the nation. Through keeping costs low and dealing in great volume they turn a profit. They also breed terrible cats with physiques that do not meet the breed standards and have edgy, unpredictable temperaments. These cats pollute their respective breeds' gene pools and give the art and science of breeding a bad name.

The bottom line is that you won't become a millionaire as a cat breeder and probably won't even break even. Profit, therefore, never becomes a motivation for starting a cat breeding program.

Just one litter?

SOME CAT OWNERS WILL SAY,

"But I just want to let my female have one litter of kittens, just to let my children experience the miracle of birth. What's wrong with that?"

■ **They may be beautiful**, *but finding homes for a litter of kittens can be difficult.*

The sad fact is that too many cat owners decide to do just this. Afterward, when the mystery and wonder have worn off, the four or five kittens must find homes. Unfortunately, because too many owners allow their female cats to have kittens, there are far too many to go around. Most of them end up at shelters, where many thousands of healthy, lovely cats are put down each week simply because they do not have homes.

Your desire to allow your kids to experience the miracle of birth turns into the useless slaughter of more cats and kittens than you could count in a lifetime. That, in my opinion, is not worth it, especially if you hold cats dear.

A simple summary

✔ For reputable breeders, breeding is a passion that consumes their lives and their homes.

✔ Breeders must have a serious knowledge of biology and genetics, cat midwifery, and more before they even start breeding cats.

✔ The emotional and financial toll of breeding cats be very high.

✔ Anyone who gets rich breeding cats is not doing it responsibly and well.

✔ A breeder is responsible for the life of every kitten he or she breeds.

✔ Millions of healthy, homeless cats are put down every year. Do you really want to add to the problem?

Chapter 19

Showing Off at Cat Shows

CATS HAVE BEEN DISPLAYED in public forums since the 16th century, and the first modern cat show took place in London in 1871 at Crystal Palace. Basically a contest of beauty, health, and temperament, the best representatives of catdom can be seen at cat shows. Cat shows also serve as venues for breeders and buyers to see and possibly acquire a cat or kitten descended from one of the champions on display. This chapter will give you the basics of showing cats and will help you decide whether or not you want to give it a go with your tame little tiger. From eligibility and basic show procedures to dealing with judges and health issues, it's all covered here.

In this chapter...
✓ Cat shows defined
✓ Should you show your cat?
✓ Entering a cat show
✓ Before the show
✓ Center stage!

A PEDIGREED CAT IS JUDGED AGAINST THE BREED STANDARD

Cat shows defined

A CAT SHOW IS BASICALLY an event at which cats are judged against the breed standard for each breed (with the exception of cats in the Household Pet category), to see how close to the ideal they can come.

Today, cat clubs and associations the world over sponsor cat shows. They are a great way for the public to see the best examples of feline beauty and comportment and for breeders and those in the cat business to meet with their contemporaries.

Cat shows also are a great place for prospective buyers to meet with qualified cat breeders; in fact, cat shows are one big way that breeders get to advertise their prize cats. What better way to attract attention to your kittens than to win a "Best in Show" at a top cat show?

■ **The cat show** *is an ideal place to see the finest examples of a particular pedigree, including some not commonly seen. It is also a good venue for meeting qualified breeders, perhaps with a view to buying.*

All or some

Individual cat shows are categorized as either all-breed or specialty. In an all-breed show, all cats, regardless of coat length, compete for various honors. In a specialty show, only cats of similar coat length compete for awards.

Pedigreed or not

The big deal at cat shows is the pedigreed cats. But cats without a pedigree – humble alley cats – can also compete as Household Pets. These cats are judged on their overall healthy appearance, their coat patterns and colors, and their alert, lively dispositions.

The judging

The exact order of judging, and which awards are given out, varies a bit according to which registry's rules are being followed at the cat show.

■ **Nonpedigreed cats** *can be entered into the Household Pet competition. They are judged for their overall health, personality, and general disposition.*

In general, cats at a show compete against other cats of the same breed, sex, and color. Those cats are then judged for best of breed.

After the judges have picked the best cat of each breed, it is time for finals. The judges then present the top cats in each class. From these top cats, "Best Cat in Show" is awarded to one of the lucky felines.

■ **Cats of the same breed,** *such as these Bengals, compete against each other in their breed class. The winners of each individual class then compete against each other for the title of "Best Cat in Show."*

CLASSES DEFINED

Competition at Cat Fanciers' Association (CFA) shows is held in these classes:

- Kitten competition is for unneutered or neutered pedigreed kittens between the ages of 4 and 8 months.

KITTEN

- Championship competition is for unneutered pedigreed cats over the age of 8 months that have not been altered.

- Premiership competition is for neutered or spayed pedigreed cats over the age of 8 months.

SPAYED PEDIGREED CAT

- Provisional competition is for breeds that have not yet achieved Championship status. Cats in this class compete up to the awarding of Best of Breed, but are not eligible for finals until the breed has advanced to Championship status.

- Miscellaneous competition is for breeds that are not yet accepted for Provisional status, but are accepted for registration and showing in the Miscellaneous class. This class receives no actual awards.

- Household Pet competition is for all mixed-breed, or nonpedigreed cats. Entries must have all normal physical properties, and cannot be declawed. Kittens must be older than four months. Entries older than eight months must be neutered.

HOUSEHOLD PET

Should you show your cat?

IF YOU THINK YOU MIGHT *like to enter your little star in a cat show, you should ask yourself whether or not you think your cat will enjoy the experience as much as you might. A show cat needs good temperament and shouldn't be too timid or at all aggressive toward new people and situations. Often you won't actually know this until you've entered the cat.*

■ **Nervous cats** *do not make good show cats. When you are deciding whether or not to enter a show, take into account the personality of your cat.*

The show test

To test the cat, take it to a friend's home and have your friend examine the cat while it stands on a table in front of them. The friend should be a stranger to the cat, because this is what will happen when your cat is at a show. If your cat is aggressive, fearful, or simply stressed out by the experience, chances are it won't fare well in a show. If that's the case, don't worry about it. Show business isn't all it's cracked up to be anyway.

If the cat loves the attention, however, you might have a star on your hands. In that case, read on.

Most owners who show their cats train them to be hams from early kittenhood. You can do this with your kitten. Teach your cat to accept the type of handling it will receive at a cat show by regularly giving it rewards for tolerating handling.

■ **A show cat** *must accept handling from strangers, so get your pet used to other people touching it from kittenhood.*

Entering a cat show

MOST CAT SHOWS *are 2-day affairs, normally on Saturday and Sunday. Occasionally, however, clubs sponsor 1-day shows. A few of the largest shows may even be 3 days.*

For all cat shows, you must enter your pet in advance.

■ **The larger cat shows** *last 2 days or more and are scheduled months in advance. You must enter your cat prior to the show.*

Finding the shows

Upcoming cat shows are listed in many places. The magazines *Cats* and *Cat Fancy* both list show announcements from several associations at least a month or two in advance, so that's a good place to start looking. Each cat association has a newsletter, which will list show calendars many months ahead of schedule. The associations all have web sites as well; you should be able to learn about any local or national shows by logging on. Details of cat associations can be found in the Useful Addresses appendix. Alternatively, get in contact with your local cat club. Someone there will be able to help you.

If you're planning to exhibit your cat on a regular basis, belonging to a cat club can be a very valuable resource. The major cat associations can provide you with a list of local cat clubs that might be right for you and your cat. Joining one could be the best way to learn quickly about entering and competing your cat.

INTERNET

www.fanciers.com/clubs.html

You'll find cat-show information and show calendars on this site.

■ **If you have a kitten or cat** *that you would like to show, first consider joining a cat club to learn the ropes.*

CAT CLUBS

At last count, there were well over 650 cat clubs in the United States alone and hundreds more in Europe and the rest of the world. Usually organized around one specific breed of cat, each club maintains an affiliation with a major cat registry.

Why join?

Most cat lovers who intend to exhibit should join a cat club first to learn the ropes. Doing so really helps educate novice **cat fanciers** so they won't feel so overwhelmed upon going to their first cat shows. The veteran club members will make you feel right at home and make the often confusing world of cat shows seem much more accessible. They will also share with you priceless knowledge gained from years of experience.

By joining a breed club, you may learn things about your favorite cat breed that will amaze you, including the history of it development – which is often quite colorful and convoluted. The inside scoop on local and national cat shows will become available to you through the other members, as will information on the judges you might have to face (look out for the grumpy one over there). The people in the club will have similar interests as well. You and your cat could make some great friends.

■ **Joining a cat club** *will give you an opportunity to learn more about the ancestry and distinguishing features of your favorite breed, such as this white Maine Coon.*

Where can you find one?

You should be able to find a local breed club by contacting a major cat association and asking for some referrals. Check online, too; doing a search for "cat clubs" will provide you with a wealth of information. You can also talk to your veterinarian or to any local breeders you may know.

How to enter

A show announcement from the sponsoring club or association should list the name of the club, the show location, the names of the judges, the association whose rules the show will be held under, and the name of the *entry clerk*. Call him or her and ask for an entry form.

Make sure you know the closing date for entry to the show because most shows will not accept entries 1–2 weeks before a show begins, and popular shows often close much earlier than that. Try to enter as early as possible.

If you are entering your cat in the Household Pet category (or HHP), make sure you know if the show is accepting entry forms for HHPs. Some clubs and associations do not have HHP entries available at all shows.

DEFINITION

The entry clerk is the person to contact to enter a show. He or she will send you an entry form and answer any questions you might have about the event.

The entry form

Your entry form will ask you to list information about you and your cat. Some categories may apply, others may not. For example, some associations have no registration number for HHPs, while others do. Be sure to ask the entry clerk what is correct for your situation.

Information asked for on the entry form usually includes:

1. **Color and class** Your cat's color and breed should be listed on its registration certificate. Registries have specific names for the various colors and patterns, and you must use the right terms. If you aren't sure about this, consider mailing in a photo of your cat with the entry form. Also, specify whether your cat is a longhair or shorthair.

2. **Color class number** Some registration forms ask you to put down a number for the cat's color class. This is for pedigreed entries only. These numbers are listed in the show rules. If you don't have a copy of the show rules, obtain one from (you guessed it) the entry clerk.

■ **The color** *of your cat should be included on the entry form. This is a Blue-and-White Scottish Fold.*

③ **Owner information** Here you simply put down all pertinent information about yourself, such as your address and phone number. If you are showing someone else's cat, you would be designated as an agent of the owner. An agent is not listed as an owner of the cat. Agents need to fill out special sections of the form.

④ **Region** This is the area where you reside, not the region where the cat will be shown.

⑤ **Classes and titles** Here you need to mark whether your cat is in Kitten, Championship, Premiership, or HHP class. Beneath this is often an area where you list what titles, if any, your cat has won.

Registration for a single cat will generally run from $35 to $50 for most 2-day shows.

A WORD ABOUT HOUSEHOLD PET COMPETITIONS

I think it's great that mixed-breed cats can compete in cat shows.

Judging in the HHP classes is different than in the purebred classes, however. Since there are no breed standards to work with, judges score these cats on their temperament, health, and appearance.

Owners of HHPs are almost always more at ease than those showing pedigreed cats, as the results will not affect a breeder's future earnings or reputation. It's just all fun for most owners out there in the HHP ring.

In CFA HHP rings, favored cats are awarded Merit ribbons. These competitions are fairly unpredictable and often a cat with a unique look or personality will capture the judge's attentions.

HOUSEHOLD PET

Confirming your entry

After you have bravely entered the show, you will receive a confirmation letter listing your information, such as your cat's name, breed, color class, title, breeder's name, and owner's name. Be sure that everything is correct. If something is not, call the good old entry clerk.

You should also receive directions to the show, as well as information about what accommodations may be close by.

My suggestion is to make reservations early, since the hotels will quickly fill up with other contestants.

Before the show

BEFORE YOU *even go near the show, make sure your cat is in top health. It should be up-to-date on all of its vaccinations and should be tested for feline leukemia, a highly infectious killer of cats. Your cat should also be free of all external parasites.*

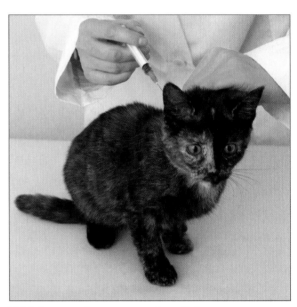

■ **Make sure that your cat** *has all the necessary vaccinations before entering it in a cat show.*

Vaccinations

Make sure you tell your veterinarian that you intend entering your cat in shows because this must be taken into consideration when you're both deciding what vaccinations your cat needs. You will need to take up to date vaccination certificates with you to the show.

Many shows now require you to have proof of a rabies vaccination in order to compete.

A good bath

A few days before the show, it's a good idea to bathe your cat. Be sure to give your cat's coat at least a day or two before the show for the oils in its skin to return a nice sheen to the coat.

Be sure to clean your cat's ears and eyes before the show, because nothing is as embarrassing as when a judge makes a disdainful face over goopy ears or runny eyes. Trim the nails, too; the judge will appreciate that.

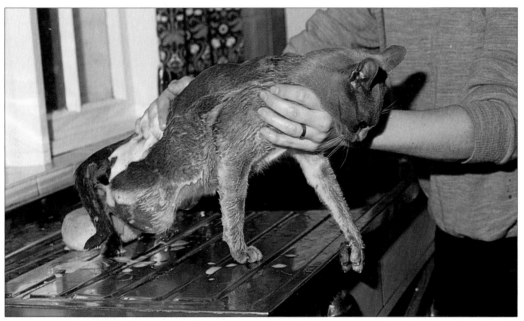

■ **Bathe your cat** *before taking it to a show to ensure that its coat is clean and shiny. Maintaining a show cat requires a great deal of time and commitment from its owner.*

What to pack

You can't just show up with your cat and a smile on your face. What supplies must you bring with you? Here is a list of items I think are essential for a private owner (one who is not a breeder) to bring to a cat show. The following is the bare minimum:

- Your confirmation letter from the entry clerk.
- A current rabies certificate and proof of a negative feline leukemia (FeLV) test.
- An exhibition cage measuring at least 20 inches square (if one is not provided by the show; make sure that you ask the entry clerk about this beforehand).
- Attractive curtains for your cat's cage, to lend a bit of privacy to your cat and to keep it from becoming stressed by all of the activity. Make them from an old bed sheet, or buy them from a cage retailer.

- A grooming table. Many different designs are available from quality pet supply stores.
- Cat food and food dishes.
- Water, especially if the show is far from your home, because your cat could become nauseous from the foreign-tasting water where the show is being held.
- Grooming supplies, including brush and comb, scissors, cotton swabs and baby oil, shampoo and conditioner, and nail clippers.
- Portable litter box and litter. Leave the home litter box where it is and use a large rubber pan instead, such as a piece of Tupperware. Be sure to include a scooper and plastic bags.
- Paper towels.
- Cage floor covering. A section of indoor-outdoor carpeting works well.
- A disinfectant cleaner that is nontoxic to cats.
- A small, snuggly cat bed that will easily fit inside the cage.
- A few of your cat's favorite toys.
- Treats for your cat.
- A feline first-aid kit.
- Last, but not least, the star, in a well-constructed cat carrier.

Trivia...

By far the most widely shown cat the world over is the Persian. This has been true ever since the late 19th century, when it eclipsed the Angora as the most popular breed.

■ **A sturdy cat carrier** *is a must for transporting your prize feline to and from cat shows. Line it with a cosy, soft blanket for your cat's comfort. Fresh water should also be available at all times.*

Center stage!

THE TIME HAS FINALLY COME. You and your little star are on your way to the show. When you get there, you will need to check in properly. First, go to the entry clerk and tell him or her who you are. You will be given a copy of the show catalog and an indication of where you should put your cage. You must place your entry number on the cage.

Listen up

After you are all set up and your cat is looking as good as possible, you will have little to do until your number is called to a ring. Make sure you're aware of the schedule and check progress frequently. When your class or number is called, get your cat out of its cage and bring it to the ring.

Be sure to read through the show catalog. It lists all of the cats competing in the show, including yours, as well as the schedule of judging.

While you wait

Some exhibitors work powder into the coats of their cats while preparing for the show. Using a corn starch-based powder can add fullness to a longhaired cat's coat or give a nice sheen to a shorthaired coat. The powder soaks up excess oils in the hair that might give the coat a sloppy look. If you're using powder, be sure to brush all traces of it out of the coat before entering the ring.

Your turn

When you're called, go to the appropriate ring and place your cat in its designated judging cage, which will have the cat's number on top.

Now comes the actual judging. Your little darling is on its own, because you must wait outside the ring. Your cat will be examined by the judge to see how close it comes to the standard. Just relax, and don't talk. It will all be over quickly. Just cross your fingers and don't get huffy if your cat doesn't do well.

When the judge is finished, go to the cage, gather any ribbons awarded, remove your cat, and leave promptly.

It's an all-day thing

Most shows have a rule preventing you from leaving the show hall until a specific time. In a 2-day show, you may leave your cage and supplies at the hall overnight. Just be sure to take anything of value (including your cat) back to the hotel with you.

Never leave your cat in its cage unattended at the show.

Get another exhibitor nearby to watch the cat while you go to the bathroom, get something to eat, or watch the other cats in the ring.

SHOW-RING ETIQUETTE

Here is a list of do's and don'ts relating to cat-show judges and how to interact with them. Knowing the proper protocol can be every helpful, so read carefully!

- Don't speak to the judge at any time during the judging, unless he or she specifically asks you a question.
- Don't speak to the judge while you are placing or retrieving your cat from a ring.
- If you see a judge outside of the ring before the judging, don't speak to him or her.
- Do treat the judge with respect.
- Do ask the judge for his or her opinion of your cat after the judging is finished. Although some will not give it to you, most will offer their opinion if you ask politely.

These rather strict rules regarding fraternizing with the judge exist to maintain impartiality; if a judge were seen chatting with one particular contestant, cries of favoritism and foul play would be rampant. Remember, it's not easy being a judge!

■ **The judge will examine** *your cat from head to foot. He or she will judge your pet against the breed standard.*

Keep strangers away

Every so often, a visitor does something that could harm a cat, accidentally or intentionally. Don't let that happen to your cat.

Never allow a visitor at the show to handle your cat, even if he or she seems to know about cats.

A simple summary

✓ A cat show is a contest in which different classes of cats (both pedigreed and pets) compete against an ideal standard of excellence. The cats that come closest to this standard win.

✓ Enter a cat show if you have the desire and the patience to compete and if your cat has an easygoing, tolerant temperament and a good physical presence.

✓ Find an upcoming cat show by checking cat association newsletters, cat magazines, the Web, and any local cat club information.

✓ To enter, find out which cat club is sponsoring the show, then request an entry form. After filling it out, send the form back to the entry clerk, the person in charge of administering the show.

✓ Before the show, be sure to have your veterinarian give your cat a clean bill of health, to prevent other cats at the show from becoming infected with a serious illness. Also, a day or two before the show, give your cat a bath, clean its ears, and trim its nails.

✓ Be sure to bring the proper supplies to the show so you're prepared for any situation that might come up. Check in with the entry clerk, set up in your assigned location, groom your cat, then bring your cat up to be judged when called.

✓ Belonging to a cat club can be a great way to learn about cat shows before you actually attend one.

More resources

Cat Organizations and Associations

Alley Cat Allies
1801 Belmont Rd., NW, Suite 201
Washington, DC 20009
(202) 667-3630
www.alleycat.com

American Cat Fancier's Association
PO Box 203
Pt. Lookout, MO 65726
(417) 334-5430
www.afcacat.com

American Society for the Prevention of
Cruelty to Animals
441 E. 92nd St.
New York, NY 10128
(212) 876-7700
www.aspca.org

Canadian Cat Association
289 Rutherford Rd. South
Unit 18
Brampton, Ontario
Canada L6W3R9
(905) 459-1481
www.cca-afc.com

Cat Fancier's Association
PO Box 1005
Manasquan, NJ 08738-1005
(732) 528-9797
www.cfainc.org

Cat Fancier's Federation
PO Box 661
Gratis, OH 45330
(937) 787-9009
www.cffinc.org

Feral Cat Coalition
9528 Miramar Rd.
PMB 160
San Diego, CA 92126
(619) 497 1599
www.feralcat.com

The Governing Body of the Cat Fancy
4–6 Penel Orlieu
Bridgewater
Somerset
TA6 3P6, United Kingdom
+44 (0) 1278 427 575
http://ourworld.compuserve.com/homepages/
GCCF-CATS

Humane Society of the United States
2100 L St. NW
Washington, DC 20037
(202) 452-1100
www.hsus.org

The International Cat Association
PO Box 2684
Harlingen, TX 78551
(956) 428-8046
www.tica.org

National Pet Alliance
PO Box 53385
San Jose, CA 95153
(408) 363 0700
www.fanciers.com/npa

Traditional Cat Association
18509 NE. 279th St.
Battleground, WA 98604
www.traditionalcats.com

Magazines

Cats
260 Madison Ave., 8th floor
New York, NY 10016
(917) 256-2305
www.catsmag.com

Cat Fancy
PO Box 6050
Mission Viejo, CA 92690
(949) 855-8822
www.catfancy.com

Cats and Kittens
7-L Dundas Circle
Greensboro, NC 27407
(336) 292-4047
www.catsandkittens.com

Books

Housecat: How to Keep Your Indoor Cat Sane and Sound
by Christine Church, IDG/Howell Book House, 1998

No, Kitty!
by Steve Duno, St. Martin's Press, 2000

Plump Pups and Fat Cats,
by Steve Duno, St. Martin's Press, 2000

The Cat's Mind
by Bruce Fogle, DVM, IDG/Howell Book House, 1995

The Encyclopedia of the Cat
by Bruce Fogle, DVM, Dorling Kindersley Publishing, 1997

The Eyewitness Handbook of Cats
by Bruce Fogle, DVM, Dorling Kindersley Publishing, 1992

Think Like a Cat
by Pam Johnson-Bennett, Penguin, 2000

The Holistic Animal Handbook
by Kate Solisti-Mattelon and Patrice Mattelon, Beyond Words Publishing, 2000

Cat Care, Naturally
by Celeste Yarnall, Charles E. Tuttle Co., 1995

Helpful web sites

THE INTERNET OFFERS YOU *a wealth of sites where you might discover all manner of information on our friend the cat, from medical or behavioral concerns, to facts on breeds, showing, or pet supplies. To make it all a bit less intimidating, I have included a list of web sites that you should find informative and entertaining. Beware, however, that due to the fast-changing nature of the Internet, some of these sites may be out of date by the time you read this. Happy surfing!*

www.acfacat.com

The American Cat Fanciers Association has information about all the breeds it recognizes.

www.annesanimalactors.com

Click here to learn about one of Hollywood's best-known animal trainers.

www.avma.org/vafstf/default.asp

This page has the latest news from the Vaccine-Associated Feline Sarcoma Task Force, a joint effort of the American Association of Feline Practitioners, the American Animal Hospital Association, the American Veterinary Medical Association, and the Veterinary Cancer Society to investigate vaccine-associated cancers. You'll find a frank discussion of the risks and benefits of vaccinating your cat.

www.awionline.org

Log on here for information on zoo-enrichment programs and how animal welfare groups are trying to make zoo life as pleasant as possible for the captive animals.

www.breedlist.com

You can learn about the personality profiles of the different cat breeds by logging onto this site.

www.catfamily.com

Log on to this site, then click on the "Cat Tips" button for great advice ranging from feeding to safety tips.

www.cattv.com/Videos forCats.htm

Check out this web site for videos featuring cavorting squirrels, chirping birds, and squeaking mice – all designed to capture the attention of your TV-watching feline.

www.cfainc.org

The Cat Fanciers' Association has information about all the breeds it recognizes, as well as cat health and behavior articles.

www.cffinc.org

The Cat Fanciers' Federation maintains this site about pedigreed cats.

www.fanciers.com

Check out this site for all sorts of great cat information, including breed descriptions, cat care advice, articles on veterinary developments, and useful lists of breeders for every cat breed – in North America and the rest of the world.

www.healthypet.com

Check out this site for all sorts of useful information on your cat's health, including tips on feline exercise.

www.holisticat.com/rawdiet.html

For more information on how to put together a properly balanced and healthy raw food diet for your cat, as well as some sample recipes, check out this site from Holisticat.

www.iapoc.com/petloss.htm

This page of the International Association of Pet Cemetaries' web site is dedicated to dealing with the loss of a pet.

www.ivillage.com/pets/features/petpourri/articles/0,4437,17000,00.html

Typing in this long address will bring you to an excellent article about how to choose a veterinarian who can become your partner in caring for your cat.

www.learnfree-pets.com/pet-rescue/

This is a great site to learn more about feline first aid.

www.lookd.com/cats/anatomy.html

Here you'll find great information on the anatomy of the domestic cat.

www.lovethatcat.com

At this site you can find books and videos on dealing with undesirable cat behaviors, as well as lots of other useful cat products, including toys, beds, and even kitty mobiles.

www.peteducation.com

Here is a great site for informative articles on cat care, veterinary articles, and pet news.

www.petmarket.com

Log onto this site, click on the "Cat Catalog" link, then click on "Videos." You will find a great instructional video on how to teach lots of tricks to your brainy cat.

www.pet-net.net/bookstore.htm

Log onto this site for a great list of books about pets. There are some specifically targeted at helping grieving pet owners and their children.

www.tica.org

The International Cat Association has information about all the breeds it recognizes.

www.21cats.org

This is a great site for information on just about everything to do with cats, including what kind of supplies and toys are best and why your kitty needs them.

users.netropolis.net/kazikat/FelineHD1.htm

The Feline Hip Dysplasia Awareness web site is the best place to go to learn more about this disorder. The site offers up-to-date information and positive support.

www.vetmed.wsu.edu/clientED/

Try this site for information on pet anatomy and veterinary terminology.

www.vetcentric.com

Log on here for answers to nearly any medical question you might have about your cat.

www.wicatclub.com

For a great assortment of articles on feline behavior and training, check out this site from Cats International.

www.Y2spay.org

If I still haven't convinced you not to breed your cat, maybe this site will.

A simple glossary

Abscess A pus-filled enclosure in the skin of the cat, the result of an infection left untreated.

Allergen A substance that provokes an allergic reaction.

Benign A growth that ceases to grow at some point, such as a cyst.

Breed standard A written description of the ideal cat of a particular breed. It covers the breed's physical proportions, coat, color, and behavior. Strictly speaking, show cats are not judged one against the other, but are judged against this standard. The cat that comes closest to embodying the standard for its breed is the winner.

Castrate Surgically removing the testes from a male cat, thus preventing an animal from reproducing.

Cat fancier A feline enthusiast, usually someone involved in showing cats.

Cattery The facility used by a cat breeder to house his or her cats.

Championship class Cat show competition for unneutered pedigreed cats over the age of 8 months.

Cilia Microscopic hairs that line the cat's inner ear chambers and help the cat determine its exact position in space.

Conditioned response A behavior an animal has been systematically conditioned to make in response to a certain stimulus.

Congenital defect An anatomical malformation that occurs while a kitten is developing within the womb or within a few weeks of birth.

Dialysis The process of removing waste materials from the blood by means of some filtering technique or mechanism.

Domestication Taming and selectively breeding wild animals for the purpose of accommodating humanity in some fashion, whether for food, service, or companionship.

Entry clerk The person to contact to enter a cat show. He or she will send you an entry form and answer any questions you might have about the event.

Euthanasia A procedure performed by a veterinarian in which an animal is painlessly killed by means of a lethal injection.

Free-feeding Keeping food in your cat's dish all the time. Though convenient, this form of feeding tends to lower a cat's food drive and is not the most healthy way to feed a cat.

Hairball A solid mass of cat hair that can form in a cat's stomach or intestines over time as a result of the pet's daily grooming.

Harness A device made of sturdy nylon cord that can be used to walk a cat on a leash. Part of it fits around the cat's midsection, while another part goes around the pet's neck. The two sections are connected atop the cat's back by a third piece, on which is attached a metal ring. A leash can be connected to this. The harness spreads the tension of the leash out so that the pet doesn't feel controlled as much or pulled around by the neck.

Hierarchy A power structure, or pecking order. At the top is the alpha, or leader, the most powerful, successful animal (usually, but not always, a male). Below him in descending order are animals with less and less power and authority. At the very bottom is the animal in the group with the least power and influence.

Household Pet class Cat show competition for all mixed-breed, or nonpedigreed cats. Entries must have all normal physical properties and cannot be declawed. Kittens must be older than 4 months. Entries older than 8 months must be neutered.

Induced ovulator Any animal, including the cat, that releases an egg in response to the act of copulation.

Insulin A hormone normally produced within the pancreas that is necessary for the metabolism of glucose, the body's fuel.

Kitten class Cat show competition for unneutered or neutered pedigreed kittens between the ages of 4 and 8 months.

Litter The absorbent material inside a litter box that soaks up the urine and hides the feces.

Litter box A rectangular plastic container filled with an absorbent granular material. It provides your cat with a place to relieve itself properly.

Malignant When a growth grows uncontrollably, without stopping. This is a true cancer.

Metastasize When part of a cancerous tumor breaks off and travels to other areas of the body, where it can take root and cause more uncontrolled growths.

Miscellaneous class Cat show competition for breeds that are not yet accepted for Provisional status, but are accepted for registration and showing in the Miscellaneous class. This class receives no actual awards.

Mixed-breed cat Any domestic feline whose lineage includes a mixture of breeds or other mixed-breeds.

Neuter To remove the primary reproductive organs, preventing an animal from reproducing. See also *spay* and *castrate*.

Obligate carnivore An animal that is obliged to eat meat. Cats must get their vitamin A, arginine, niacin, vitamin D, and taurine directly from animal sources. They cannot live without these nutrients in their diet.

Old age How old is an old cat? The Academy of Feline Medicine recommends beginning a senior preventive health care program by 7 to 11 years of age. At 12, almost all cats start experiencing the effects of aging.

Osteoarthritis A degenerative condition that causes cartilage at the end of joints to wear away, causing pain, swelling, and sometimes unwanted bone growth.

Papillae Hook-shaped protuberances covering the cat's tongue used by wild cats to strip meat off a bone. They also help the domestic cat groom itself.

Pedigree A written record provided to a buyer by the breeder that documents a cat or kitten's family history, showing what level of competition each of its ancestors attained.

Pedigreed cat A domestic cat whose lineage (or pedigree) includes only purebred ancestors and whose breed is accepted for competition by one of the several cat associations.

Pinna The external part of the cat's ear – the triangle that sticks up. The two pinnas can rotate independently of one another.

Plaque A hard, organic material that slowly forms on teeth when they are not properly cleaned. Food particles, bacteria, and saliva combine to form plaque, which can cause tooth decay and gum disease.

Premiership Cat show competition for neutered or spayed pedigreed cats over the age of 8 months.

Provisional class Cat show competition for breeds that have not yet achieved Championship status. Cats in this class compete up to the awarding of Best of Breed but are not eligible for finals until the breed has advanced to Championship status.

Pulse The number of times your cat's heart beats per minute.

Queen An unneutered female cat whose job it is to give birth to the kittens.

Quick The vein that runs through each nail on the cat. If you cut the quick when you're trimming the cat's nails, you'll hurt the cat and the nail will bleed.

Respiration The lungs' regular intake of oxygen and exhalation of carbon dioxide

Retrovirus Instead of injecting DNA into a host cell in order to take over its reproductive abilities, the way a standard virus does, a retrovirus uses RNA instead. Basically, RNA is a simpler form of DNA. The AIDS virus (HIV) is a retrovirus, as are several other viruses that target the immune system.

Rheumatoid arthritis Rare in cats, this disorder of the immune system attacks healthy joints and tissues, resulting in pain, swelling, and deformity.

Scooper A long-handled device that looks like a slotted plastic shovel and is designed to scoop out clumps of litter that have absorbed cat waste.

Semicircular canals Fluid-filled chambers inside the cat's ears that help it precisely determine its motion.

Separation anxiety When a cat shows increased fearfulness and stress when its owners leave the home.

Spay Surgically removing the ovaries and uterus from a female cat, preventing an animal from reproducing.

Stone A small, hard object that can form in the cat's bladder, urethra, or kidney. Consisting of minerals such as calcium or magnesium plus mucus, these stones can vary in size from the microscopic to the size of a dime, or even larger.

Tapetum A mirror-like apparatus located behind the retina, its job is to reflect back onto the retina as much available light as possible, including light that wasn't absorbed by the retina the first time around. Although the cat cannot see in total darkness, the tapetum enables cats to see in light levels that are so low they would seem to us to be completely dark.

Taurine An essential amino acid your cat needs to properly form protein in its body. Since it is not naturally formed within a cat's system, the cat's diet must supply the cat with taurine each day of its life.

Temperament How a cat behaves in a general sense.

Tom An unneutered male cat whose job it is to impregnate the female.

Venom A poisonous, liquid substance often secreted by snakes, scorpions, bees, and spiders. It is injected into a prey animal or enemy, chiefly by biting or stinging.

Vertebrate Any animal with a backbone.

Virus A microscopic organism that contains genetic information but cannot reproduce itself. To replicate, a virus must invade another cell, insert its own DNA into the unfortunate host, then take over that cell's reproductive machinery.

A simple home-cooking recipe for cats

The amount of food prepared with this recipe should last about 5 days for an adult cat of normal size. Your cat may eat more or less at each meal; use common sense to decide on serving size. Because this mixture is slightly lower in calories than dry cat food, you will need to serve slightly more of it in comparison.

Also, I recommend you give your cat a vitamin-mineral supplement once a day.

3 cups raw or lightly cooked ground meat (beef, chicken, turkey, or lamb)
1 cup raw or slightly cooked organ meat (kidney, liver, heart, lung)
1 raw turkey neck, ground or finely chopped (be sure not to cook)
1 cup well-cooked grains (oats, rice, barley, or cornmeal)
1/2 cup well-cooked vegetables (broccoli, zucchini, carrots, squash, or green beans)
1 raw egg
1 teaspoon olive oil or flax seed oil

Mix all ingredients together, then divide into individual portions.

Yield: About 6 cups of food, with approximately 250 to 300 calories per cup.

The less you cook the ingredients, the more nutritional it will be for your cat. If you freeze the individual portions, they will keep for several weeks and you can defrost one a day. When thawing, try not to use the microwave or another cooking method, since this will reduce nutrient levels. Instead, let the food thaw overnight in the refrigerator. To warm it, place the food in a plastic bag with a zipper closure, then immerse the bag into hot (not boiling) water for 10 minutes.

Index

Acknowledgments

Author's acknowledgments

This book is dedicated to Nicki, Zac, Jake, and Louie, my spirited Seattle family.

I would like to thank Beth Adelman for a great job done; I couldn't have asked for a better editor or friend. Kudos also to LaVonne Carlson-Finnerty and Jennifer Williams, my DK family. Special thanks also to the owners and employees at the Grateful Bread Bakery and Coffee Shop in Seattle, for filling me with tea and bagels and letting me pound away on my trusty notebook computer in that most friendly corner of the world.

Publisher's acknowledgments

Dorling Kindersley would like to thank the following people for their contributions to this project: Caroline Hunt for editorial assistance; Melanie Simmonds for picture library research; Neal Cobourne for designing the jacket.

Indexer
Indexing Specialists, Hove

Picture credits
Animal Photography: 2; 50; 59; 77; 107; 111; 112; 120; 132;
    139; 151; 159; 182; 186; 193; 200; 207; 212; 228; 230; 247;
    254; 255; 257; 270; 312; 315(t); 318; 320; 323; 324; 330(t)
Animals Unlimited: 168; 191; 192; 224; 295; 310; 327(t);
    327(b); 334; 335
Gettyone Stone: Tony Stone 20; 76; 170; 282
Mary Evans Picture Library: 32
Science Photo Library: 195; 197
Telegraph Photo Library: 117; Matt Anker 164; Bavaria 322;
    Stephen W. Jones 296; L'image magic, Inc. 114;
    New Earth Pictures 103; Peter J. Oxford 16-17;
    Gary Randall 154; Hans Reinhard 96; Mike Russell 142;
    Miguel S. Salmeron 78; Al Satterwhite 299;
    Carlos Spaventa 162; Arthur Tilley 213; V.C.L. 253

All other images © Dorling Kindersley.
For further information see: www.dkimages.com